Implementing Domain-Specific Languages with Xtext and Xtend

Second Edition

Learn how to implement a DSL with Xtext and Xtend using easy-to-understand examples and best practices

Lorenzo Bettini

[PACKT] open source *

PUBLISHING   community experience distilled

BIRMINGHAM - MUMBAI

Implementing Domain-Specific Languages with Xtext and Xtend

Second Edition

First published: August 2013

Second Edition: August 2016

Production reference: 1230816

Published by Packt Publishing Ltd.
Livery Place
35 Livery Street
Birmingham B3 2PB, UK.

ISBN 978-1-78646-496-5

www.packtpub.com

Credits

Author
Lorenzo Bettini

Reviewer
Dr. Jan Koehnlein

Commissioning Editor
Amarabha Banerjee

Acquisition Editor
Reshma Raman

Content Development Editors
Divij Kotian
Sweta Basu

Technical Editor
Rutuja Vaze

Copy Editor
Charlotte Carneiro

Project Coordinator
Sheejal Shah

Proofreader
Safis Editing

Indexer
Mariammal Chettiyar

Graphics
Disha Haria

Production Coordinator
Nilesh Mohite

Cover Work
Nilesh Mohite

Foreword

In the age of the digital transformation, every business and every company eventually needs to write software in some way. After all, "software is eating the world" and business that we all thought were mature and well developed, get disrupted by small startups that are smart enough to leverage the possibilities of software (for example, Uber, AirBnb, or Tesla). It is pretty clear that in future software development will become even more important than it is today. In order to meet the ever increasing demand of software systems, we need to find ways to enable more people to participate and contribute in software development.

Domain-Specific Languages (DSL) are a way to define powerful interfaces for domain experts to help them participating in software development process. DSLs not only help to do more with less code, but also significantly improves communication between stakeholders. Furthermore, it reduces maintenance costs greatly as it decouples technical aspects from domain aspects.

Xtext is the one-stop solution for building DSLs, and is widely used in industry and research. It not only lets you define a parser, but also provides you with a full environment, including rich IDEs and text editors to support your DSL. It is everything you need to help professionals work efficiently.

Lorenzo has written an excellent book on DSL engineering with Xtext, that is both a great reference as well as a good way to learn the most important parts of the framework. If you are a software developer that wants to add an important and powerful new weapon to your tool belt, I can only recommend reading this book and diving into the possibilities of language engineering.

Sven Efftinge

Founder of Xtext and Xtend

About the Author

Lorenzo Bettini is an associate professor in computer science at the Dipartimento di Statistica, Informatica, Applicazioni "Giuseppe Parenti," Università di Firenze, Italy. Previously, he was a researcher in computer science at Dipartimento di Informatica, Università di Torino, Italy. He also was a Postdoc and a contractual researcher at Dipartimento di Sistemi e Informatica, Università di Firenze, Italy. He has a masters degree summa cum laude in computer science and a PhD in "Logics and Theoretical Computer Science." His research interests cover design, theory, and the implementation of programming languages (in particular, object-oriented languages and network-aware languages). He has been using Xtext since version 0.7. He has used Xtext and Xtend for implementing many domain-specific languages and Java-like programming languages. He also contributed to Xtext, and he recently became an Xtext committer. He is the author of the first edition of the book "Implementing Domain-Specific Languages with Xtext and Xtend", published by Packt Publishing (August 21, 2013). He is also the author of about 80 papers published in international conferences and international journals. You can contact him at http://www.lorenzobettini.it.

Acknowledgments

First of all, I would like to thank the reviewer of this book, Jan Koehnlein. His constructive criticism, extensive suggestions, and careful error reporting helped extremely in improving the book. Since this is a second edition, which contains some material from the previous edition, I am also grateful to the reviewers of the first edition, Henrik Lindberg, Pedro J. Molina, and Sebastian Zarnekow.

I'm also grateful to all the people from Packt I dealt with, Sweta Basu and Reshma Raman. I would also like to thank Divij Kotian and Rutuja Vaze for their continuous support throughout the book.

This book would not have been possible without the efforts that all the skilled Xtext developers have put in this framework. Most of them are always present in the Xtext forum and are very active in providing help to the users. Many other people not necessarily involved with Xtext development are always present in the forum and are willing to provide help and suggestions in solving typical problems about Xtext. They also regularly write on their own blogs about examples and best practices with Xtext. Many contents in this book are inspired by the material found on the forum and on such blogs. The list would be quite long, so I will only mention the ones with whom I interacted most: Christian Dietrich, Moritz Eysholdt, Dennis Huebner, Jan Koehnlein, Anton Kosyakov, Henrik Lindberg, Ed Merks, Holger Schill, Miro Spoenemann, and Karsten Thoms.

I am particularly grateful to Sebastian Zarnekow, one of the main Xtext committers. In the last few years, he has always been willing to help me to get familiar with most of the things about Xtext and Xbase internals I know today.

A very special thank you to Sven Efftinge, the project lead of Xtext, for creating such a cool and impressive framework. Not to mention the nice foreword Sven wrote for this second edition. I am also grateful to Sven for nominating me as an Xtext committer.

I am grateful to itemis Schweiz for sponsoring the writing of this book, and in particular, I am thankful to Serano Colameo.

Last but not least, a big thank you to my parents for always supporting me through all these years. A warm thank you to my Silvia, the "rainbow" of my life, for being there and for not complaining about all the spare time that this book has stolen from us.

About the Reviewer

Dr. Jan Koehnlein has earned several years of experience in the development of programming tools. That involves language design, modeling, combining textual and graphical notations, and the integration into an IDE on various platforms.

Jan has been a committer to the Eclipse projects Xtext and Xtend right from their beginnings. In addition, he designed FXDiagram, an open source framework to visualize any kind of model with a strong focus on user experience and a modern look and feel.

Jan is a well-known speaker at international conferences, and he has published a number of articles in magazines. He also gives trainings and lectures on Xtext and surrounding technologies.

In 2016, Jan and two friends founded the company TypeFox. It is specialized in the development of tools and languages for software engineers and other domain experts, providing everything from contract work, to professional support, consulting, and workshops.

In his private life, Jan is a passionate father. He loves photography and kayaking.

www.PacktPub.com

eBooks, discount offers, and more

Did you know that Packt offers eBook versions of every book published, with PDF and ePub files available? You can upgrade to the eBook version at www.PacktPub.com and as a print book customer, you are entitled to a discount on the eBook copy. Get in touch with us at customercare@packtpub.com for more details.

At www.PacktPub.com, you can also read a collection of free technical articles, sign up for a range of free newsletters and receive exclusive discounts and offers on Packt books and eBooks.

https://www2.packtpub.com/books/subscription/packtlib

Do you need instant solutions to your IT questions? PacktLib is Packt's online digital book library. Here, you can search, access, and read Packt's entire library of books.

Why subscribe?

- Fully searchable across every book published by Packt
- Copy and paste, print, and bookmark content
- On demand and accessible via a web browser

Table of Contents

Preface

Xtext is an open source Eclipse framework for implementing Domain Specific Languages together with their integration in the Eclipse IDE. Xtext allows you to implement languages quickly by covering all aspects of a complete language infrastructure, starting from the parser, code generator, or interpreter, up to a full Eclipse IDE integration, with all the typical IDE features such as editor with syntax highlighting, code completion, error markers, automatic build infrastructure, and so on.

This book will incrementally guide you through the very basics of DSL implementation with Xtext and Xtend, such as grammar definition, validation, and code generation. The book will then cover advanced concepts such as unit testing, type checking, and scoping. Xtext comes with good and smart default implementations for all these aspects. However, every single aspect can be customized by the programmer.

Although Java can be used for customizing the implementation of a DSL, Xtext fosters the use of Xtend, a Java-like programming language completely interoperable with the Java type system which features a more compact and easier to use syntax and advanced features such as type inference, extension methods, multi-line template strings and lambda expressions. For this reason, we will use Xtend throughout the book.

Most of the chapters have a tutorial nature and will describe the main concepts of Xtext through uncomplicated examples. The book also uses test driven development extensively. The last chapters will describe more advanced topics such as Continuous Integration and Xbase, a reusable Java-like expression language that ships with Xtext which can be used in your DSLs.

This book aims at being complementary to the official documentation, trying to give you enough information to start being productive in implementing a DSL with Xtext. This book will try to teach you some methodologies and best practices when using Xtext, filling some bits of information that are not present in the official documentation.

The chapters are meant to be read in order, since they typically refer to concepts that were introduced in the previous chapters.

All the examples shown in the book are available online, see the section *Downloading the example code*. We strongly suggest that you first try to develop the examples while reading the chapters and then compare their implementations with the ones provided by the author.

What this book covers

After a small introduction to the features that a DSL implementation should cover, including integration in an IDE, the book will introduce Xtend since it will be used in all the examples. The book proceeds by explaining the main concepts of Xtext. For example, validation, code generation, and customizations of runtime and UI aspects. The book will then show how to test a DSL implemented in Xtext with JUnit in order to follow a Test Driven Development strategy that will help you to quickly implement cleaner and more maintainable code. The test-driven approach is used in the rest of the book when presenting advanced concepts such as type checking and Scoping. The book also shows how to build a DSL with Continuous Integration mechanisms and how to produce a release of your DSL so that others can install it in Eclipse. At the end of the book Xbase is introduced. Finally, the book describes some advanced topics and mechanisms that can be used when implementing an Xtext DSL.

Chapter 1, Implementing a DSL, gives a brief introduction to Domain Specific Languages (DSL) and sketches the main tasks for implementing a DSL and its integration in an IDE. The chapter also shows how to install Xtext and gives a first idea of what you can do with Xtext.

Chapter 2, Creating Your First Xtext Language, shows a first example of a DSL implemented with Xtext and gives an introduction to some features of the Xtext grammar language. The chapter describes the typical development workflow of programming with Xtext and provides a small introduction to EMF (Eclipse Modeling Framework), a framework on which Xtext is based.

Chapter 3, Working with the Xtend Programming Language, describes the main features of the Xtend programming language, a Java-like language interoperable with the Java type system. We will use Xtend in all the other chapters, to implement every aspect of an Xtext DSL.

Chapter 4, Validation, describes validation, in particular, the Xtext mechanism to implement validation, that is, the validator. This chapter is about implementing additional constraint checks that cannot be done at parsing time. It also shows how to implement quickfixes corresponding to the errors generated by the validator.

Chapter 5, Code Generation, shows how to write a code generator for an Xtext DSL using the Xtend programming language. The chapter also shows how a DSL implementation can be exported as a Java standalone command-line compiler.

Chapter 6, Customizing Xtext Components, describes the main mechanism for customizing Xtext components, Google Guice, a Dependency Injection framework. In particular, the chapter shows how to customize both the runtime and the UI aspects of an Xtext DSL.

Chapter 7, Testing, describes how to test a DSL implementation using JUnit and the additional utility classes provided by Xtext. The chapter shows the typical techniques for testing both the runtime and the UI aspects of a DSL implemented in Xtext.

Chapter 8, An Expression Language, covers the implementation of a DSL for expressions, including arithmetic, boolean, and string expressions. The chapter shows how to deal with recursive rules and with typical problems when writing Xtext grammars. The implementation will be described incrementally and in a test-driven way. The chapter also shows how to implement a type system for checking that expressions are correct with respect to types and how to implement an interpreter for these expressions. Some hints for optimizing the performance of a DSL implementation are also presented.

Chapter 9, Type Checking, covers the implementation of a small object-oriented DSL, which can be seen as a smaller version of Java that we call SmallJava. This chapter shows how to implement some type checking techniques that deal with object-oriented features, such as inheritance and subtyping. The chapter also describes some good practices in Xtext DSL implementations.

Chapter 10, Scoping, covers the main mechanism behind visibility and cross-reference resolution in Xtext. Since scoping and typing are often strictly connected and inter-dependent especially for object-oriented languages, the chapter is based on the SmallJava DSL introduced in the previous chapter. The chapter describes both local and global scoping and how to customize them.

Chapter 11, Continuous Integration, describes how you can release your DSL implementation by creating an Eclipse update site so that others can install it in Eclipse. The chapter also describes how to build and test your DSL implementation on a continuous integration server, using Maven/Tycho or Gradle. We will also show how to have a web application with a web editor for your DSL, and how your DSL implementation can be easily ported to IntelliJ.

Chapter 12, Xbase, describes Xbase a reusable expression language interoperable with Java. By using Xbase in your DSL, you will inherit all the Xbase mechanisms for performing type checking according to the Java type system and the automatic Java code generation.

Chapter 13, Advanced Topics, describes a few advanced topics concerning an Xtext DSL implementation, and some advanced techniques. In the first part of the chapter we will show how to manually maintain the Ecore model for the AST of an Xtext DSL. We will show how to create an Xtext DSL starting from an existing Ecore model, how to switch to a manually maintained Ecore model, starting from the one generated by Xtext, and how to use Xcore to maintain the Ecore model for the AST. In the last section we will show how to extend an Xbase DSL with new expressions, customizing the Xbase type system and the Xbase compiler in order to handle the new Xbase expressions.

Chapter 14, Conclusions, concludes the book by providing a few references to some additional material available online.

What you need for this book

The book assumes that you have a good knowledge of Java; it also assumes that you are familiar with Eclipse and its main features. Existing basic knowledge of a compiler implementation would be useful, though not strictly required, since the book will explain all the stages of the development of a DSL.

Who this book is for

This book is for programmers who want to learn about Xtext and how to use it to implement a DSL or a programming language together with the Eclipse IDE tooling.

Conventions

In this book, you will find a number of text styles that distinguish between different kinds of information. Here are some examples of these styles and an explanation of their meaning.

Code words in text, database table names, folder names, filenames, file extensions, pathnames, dummy URLs, user input, and Twitter handles are shown as follows: "We can include other contexts through the use of the `include` directive."

A block of code is set as follows:

```java
public static void main(String args[]) {
    System.out.println("Hello world");
```

Where **keywords** of the languages are typeset in bold, and references to static members are typeset in italics (for example, Java static methods).

When we wish to draw your attention to a particular part of a code block, the relevant lines or items are set in bold:

```xml
<plugin>
  <groupId>org.codehaus.mojo</groupId>
  <artifactId>exec-maven-plugin</artifactId>
  <version>1.4.0</version>
  <executions>
    <execution>
      <!-- new execution for generating EMF classes -->
      <id>mwe2GenerateEMFClasses</id>
```

Any command-line input or output is written as follows:

```
mvn org.eclipse.tycho:tycho-versions-plugin:set-version
  -DnewVersion=1.1.0-SNAPSHOT -Dtycho.mode=maven
```

Bibliographic references are of the form "Author" "year" when there is a single author, or "First author" et al. "year" when there is more than one author. Bibliographic references are used for books, printed articles or articles published on the web. The Bibliography can be found at the end of the book.

New terms and **important words** are shown in bold. Words that you see on the screen, for example, in menus or dialog boxes, appear in the text like this: "Clicking the **Next** button moves you to the next screen." When the user is requested to select submenus, we separate each menu with a pipe, like this: "To create a new project, navigate to **File | New | Project...**".

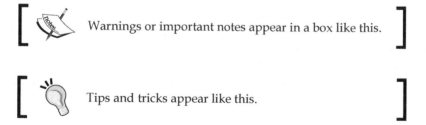

Warnings or important notes appear in a box like this.

Tips and tricks appear like this.

Reader feedback

Feedback from our readers is always welcome. Let us know what you think about this book — what you liked or disliked. Reader feedback is important for us as it helps us develop titles that you will really get the most out of.

To send us general feedback, simply e-mail `feedback@packtpub.com`, and mention the book's title in the subject of your message.

If there is a topic that you have expertise in and you are interested in either writing or contributing to a book, see our author guide at `www.packtpub.com/authors`.

Customer support

Now that you are the proud owner of a Packt book, we have a number of things to help you to get the most from your purchase.

Downloading the example code

You can download the example code files from your account at `http://www.packtpub.com` for all the Packt Publishing books you have purchased. If you purchased this book elsewhere, you can visit `http://www.packtpub.com/support` and register to have the files e-mailed directly to you.

The example code for this book is also available on a Git repository at

`https://github.com/LorenzoBettini/packtpub-xtext-book-2nd-examples`.

We suggest you to monitor this git repository, since it will always contain the most up-to-date version of the examples.

Errata

Although we have taken every care to ensure the accuracy of our content, mistakes do happen. If you find a mistake in one of our books — maybe a mistake in the text or the code — we would be grateful if you could report this to us. By doing so, you can save other readers from frustration and help us improve subsequent versions of this book. If you find any errata, please report them by visiting `http://www.packtpub.com/submit-errata`, selecting your book, clicking on the **Errata Submission Form** link, and entering the details of your errata. Once your errata are verified, your submission will be accepted and the errata will be uploaded to our website or added to any list of existing errata under the Errata section of that title.

To view the previously submitted errata, go to `https://www.packtpub.com/books/content/support` and enter the name of the book in the search field. The required information will appear under the **Errata** section.

The Errata is also available on the Git repository of the examples of the book `https://github.com/LorenzoBettini/packtpub-xtext-book-2nd-examples`.

Piracy

Piracy of copyrighted material on the Internet is an ongoing problem across all media. At Packt, we take the protection of our copyright and licenses very seriously. If you come across any illegal copies of our works in any form on the Internet, please provide us with the location address or website name immediately so that we can pursue a remedy.

Please contact us at `copyright@packtpub.com` with a link to the suspected pirated material.

We appreciate your help in protecting our authors and our ability to bring you valuable content.

Questions

If you have a problem with any aspect of this book, you can contact us at `questions@packtpub.com`, and we will do our best to address the problem.

Preface to the second edition

Since the very beginning, Xtext has always been a continuously evolving software. Each new version of Xtext comes with many new features and bugfixes.

When I wrote the first edition of the book, which was published in August 2013, Xtext 2.4.0 had been recently released. Since then, all the features introduced in each new release of Xtext aimed at making DSL implementation easier and at improving the user experience.

All these things came with a small price though — the contents of the book were getting stale in time, and they did not respect the features of Xtext in the new releases anymore.

In all these years, Xtext has always been my daily framework since my research is based on programming language design, theory, and most of all, implementation. I've been implementing lots of DSLs since the first edition of the book and doing that I've also learned many more aspects of Xtext and new best practices. I've also started to contribute more actively to the Xtext code base, and I can proudly announce that I recently became an Xtext committer.

Thus, at the end of 2015, I decided to propose to Packt a second edition of the book and they reacted very positively.

While working on this second edition, I updated all the contents of the previous edition in order to make them up to date with respect to what Xtext provides in the most recent release (at the time of writing, it is 2.10). All the examples have been rewritten from scratch. With respect to the examples of the first edition, many parts of the DSLs have been modified and improved, focusing on efficient implementation techniques and the best practices I learned in these years. Thus, while the features of most of the main example DSLs of the book is the same as in the first edition, their implementation is completely new. In the last chapters, many more examples are also introduced.

In particular, *Chapter 11*, *Continuous Integration*, which in the previous edition was called *Building and Releasing*, has been completely rewritten and it is now based on Maven/Tycho instead of Buckminster, since Xtext now provides a project wizard that also creates a Maven/Tycho build configuration for your Xtext DSL. This new chapter also briefly describes the new Xtext features that allow you to port your DSL editor on the web and also on IntelliJ. I also added a brand new chapter at the end of the book, *Chapter 13*, *Advanced Topics*, is loaded with much more advanced material and techniques that are useful when your DSL grows in size and features. For example, the chapter will show how to manually maintain the Ecore model for the AST of your DSL in several ways, including Xcore. This chapter also presents an example that extends Xbase, including the customization of its type system and compiler. An introduction to Xbase is still presented in *Chapter 12*, *Xbase*, as in the previous edition, but with more details.

As in the previous edition, the book fosters unit testing a lot. An entire chapter, *Chapter 7*, *Testing*, is devoted to testing all aspects of an Xtext DSL implementation. I also kept the same tutorial nature of most chapters as in the previous edition.

Summarizing, while the title and the subject of most chapters is still the same, their contents has been completely reviewed, extended, and hopefully, improved.

If you enjoyed the first edition of the book and found it useful, I hope you'll like this second edition even more.

Lorenzo Bettini

1
Implementing a DSL

In this chapter, we will provide a brief introduction on **Domain-Specific Languages** (**DSLs**) and the issues concerning their implementation, especially in the context of an **Integrated Development Environment** (**IDE**). In the initial part of the chapter, we will sketch the main tasks for implementing a DSL and its integration in an IDE. At the end of the chapter, we will also show you how to install Xtext and will give you a glimpse of what you can do with Xtext. It is an Eclipse framework for the development of DSLs that covers all aspects of a language implementation, including its integration in the Eclipse IDE.

This chapter will cover the following topics:

- An introduction to DSLs
- The main steps for implementing a DSL
- The typical IDE tooling for a DSL
- The very first demo of Xtext

Domain-Specific Languages

Domain Specific Languages, abbreviated to **DSLs**, are programming languages or specification languages that target a specific problem domain. They are not meant to provide features for solving all kinds of problems. You probably will not be able to implement all programs you can implement with, for instance, Java or C, which are known as **General Purpose Languages** (**GPL**). On the other hand, if your problem's domain is covered by a particular DSL, you will be able to solve that problem easier and faster using that DSL instead of a GPL.

Some examples of DSLs are SQL (for querying relational databases), Mathematica (for symbolic mathematics), HTML, and many others you have probably used in the past. A program or specification written in a DSL can then be interpreted or compiled into a GPL. In other cases, the specification can represent simple data that will be processed by other systems.

For a wider introduction to DSLs, you should refer to the books *Fowler 2010*, *Ghosh 2010*, and *Voelter 2013*.

Need for a new language

You may now wonder why you need to introduce a new DSL for describing specific data, models, or applications, instead of using XML, which allows you to describe data in a machine in human-readable form. There are so many tools now that allow you to read, write, or exchange data in XML without having to parse such data according to a specific syntax such as an **XML Schema Definition** (**XSD**). There is basically only one syntax (the XML tag syntax) to learn, and then all data can be represented with XML.

Of course, this is also a matter of taste, but many people, including myself, find that XML is surely machine readable, but not so much human-readable. It is fine to exchange data in XML, if the data in that format is produced by a program. But often, people (programmers and users) are requested to specify data in XML manually; for instance, for specifying an application's specific configuration.

If writing an XML file can be a pain, reading it back can be even worse. In fact, XML tends to be verbose, and it fills documents with too much additional syntax noise due to all the tags. The tags help a computer to process XML, but they surely distract people when they have to read and write XML files.

Consider a very simple example of an XML file describing people:

```
<people>
  <person>
    <name>James</name>
    <surname>Smith</surname>
    <age>50</age>
  </person>
  <person employed="true">
    <name>John</name>
    <surname>Anderson</surname>
    <age>40</age>
  </person>
</people>
```

It is not straightforward for a human to grasp the actual information about a person from such a specification—a human is distracted by all those tags. Also, writing such a specification may be a burden. An editor might help with some syntax highlighting and early user feedback concerning validation, but still there are too many additional details.

JSON (JavaScript Object Notation) could be used as a less verbose alternative to XML. However, the burden of manually reading, writing, and maintaining specifications in JSON is only slightly reduced with respect to XML.

The following version is written in an ad hoc DSL:

```
person {
  name=James
  surname=Smith
  age=50
}
person employed {
  name=John
  surname=Anderson
  age=40
}
```

This contains less noise, and the information is easier to grasp. We could even do better and have a more compact specification:

```
James Smith (50)
John Anderson (40) employed
```

After all, since this DSL only lets users describe the name and age of people, why not design it to make the description both compact, easy to read and write?

Implementing a DSL

For the end user, using a DSL is surely easier than writing XML code. However, the developer of the DSL is now left with the task of implementing it.

Implementing a DSL means developing a program that is able to read text written in that DSL, parse it, process it, and then possibly interpret it or generate code in another language. Depending on the aim of the DSL, this may require several phases, but most of these phases are typical of all implementations.

In this section, we only sketch the main aspects of implementing a DSL. For a deeper introduction to language implementations and the theory behind, we refer the interested reader to the book *Aho et al. 2007*.

 From now on, throughout the book, we will not distinguish, unless strictly required by the context, between *DSL* and *programming language.*

Parsing

First of all, when reading a program written in a programming language, the implementation has to make sure that the program respects the syntax of that language.

To this aim, we need to break the program into tokens. Each token is a single atomic element of the language; this can be a **keyword** (such as class in Java), an **identifier** (such as a Java class name), or a **literal**, that is, a fixed value. Examples of literals are **string literals**, typically surrounded by quotes, **integer literals**, and **boolean** literals (for example, true and false). Other kinds of tokens are **operators** (such as arithmetic and comparison operators) and **separators** (such as parentheses and terminating semicolons).

For instance, in the preceding example, employed is a keyword, the parentheses are separators, James is an identifier, and 50 is an integer literal.

The process of converting a sequence of characters into a sequence of tokens is called **lexical analysis**, and the program or procedure that performs such analysis is called a **lexical analyzer, lexer,** or simply a **scanner**. This analysis is usually implemented by using **regular expressions** syntax.

Having the sequence of tokens from the input file is not enough, we must make sure that they form a valid statement in our language; that is, they respect the syntactic structure expected by the language. This phase is called **parsing** or **syntactic analysis**. The program or procedure that performs such analysis is called a **parser**.

Let's recall the DSL to describe the name and age of various people and a possible input text:

```
James Smith (50)
John Anderson (40) employed
```

In this example, each line of the input must respect the following structure:

- two identifiers
- the separator (
- one integer literal
- the separator)
- the optional keyword `employed`

In our language, tokens are separated by white spaces, and lines are separated by a newline character.

You can now deduce that the parser relies on the lexer. In fact, the parser asks the lexer for tokens and tries to build valid statement of the language.

If you have never implemented a programming language, you might be scared at this point by the task of implementing a parser, for instance, in Java. You are probably right, since this is not easy. The DSL we just used as an example is very small and still it would require some effort to implement. What if your DSL has to deal also with, say, arithmetic expressions? In spite of their apparently simple structure, arithmetic expressions are recursive by their own nature; thus a parser implemented in Java would have to deal with recursion as well, and, in particular, it should avoid possible endless loops.

There are tools to deal with parsing so that you do not have to implement a parser by hand. In particular, there are DSLs to specify the grammar of the language, and from this specification, they automatically generate the code for the lexer and parser. For this reason, these tools are called **parser generators** or **compiler-compilers**. In this context, such specifications are called grammars. A **grammar** is a set of rules that describe the form of the elements that are valid according to the language syntax.

Here are some examples of tools for specifying grammars.

Bison *and* **Flex** (*Levine 2009*) are the most famous in the C context: from a high level specification of the syntactic structure (Bison) and lexical structure (Flex) of a language, they generate the parser and lexer in C, respectively. Bison is an implementation of **Yacc** (Yet Another Compiler-compiler, *Brown et al.* 1995), and there are variants for other languages as well, such as **Racc** for Ruby.

In the Java world, the most well-known is probably **ANTLR (ANother Tool for Language Recognition)** pronounced Antler, (see the book *Parr* 2007). This allows the programmer to specify the grammar of the language in one single file (without separating the syntactic and lexical specifications in different files), and then it automatically generates the parser in Java.

Just to have an idea of what the specification of grammars looks like in ANTLR, here is a very simplified grammar for an expression language for arithmetic expressions with sum and multiplication (as we will see in *Chapter 9, Type Checking* we cannot write a recursive rule such as the one shown in the following snippet):

```
expression
  : INT
  | expression '*' expression
  | expression '+' expression
  ;
```

Even if you do not understand all the details, it should be straightforward to get its meaning—an expression is either an integer literal or (recursively) two expressions with an operator in between (either * or +).

From such a specification, you automatically get the Java code that will parse such expressions.

The Abstract Syntax Tree (AST)

Parsing a program is only the first stage in a programming language implementation. Once the program is checked as correct from the syntactic point of view, the implementation will have to do something with the elements of the program.

First of all, the overall correctness of a program cannot always be determined during parsing. One of the correctness checks that cannot be performed during parsing is type checking, that is, checking that the program is correct with respect to types. For instance, in Java, you cannot assign a string value to an integer variable, or you can only assign instances of a variable's declared type or subclasses thereof.

Trying to embed type checking in a grammar specification could either make the specification more complex, or it could be simply impossible, since some type checks can be performed only when other program parts have already been parsed.

Type checking is part of the **semantic analysis** of a program. This often includes managing the **symbol table**, that is, for instance, handling the variables that are declared and that are visible only in specific parts of the program (think of fields in a Java class and their visibility in methods).

For these reasons, during parsing, we should also build a representation of the parsed program and store it in memory so that we can perform the semantic analysis on the memory representation without needing to parse the same text over and over again. A convenient representation in memory of a program is a tree structure called the **Abstract Syntax Tree (AST)**. The AST represents the abstract syntactic structure of the program. Being abstract, the tree representation does not represent many details of the original program, such as grouping parentheses and formatting spaces. In this tree, each node represents a construct of the program.

Once the AST is stored in memory, we will not need to parse the program anymore, and we can perform all the additional semantic checks on the AST. If all the checks succeed, we can use the AST for the final stage of the implementation, which can be the interpretation of the program or code generation.

In order to build the AST, we need two additional things.

First of all, we need the **code** for representing the nodes of such a tree. If we are using Java, this means that we need to write some Java classes, typically one for each language construct. For instance, for the expression language, we might write one class for the integer literal and one for the binary expression. Remember that since the grammar is recursive, we need a base class for representing the abstract concept of an expression. For example:

```java
public interface Expression { }

public class Literal implements Expression {
  Integer value;
  // constructor and set methods...
}

public class BinaryExpression implements Expression {
  Expression left, right;
  String operator;
  // constructor and set methods...
}
```

Then, we need to **annotate** the grammar specification with **actions** that construct the AST during the parsing. These actions are basically Java code blocks embedded in the grammar specification itself. The following is just an (simplified) example, and it does not necessarily respect the actual ANTLR syntax:

```
expression:
  INT { $value = new Literal(Integer.parseInt($INT.text)); }
| left=expression '*' right=expression {
  $value = new BinaryExpression($left.value, $right.value);
```

```
        $value.setOperator("*");
    }
  | left=expression '+' right=expression {
        $value = new BinaryExpression($left.value, $right.value);
        $value.setOperator("+");
    }
  ;
```

IDE integration

Even if you have implemented your DSL, that is, the mechanisms to read, validate, and execute programs written in your DSL, your work cannot really be considered finished.

Nowadays, many programmers are accustomed to use powerful IDEs such as Eclipse. For this reason, a DSL should be shipped with good IDE support. This will increase the likelihood of your DSL being adopted and successful.

If your DSL is supported by all the powerful features in an IDE such as a syntax-aware editor, immediate feedback, incremental syntax checking, suggested corrections, auto-completion, and so on, then it will be easier to learn, use, and maintain.

In the following sections, we will see the most important features concerning IDE integration. In particular, we will assume Eclipse as the underlying IDE (since Xtext is mainly an Eclipse framework).

Syntax highlighting

The ability to see the program colored and formatted with different visual styles according to the elements of the language (for example, comments, keywords, strings, and so on) is not just *cosmetic*.

First of all, it gives immediate feedback concerning the syntactic correctness of what you are writing. For instance, if string constants (typically enclosed in quotes) are rendered as red, and you see that at some point in the editor the rest of your program is all red, you may soon get an idea that somewhere in between you forgot to insert the closing quotation mark.

Background validation

The programming cycle consisting of writing a program with a text editor, saving it, switching to the command line, running the compiler, and in the case of errors, shifting back to the text editor is surely not productive.

The programming environment should not let the programmer realize about errors too late. On the contrary, it should continuously check the program in the background while the programmer is writing, even if the current file has not been saved yet. The sooner the environment can tell the programmer about errors, the better it is. The longer it takes to realize that there is an error, the higher the cost in terms of time and mental effort to correct it.

Error markers

When your DSL parser and checker issue some errors, the programmer should not have to go to the console to discover such errors. Your implementation should highlight the parts of the program with errors directly in the editor by underlining (for instance, in red) only the parts that actually contain the errors. It should also put some error markers with an explicit message on the left of the editor in correspondence to the lines with errors, and should also fill the **Problems** view with all these errors. The programmer will then have the chance to easily spot the parts of the program that need to be fixed.

Content assist

Content assist is the feature that automatically, or on demand, provides suggestions on how to complete the statement/expression the programmer just typed. The proposed content should make sense in that specific program context in order to be effectively useful. For instance, when editing a Java file, after the keyword new, Eclipse proposes only Java class names as possible completions.

Again, this has to do with productivity. It does not make much sense to be forced to know all the syntax of a programming language by heart (especially for DSLs, which are not common languages such as Java), neither to know all the language's library classes and functions.

In Eclipse, the content assist is usually accessed with the keyboard shortcut *Ctrl + Space bar*.

Hyperlinking

Hyperlinking is a feature that makes it possible to navigate between references in a program. For example, from a variable to its declaration, or from a function, call to the function definition. If your DSL provides declarations of any sort (for instance, variable declarations or functions) and a way to refer to them (for instance, referring to a variable or invoking a declared function), then it should also provide **Hperlinking** from a token referring to a declaration. It should be possible to directly jump to the corresponding declaration. This is particularly useful if the declaration is in a file different from the one being edited. In Eclipse, this corresponds to pressing *F3* or using *Ctrl + click*.

Hovering is a similar IDE feature — if you need some information about a specific program element, just hovering on that element should display a pop-up window with some documentation about that element.

Quickfixes

If the programmer made a mistake and your DSL implementation is able to fix it somehow, why not help the programmer by offering suggested quickfixes?

As an example, in the Eclipse Java editor, if you invoke a method that does not exist in the corresponding class, you are provided with some quickfixes. For instance, you are given a chance to fix this problem by actually creating such a method. This is typically implemented by a context menu available from the error marker.

In a test-driven scenario this is actually a methodology. Since you write tests before the actual code to test, you can simply write the test that invokes a method that does not exist yet, and then employ the quickfix to let the IDE create that method for you.

Outline

If a program is big, it is surely helpful to have an **outline** of it showing only the main components. Clicking on an element of the outline should bring the programmer directly to the corresponding source line in the editor.

Furthermore, the outline can also include other pieces of information such as types and structure that are not immediately understood by just looking at the program text. It is handy to have a view that is organized differently, perhaps sorted alphabetically to help with navigation.

Automatic build

In an Eclipse Java project, when you modify one Java file and save it, you know that Eclipse will automatically compile that file and, consequently, all the files that depend on the file you have just modified. There is no need to manually call the Java compiler.

Summarizing DSL implementation

In this section, we briefly and informally introduced the main steps to implement a DSL.

The IDE tooling can be implemented on top of Eclipse, which already provides a comprehensive framework.

Indeed, all the features of the Eclipse Java editor, which is part of the project **JDT** (**Java Development Tools**), are based on the Eclipse framework; thus, you can employ all the mechanisms offered by Eclipse to implement the same features for your own DSL.

Unfortunately, this task is not really easy, it certainly requires a deep knowledge of the internals of the Eclipse framework and lot of programming.

Finally, the parser and the checker will have to be connected to the Eclipse editing framework.

To make things a little bit worse, if you learned how to use all these tools (and this requires time) for implementing a DSL, when it comes to implement a new DSL, your existing knowledge will help you, but the time to implement the new DSL will still be huge.

All these learning and timing issues might push you to stick with XML, since the effort to produce a new DSL does not seem to be worthwhile. Indeed, there are many existing parsing and processing technologies for XML for different platforms that can be used, not to mention existing editors and IDE tooling for XML.

But what if there was a framework that lets you achieve all these tasks in a very quick way? What if this framework, once learned (yes, you cannot avoid learning new things), lets you implement new DSLs even quicker than the previous ones?

Enter Xtext

Xtext is an Eclipse framework for implementing programming languages and DSLs. It lets you implement languages quickly, and most of all, it covers all aspects of a complete language infrastructure, starting from the parser, code generator, or interpreter, up to a complete Eclipse IDE integration with all the typical IDE features we discussed previously.

The really amazing thing about Xtext is that, to start a DSL implementation, it only needs a grammar specification similar to ANTLR. You do not have to annotate the rules with actions to build the AST, since the creation of the AST (and the Java classes to store the AST) is handled automatically by Xtext itself. Starting from this specification, Xtext will automatically generate all the mechanisms sketched previously. It will generate the lexer, the parser, the AST model, the construction of the AST to represent the parsed program, and the Eclipse editor with all the IDE features!

Xtext comes with good and smart default implementations for all these aspects, and indeed most of these defaults will surely fit your needs. However, every single aspect can be customized by the language designer.

With all these features, Xtext is easy to use. It produces a professional result quickly, and it is even fun to use.

Since version 2.9.0, Xtext allows you to seamlessly port your DSL implementation and IDE tooling to **IntelliJ** and also to embed your DSL editor in a web application.

Installing Xtext

We will use the latest version of Eclipse. At the time of writing this book, the latest version of Eclipse is 4.6, named **Neon**. This version requires Java 8, so you will also have to make sure that you have Java 8 installed (see `https://www.eclipse.org/downloads`).

Xtext is an Eclipse framework; thus, it can be installed into your Eclipse installation using the update site as follows:

```
http://download.eclipse.org/modeling/tmf/xtext/updates/composite/
releases
```

Just copy this URL into the dialog you get when you navigate to **Help | Install New Software...** in the textbox **Work with** and press *Enter*; after some time (required to contact the update site), you will be presented with lots of possible features to install, grouped by categories. Navigate to the **Xtext** category and select the **Xtext Complete SDK** feature.

Alternatively, an Eclipse distribution for DSL developers based on Xtext is also available from the main Eclipse downloads page, `http://www.eclipse.org/downloads`, called **Eclipse IDE for Java and DSL Developers**.

Using Xtext with IntelliJ will be discussed later in *Chapter 11, Continuous Integration*.

 At the time of writing this book, the current version of Xtext was 2.10, and this is the version used in this book.

Let's try Xtext

Hopefully, by now you should be eager to see for yourself what Xtext can do! In this section, we will briefly present the steps to write your first Xtext project and see what you get. Do not worry if you have no clue about most of the things you will see in this demo; they will be explained in the coming chapters.

Perform the following steps:

1. Start Eclipse and navigate to **File | New | Project...**; in the dialog, navigate to the **Xtext** category and select **Xtext Project**. Refer to the following screenshot:

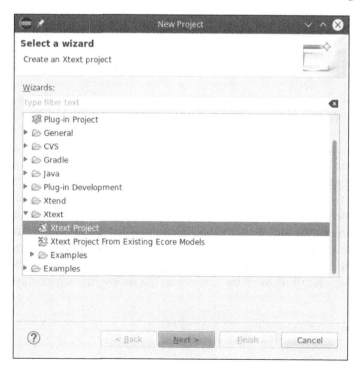

2. In the next dialog, you can leave all the defaults and press **Finish**:

3. The wizard will create several Eclipse projects and will open the file MyDsl. xtext, which is the grammar definition of the new DSL we are about to implement. You do not need to understand all the details of this file's contents for the moment. But if you understood how the grammar definitions work from the examples in the previous sections, you might have an idea of what this DSL does. It accepts lines starting with the keyword Hello followed by an identifier, then followed by !. Refer to the following screenshot:

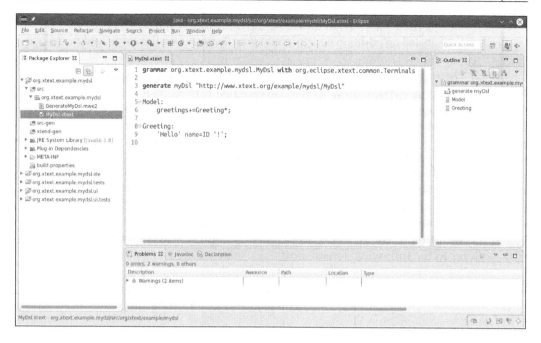

4. Now, it is time to start the first Xtext generation, so navigate to the file `MyDsl.xtext` in the `org.xtext.example.mydsl` project, right-click on it, and navigate to **Run As | Generate Xtext Artifacts**. The output of the generation will be shown in the **Console** view. You will note that a file will be downloaded from the Internet (thus, an Internet connection is required at this stage): "downloading file from `http://download.itemis.com/antlr-generator-3.2.0-patch.jar` ...". This JAR will be downloaded and stored in your project once and for all as `.antlr-generator-3.2.0-patch.jar` (this file cannot be delivered together with Xtext installation: its license, BSD, is not compatible with the Eclipse Public License. Note however that such a jar is not needed at runtime). Note that since this file starts with a dot, it is automatically hidden from the Eclipse **Package Explorer**, just like the files `.classpath` and `.project`. You can make them visible by removing the filter `.*` resources in the **Package Explorer**. Wait for that file to be downloaded, and once you read **Done** in the console, the code generation phase is finished, and you will note that all the projects now contain much more code. Of course, you will have to wait for Eclipse to build the projects and you need to make sure that **Project | Build Automatically** is enabled.

If you want to avoid downloading this additional JAR, you need to install an additional feature into your Eclipse. Use this update site:

`http://download.itemis.com/updates/releases/`

Navigate to the **Xtext Antlr** category and install the feature **Xtext Antlr SDK Feature**. When you restarted Eclipse, if you create a new Xtext project from scratch and you run **Generate Xtext Artifacts**, then the additional JAR is not needed anymore.

5. Your DSL implementation is now ready to be tested! Since what the wizard created for you are Eclipse plug-in projects, you need to start a new Eclipse instance to see your implementation in action. To do so, right-click on the `org.xtext.example.mydsl` project and navigate to **Run As | Run Configurations...**; in the dialog, select **Eclipse Application**, and then the **New** button to create a new launch configuration. Select it and click on **Run**. Refer to the following screenshot:

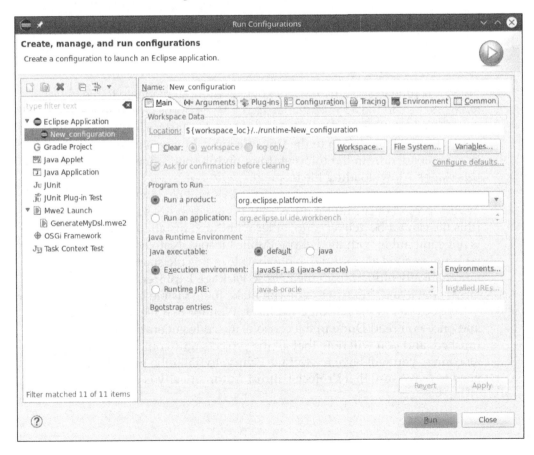

If for any reason, you are using an earlier version than Java 8, before you start the new Eclipse instance, you must make sure that the launch configuration has enough **PermGen size**; otherwise, you will experience *out of memory* errors. You need to specify this VM argument in your launch configuration's **Arguments** tab, in the box **VM arguments**: `-XX:MaxPermSize=256m`.

6. A new Eclipse instance will be run and a new workbench will appear (you may have to close the **Welcome View**). In this instance, your DSL implementation is available. Make sure you are using the **Plug-in Development** perspective or the **Java perspective** (you select the perspective with **Window | Perspective | Open Perspective**). Let's create a new **General** project (**File | New | Project... | General | Project**) and call it, for instance, `sample`. Inside this project, create a new file (**File | New | File**); the name of the file is not important, but the file extension must be `mydsl` (remember that this was the extension we chose in the Xtext new project wizard). As soon as the file is created, it will also be opened in a text editor, and you will be asked to convert the project to an Xtext project. You should accept that to make your DSL editor work correctly in Eclipse.

7. Now, try all the things that Xtext created for you! The editor features syntax highlighting. You can see that by default Xtext DSLs are already set up to deal with Java-like comments such as // and /* */. You also get immediate error feedback with error markers in the relevant parts of the file, even if you have not saved the file yet. The error markers will also appear in the **Problems** view and in the corresponding file in the **Package Explorer** as you soon as you save the file. The outline view is automatically synchronized with the elements in the text editor. The editor also features code completion. All of these features have been automatically generated by Xtext starting from a grammar specification file:

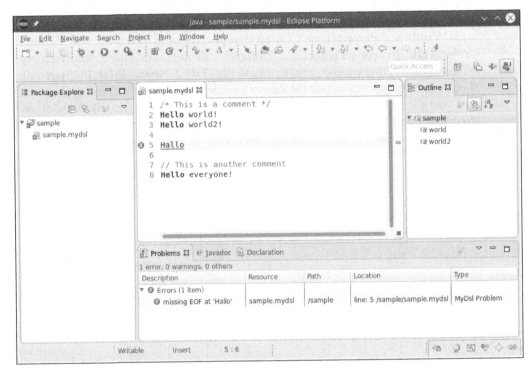

This short demo should have convinced you about the powerful features of Xtext. Implementing the same features manually would require a huge amount of work. The result of the code generated by Xtext is so close to what Eclipse provides you for Java that your DSLs implemented in Xtext will be of high-quality and will provide the users with all the IDE tooling benefits.

The aim of this book

Xtext comes with a lot of nice documentation; you can find it in your Eclipse help system or online at `https://www.eclipse.org/Xtext/documentation/`.

This book aims at being complementary to the official documentation, trying to give you enough information to start being productive in implementing DSLs with Xtext. This book will try to teach you some methodologies and best practices when using Xtext, filling some bits of information that are not present in the official documentation. This book will also focus on automatic testing methodologies so that your DSL implementation will have a solid JUnit test suite. This will help you develop your Xtext DSL faster, with better confidence, and to keep it maintainable. Most chapters will have a tutorial nature and will provide you with enough information to make sure you understand what is going on. However, the official documentation should be kept at hand to learn more details about the mechanisms we will use throughout the book.

The source codes of the examples shown in this book are available online as a **Git** repository at `https://github.com/LorenzoBettini/packtpub-xtext-book-2nd-examples`.

We strongly suggest that you try to implement the examples yourself from scratch while reading the chapters of the book. Then, you can compare your implementation with the sources you find on the Git repository.

We will maintain the source code of the examples up-to-date with respect to future releases of Xtext. In the main README file at the preceding URL, we will also document possible updates to the source code and to the contents of the book itself.

We do not commit the generated files into the Git repository, for example, the `src-gen` and `xtend-gen` folders; thus, for each example in the repository, you will need to generate the Xtext artifacts yourself, using the procedure you used when creating the first project. In the README file, we also document an automated procedure, using the **Eclipse Installer Oomph**, for having an Eclipse with all the required plug-ins for developing with Xtext and a workspace with all the sources of the examples and the corresponding generated files.

Summary

In this chapter, we introduced the main concepts related to implementing a DSL, including IDE features. At this point, you should also have an idea of what Xtext can do for you.

In the next chapter, we will use an uncomplicated DSL to demonstrate the main mechanisms and to get you familiar with the Xtext development workflow.

2
Creating Your First Xtext Language

In this chapter, we will develop a DSL with Xtext and learn how the Xtext grammar language works. We will see the typical development workflow of programming with Xtext when we modify the grammar of the DSL. The chapter will also provide a small introduction to **EMF (Eclipse Modeling Framework)** a framework that Xtext relies on to build the AST of a program.

This chapter will cover the following topics:

- A DSL for entities
- The Xtext generator
- The Eclipse Modeling Framework
- Improvements to the DSL

A DSL for entities

We will now implement a simple DSL to model entities, which can be seen as simple Java classes. Each entity can have a super type entity (you can think of it as a Java superclass) and some attributes (similar to Java fields). This example is a variant of the domain model example that can be found in the Xtext documentation.

Creating the project

First of all, we will use the Xtext project wizard to create the projects for our DSL. We have already experimented with this at the end of *Chapter 1, Implementing a DSL.*

1. Start Eclipse and navigate to **File | New | Project...**. In the dialog, navigate to the **Xtext** category and select **Xtext Project**.

2. In the next dialog, you should specify the following names:
   - **Project name:** org.example.entities
   - **Name:** org.example.entities.Entities
   - **Extensions:** entities

3. Press **Finish**.

The wizard will create several projects and it will open the file Entities.xtext, which is the grammar definition.

The main dialog of the wizard is shown in the following screenshot:

Xtext projects

The Xtext wizard generates several projects (with a name based on the **Project name** you specified in the wizard). In our example we have the following:

- `org.example.entities`: This is the main project that contains the grammar definition and all the runtime components that are independent from the UI.

- `org.example.entities.ide`: This contains the components related to the UI that are independent from Eclipse (as we will see in *Chapter 11, Continuous Integration*, this is useful for targeting IntelliJ and web integration).

- `org.example.entities.tests`: This contains the JUnit tests that do not depend on any UI.

- `org.example.entities.ui.tests`: This contains the JUnit tests that depend on the Eclipse UI.

- `org.example.entities.ui`: This contains the components related to the Eclipse UI (the Eclipse editor and features related to the Eclipse tooling).

We will describe UI mechanisms in *Chapter 6, Customizing Xtext Components,* and unit tests in *Chapter 7, Testing*.

Modifying the grammar

As you may recall from *Chapter 1, Implementing a DSL*, a default grammar is generated by Xtext. In this section, you will learn what this generated grammar contains, and we will modify it to contain the grammar for our Entities DSL. The default generated grammar looks like the following:

```
grammar org.example.entities.Entities with org.eclipse.xtext.common.
Terminals

generate entities "http://www.example.org/entities/Entities"

Model:
  greetings+=Greeting*;

Greeting:
  'Hello' name = ID '!';
```

The first line declares the name of the language and of the grammar. This corresponds to the fully qualified name of the `.xtext` file; the file is called `Entities.xtext`, and it is in the `org.example.entities` package.

The declaration of the grammar also states that it reuses the grammar `Terminals`, which defines the grammar rules for common things such as quoted strings, numbers, and comments, so that in our language we will not have to define such rules. The grammar `Terminals` is part of the Xtext library. In *Chapter 12, Xbase* we will see another example of Xtext library grammar — the Xbase grammar.

The `generate` declaration defines some generation rules for EMF, and we will discuss this later.

After the first two declarations, the actual rules of the grammar will be specified. For the complete syntax of the rules, you should refer to the official Xtext documentation (`https://www.eclipse.org/Xtext/documentation`). For the moment, all the rules we will write will have a name, a colon, the actual syntactic form accepted by that rule, and are terminated by a semicolon.

Now we modify our grammar, as follows:

```
grammar org.example.entities.Entities with
  org.eclipse.xtext.common.Terminals

generate entities "http://www.example.org/entities/Entities"

Model: entities += Entity*;

Entity:
  'entity' name = ID ('extends' superType=[Entity])? '{'
    attributes += Attribute*
  '}'
;

Attribute:
  type=[Entity] array?=('[]')? name=ID ';' ;
```

The first rule in every grammar defines where the parser starts and the type of the root element of the model of the DSL, that is, of the AST. In this example, we declare that an Entities DSL program is a collection of `Entity` elements. This collection is stored in a `Model` object, in particular in a feature called `entities`. As we will see later, the collection is implemented as a list. The fact that it is a collection is implied by the `+=` operator. The star operator, `*`, states that the number of the elements (in this case `Entity`) is arbitrary. In particular, it can be any number `>= 0`. Therefore, a valid `Entities` program can also be empty and contain no `Entity`.

If we wanted our programs to contain at least one `Entity`, we should have used the operator + instead of *.

The shape of `Entity` elements is expressed in its own rule:

```
Entity:
    'entity' name = ID ('extends' superType=[Entity])? '{'
        attributes += Attribute*
    '}'
;
```

First of all, string literals, which in Xtext can be expressed with either single or double quotes, define keywords of the DSL. In this rule, we have the keywords `entity`, `extends`, `'{'`, and `'}'`.

Therefore, a valid entity declaration statement starts with the `'entity'` keyword followed by an `ID`. There is no rule defining `ID` in our grammar because that is one of the rules that we inherit from the `Terminals`.

The parsed `ID` will be assigned to the feature `name` of the parsed `Entity` model element.

 If you are curious to know how an `ID` is defined, you can *Ctrl + click* or press *F3*, on the `ID` in the Xtext editor, and that will bring you to the grammar `Terminals`, where you can see that an `ID` starts with an optional `'^'` character, followed by a letter (`'a'..'z'|'A'..'Z'`), a `'$'` character, or an underscore `'_'` followed by any number of letters, `'$'` characters, underscores, and numbers (`'0'..'9'`):

```
'^'? ('a'..'z'|'A'..'Z'|'$'|'_')  ('a'..'z'|'A'..
'Z'|'$'|'_'|'0'..'9')*;
```

The optional `'^'` character is used to escape an identifier if there are conflicts with existing keywords.

The `( )?` operator declares an optional part. Therefore, after the `ID`, you can write the keyword `extends` and the name of an `Entity`. This illustrates one of the powerful features of Xtext, that is, **cross-references**. In fact, what we want after the keyword `extends` is not just a name, but the name of an existing `Entity`. This is expressed in the grammar using square brackets and the type we want to refer to. Xtext will automatically resolve the cross-reference by searching in the program for an element of that type (in our case, an `Entity`) with the given name. If it cannot find it, it will automatically issue an error. Note that, in order for this mechanism to work, the referred element must have a feature called `name`. As we will see in the following section, the automatic code completion mechanism will also take into consideration cross-references, thus proposing elements to refer to.

By default, cross-references and their resolutions are based on the feature name and on an ID. This behavior can be customized as we will see in *Chapter 10, Scoping*.

Then, the curly brackets '{' '}' are expected and within them Attribute elements can be specified (recall the meaning of += and *). These Attribute elements will be stored in the attributes feature of the corresponding Entity object.

The shape of Attribute elements is expressed in its own rule:

```
Attribute:
    type=[Entity] array?=('[]')? name=ID ';';
```

The rule for Attribute requires an Entity name (as explained previously, this is a cross-reference) that will be stored in the type feature and an ID that will be stored in the name feature of the attribute. It must also be terminated with ;. Note that, after the type, an optional '[]' can be specified. In this case, the type of the attribute is considered an array type, and the feature array will be true. This feature is boolean since we used the ?= assign operator, and after such an operator, we specify an optional part.

Let's try the Editor

At the end of *Chapter 1, Implementing a DSL*, we saw how to run the Xtext generator. You should follow the same steps, but instead of right-clicking on the .xtext file and navigating to **Run As | Generate Xtext Artifacts**, we right-click on the .mwe2 file (in our example it is GenerateEntities.mwe2) and navigate to **Run As | MWE2 Workflow**. (Refer to *Chapter 1, Implementing a DSL*, concerning the additional downloaded JAR file, and for the tip to avoid that).

After the generation has finished and after Eclipse has built the entire workspace, we can run a new Eclipse instance to try our DSL (refer to *Chapter 1, Implementing a DSL*, for the procedure to run a new Eclipse instance).

A new Eclipse instance will be run and a new workbench will appear. In this instance, our Entities DSL implementation is available. So, let's create a new general project (call it, for instance, `sample`). Inside this project, create a new file. The name of the file is not important, but the file extension must be `entities` (remember that this was the extension we chose in the **Xtext Project** wizard). As soon as the file is created, it will also be opened in a text editor, and you will be asked to convert the project to an Xtext project. You should accept that to make your DSL editor work correctly in Eclipse.

The editor is empty, but there is no error since an empty program is a valid Entities program (remember how the `Model` rule was defined with the cardinality `*`). If you access content assist, with *Ctrl + Space*, you will get no proposal. Instead, the `entity` keyword is inserted for you. This is because the generated content assist is smart enough to know that in that particular program context there is only one valid thing to do — start with the keyword `entity`.

After that you get an error (refer to the following screenshot), since the entity definition is still incomplete. You can see that the syntax error tells you that an identifier is expected instead of the end of file:

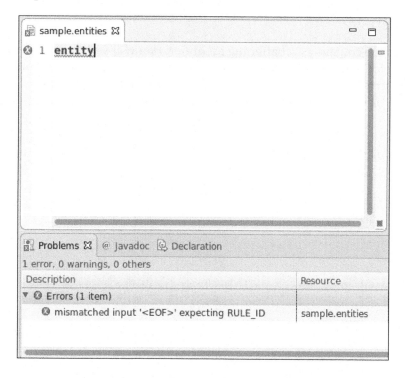

If you access the content assist again, you will get a hint that an identifier is expected (refer to the following screenshot), so let's write an identifier:

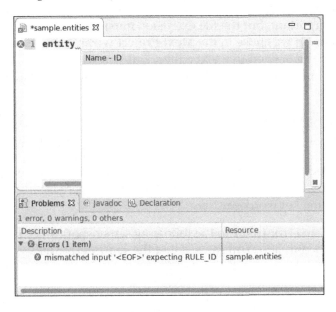

If you access the content assist after the identifier, you will see that you get two proposals (refer to the following screenshot). Again, the generated content assist knows that, in that program context, you can continue either with an extends specification or with an open curly bracket. Refer to the following screenshot:

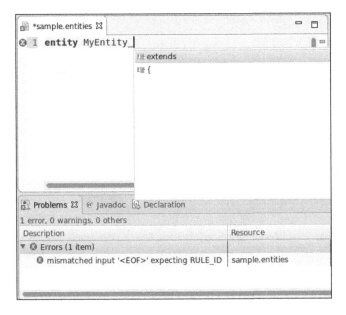

If you choose the open curly bracket, {, and press *ENTER*, you will note some interesting things in the generated editor (refer to the following screenshot):

- The editor automatically inserts the corresponding closing curly bracket.
- Inserting a newline between the brackets correctly performs indentation and moves the cursor to the right position.
- The folding on the left of the editor is automatically handled.
- The error marker turned gray, meaning that the problems in the current program are solved, but it has not been saved yet. Saving the file makes the error marker go away and the **Problems** view becomes empty.

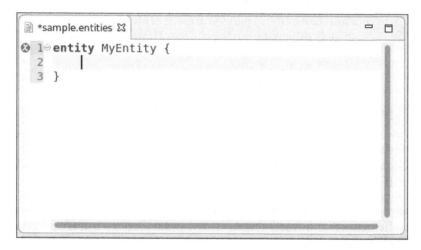

Continue experimenting with the editor. In particular, in the context where an entity reference is expected, that is, after the `extends` keyword or when declaring an attribute, you will see that the content assist will provide you with all the `Entity` elements defined in the current program.

> We should not allow an `entity` to extend itself. Moreover, the hierarchy should be acyclic. However, there is no way to express these constraints in the grammar. These issues have to be dealt with by implementing a custom `Validator` (*Chapter 4, Validation*) or a custom Scoping mechanism (*Chapter 10, Scoping*).

We would also like to stress that all these mechanisms, which are quite hard to implement manually, have been automatically generated by Xtext starting from the grammar definition of our DSL.

The Xtext generator

Xtext uses the **MWE2 (Modeling Workflow Engine 2)** DSL to configure the generation of its artifacts. The generated .mwe2 file already comes with good defaults; thus, for the moment, we will not modify it. However, it is interesting to know that by tweaking this file we can request the Xtext generator to generate support for additional features, as we will see later in this book.

 In order to deal with additional platforms besides Eclipse, such as IntelliJ and Web editors (*Chapter 11, Continuous Integration*), in Xtext 2.9, a brand new generator infrastructure has been introduced, which also aims at simplifying the overall configuration of the generated artifacts. This new generator is completely different from the old one. However, the old generator is still present in Xtext so that projects created before Xtext 2.9 still work and do not need to migrate to the new generator immediately. This book will always use the new generator.

During the MWE2 workflow execution, Xtext will generate artifacts related to the UI editor for your DSL, but most important of all, it will derive an ANTLR specification from the Xtext grammar with all the actions to create the AST while parsing. The classes for the nodes of the AST will be generated using the EMF framework (as explained in the next section).

The generator must be run after every modification to the grammar (the .xtext file). The whole generator infrastructure relies on the **Generation Gap Pattern** (*Vlissides* 1996). Indeed, code generators are fine, but when you have to customize the generated code, subsequent generations may overwrite your customizations. The Generation Gap Pattern deals with this problem by separating the code that is generated (and can be overwritten) from the code that you can customize (without the risk of being overwritten). In Xtext, the generated code is placed in the source folder src-gen (this holds for all the Xtext projects). What is inside that source folder should never be modified, since on the next generation it will be deleted and rewritten. The programmer can instead safely modify everything in the source folder src. On the first generation, Xtext will also generate a few **stub classes** in the source folder src to help the programmer with a starting point. These classes are never regenerated and can thus safely be edited without the risk of being overwritten by the generator. Some stub classes inherit from default classes from the Xtext library, while other stub classes inherit from classes that are in src-gen.

Most generated stub classes in the `src` folder are **Xtend** classes. The Xtend programming language will be introduced in the next chapter, thus, for the moment, we will not look at these stub classes.

There is one exception to the previously described generation strategy, which concerns the `plugin.xml` file (in the runtime and in the UI plugins); further Xtext generations will generate the file `plugin.xml_gen` in the root directory of your projects. It is up to you to check whether something has changed by comparing it with `plugin.xml`. In that case, you should manually merge the differences. This can be easily done using Eclipse: select the two files, right-click on them, and navigate to **Compare With | Each Other**, as illustrated in the following screenshot:

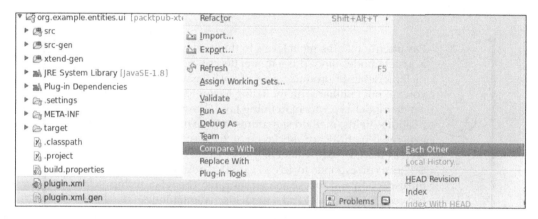

In general, checking the differences between `plugin.xml` and `plugin.xml_gen` is only needed either when you have modified the `.mwe2` file or when you are using a new version of Xtext, which can introduce new features. If you add something to the `plugin.xml` file, in order to facilitate the comparison, it is best practice to append your custom additions to the end of the file.

Finally, after running the MWE2 workflow, since the grammar has changed, new classes can be introduced or some existing classes can be modified. Thus, it is necessary to restart the other Eclipse instance where you are testing your editor.

The Eclipse Modeling Framework (EMF)

The **EMF (Eclipse Modeling Framework)** (*Steinberg et al*, 2008), `http://www.eclipse.org/modeling/emf`, provides code generation facilities for building tools and applications based on structured data models. Most of the Eclipse projects that in some way deal with modeling are based on EMF since it simplifies the development of complex software applications with its mechanisms. The model specification (**metamodel**) can be described in XMI, XML Schema, **Unified Modeling Language (UML)**, Rational Rose, or annotated Java. It is also possible to specify the metamodel programmatically using **Xcore**, which was implemented in Xtext. Typically, a metamodel is defined in the **Ecore** format, which is similar to an implementation of a subset of UML class diagrams.

Pay attention to the meta levels in this context—an `Ecore` model is a metamodel, since it is a model describing a model. Using the metamodel EMF produces a set of Java classes for the model. If you are not familiar with modeling technologies, you can think of a metamodel as a way of defining Java classes, that is, hierarchy relations, fields, method signatures, and so on. All Java classes generated by EMF are subclasses of `EObject`, which can be seen as the EMF equivalent of `java.lang.Object`. Similarly, `EClass` corresponds to `java.lang.Class` for dealing with introspection and reflection mechanisms. The relationship between a metamodel and a model is instantiation.

Xtext relies on EMF for creating the AST, Abstract Syntax Tree, which we talked about in *Chapter 1, Implementing a DSL*. From your grammar specification, Xtext will automatically infer the EMF metamodel for your language. You can refer to the Xtext documentation for all the details about metamodel inference. For the moment, you can consider this simplified scenario—for each rule in your grammar, an EMF Java interface and the corresponding implementation class will be created with a field for each feature in the rule, together with a `getter` and `setter`. For instance, for the `Entity` rule, we will have the corresponding Java interface (and the corresponding implementation Java class):

```
public interface Entity extends EObject {
  String getName();
  void setName(String value);
  Entity getSuperType();
  void setSuperType(Entity value);
  EList<Attribute> getAttributes();
}
```

Since these Java artifacts are generated, they are placed in the corresponding package in the src-gen folder. Refer to the following screenshot, where you can also see some expanded Java interfaces generated by EMF:

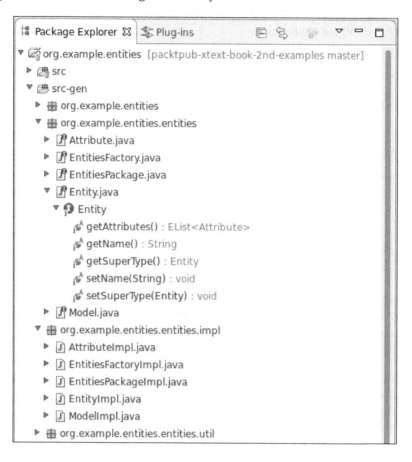

The generated EMF metamodel is placed in the directory `model/generated`. You can have a look at the generated `Entities.ecore` by opening it with the default EMF Ecore editor. Although you may not know the details of the description of a metamodel in EMF, it should be quite straightforward to grasp the meaning of it. Refer to the following screenshot:

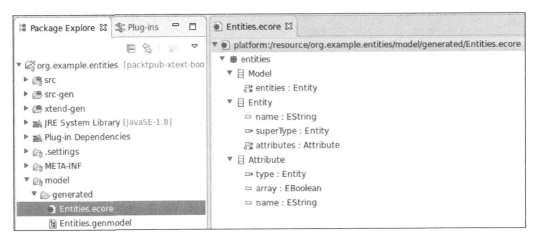

The inference of the metamodel and the corresponding EMF code generation is handled transparently and automatically by Xtext. However, Xtext can also use an existing metamodel that you maintain yourself. We will show an example of a DSL with a manually maintained metamodel in *Chapter 13*, *Advanced Topics*.

Since the model of your DSL programs are generated as instances of these generated EMF Java classes, a basic knowledge of EMF is required. As soon as you have to perform additional constraint checks for your DSL and to generate code, you will need to inspect this model and traverse it.

It is easy to use the generated Java classes since they follow conventions. In particular, instances of EMF classes must be created through a static factory, which results from EMF generation itself, thus, there is no constructor to use. Initialization of fields, that is, features, is performed using getters and setters. A collection in EMF implements the `EList` interface, which is an extension of the standard library `java.util.List`. With only these notions in mind, it is easy to programmatically manipulate the model of your program. For instance, this Java snippet programmatically creates an `Entities` model that corresponds to an `Entities` DSL program:

```java
import org.example.entities.entities.Attribute;
import org.example.entities.entities.EntitiesFactory;
import org.example.entities.entities.Entity;
import org.example.entities.entities.Model;
```

```
public class EntitiesEMFExample {

  public static void main(String[] args) {
    EntitiesFactory factory = EntitiesFactory.eINSTANCE;

    Entity superEntity = factory.createEntity();
    superEntity.setName("MySuperEntity");

    Entity entity = factory.createEntity();
    entity.setName("MyEntity");
    entity.setSuperType(superEntity);

    Attribute attribute = factory.createAttribute();
    attribute.setName("myattribute");
    attribute.setArray(false);
    attribute.setType(superEntity);

    entity.getAttributes().add(attribute);

    Model model = factory.createModel();
    model.getEntities().add(superEntity);
    model.getEntities().add(entity);
  }
}
```

EMF is easy to to learn, but as with any powerful tool, there is much to learn to fully master it. As hinted previously, EMF is widely used in the Eclipse world; thus you can consider it as an investment.

Improvements to the DSL

Now that we have a working DSL, we can do some improvements and modifications to the grammar.

After every modification to to the grammar, as we said in the section *The Xtext generator*, we must run the MWE2 workflow so that Xtext will generate the new ANTLR parser and the updated EMF classes.

First of all, while experimenting with the editor, you might have noted that

```
MyEntity[] myattribute;
```

is a valid statement of our DSL, while the one below (note the spaces between the square brackets):

```
MyEntity[  ] myattribute;
```

produces a syntax error.

This is not good, since we do not want spaces to be relevant (although there are languages such as Python and Haskell where spaces are indeed relevant).

The problem is due to the fact that, in the `Attribute` rule, we specified `[]`, thus, no space is allowed between the square brackets; we can modify the rule as follows:

```
Attribute: type=[Entity] (array?='[' ']')? name=ID ';';
```

Since we split the two square brackets into two separate tokens, spaces between the brackets are allowed in the editor. Indeed, spaces are automatically discarded, unless they are explicit in the token definition. In general, spaces in keywords should be avoided.

> Xtext 2.8 introduced support for whitespace-aware languages, where whitespaces, for example indentations, are used to specify the structure of programs (such as in Python). We will not describe this feature in this book. We refer the interested reader to the Xtext documentation and to the example language **Home Automation** that ships with Xtext.

We can further refine the array specification in our DSL by allowing an optional length:

```
Attribute:
    type=[Entity] (array ?='[' (length=INT)? ']')? name=ID ';';
```

There is no rule defining `INT` in our grammar—we inherit this rule from the grammar `Terminals`. As you can imagine, `INT` requires a positive integer literal, thus the `length` feature in our model will have an integer type as well. Since the `length` feature is optional (note the question mark), both the following `attribute` definitions will be valid statements of our DSL:

```
MyEntity[ ] a;
MyEntity[10] b;
```

When the length is not specified, the `length` feature will hold the default integer value (`0`).

Dealing with types

The way we defined the concept of an `AttributeType` is not conceptually correct, since the `array` feature is part of `Attribute` when it should be something that concerns only the type of `Attribute`.

We can then specify the concept of `AttributeType` in a separate rule, which will also result in a new EMF class in our `model`:

```
Attribute:
  type=AttributeType name=ID ';';

AttributeType:
  entity=[Entity] (array ?='[' (length=INT)? ']')?;
```

If you run the MWE2 workflow, you will note no difference in your DSL editor, but the metamodel for your AST has changed. For example, consider this part of `EntitiesEMFExample` that we showed previously:

```
Attribute attribute = factory.createAttribute();
attribute.setName("myattribute");
attribute.setArray(false);
attribute.setType(superEntity);
```

This is no longer valid Java code and has to be changed as follows:

```
Attribute attribute = factory.createAttribute();
attribute.setName("myattribute");
AttributeType attributeType = factory.createAttributeType();
attributeType.setArray(false);
attributeType.setLength(10);
attributeType.setEntity(superEntity);
attribute.setType(attributeType);
```

As a further enhancement to our DSL, we would like to have some basic types—at the moment, only entities can be used as types. For instance, let's assume that our DSL provides three basic types—`string`, `int`, and `boolean`. Therefore, a basic type is represented by its literal representation. On the contrary, an `EntityType` (the only type concept we have used up to now) is actually a reference to an existing `Entity`. Furthermore, we want to be able to declare arrays both of `BasicType` and of `EntityType`.

For these reasons, the `array` feature still belongs to `AttributeType`, but we need to abstract over `elementType`. Thus, we modify the grammar as follows:

```
AttributeType:
  elementType=ElementType (array ?='[' (length=INT)? ']')?;

ElementType:
  BasicType | EntityType;

BasicType:
```

```
    typeName=('string'|'int'|'boolean');

EntityType:
    entity=[Entity];
```

As you can see, we introduce a rule, `ElementType`, which in turn relies on two alternative mutually exclusive rules: `BasicType` and `EntityType`. Alternative rules are separated using the pipe operator `|`. Note that rules such as `ElementType`, which delegates to other alternative rules, implicitly introduce an inheritance relation in the generated EMF classes. Thus, both `BasicType` and `EntityType` inherit from `ElementType`. In the `BasicType` rule, the string feature `typeName` will contain the corresponding keyword entered in the program.

After running the MWE2 workflow, you can try your editor and see that now you can also use the three basic types. Furthermore, in a context where a type specification is expected, the content assist will present all possible `elementType` alternatives, both `entity` types and `BasicType`. Refer to the following screenshot:

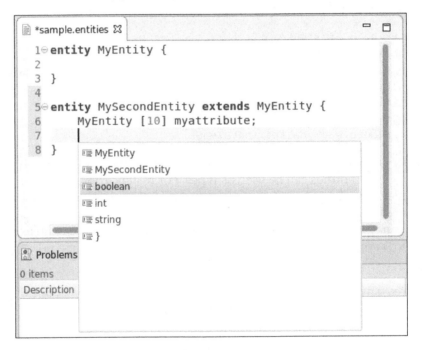

> In general, it is better not to rely on hardcoded alternatives in the grammar such as the `BasicType` we used previously. Instead, it would be better to provide a standard library for the DSL with some predefined types and functions. An application of this technique will be presented in *Chapter 10, Scoping*.

Now that our EMF model has changed again, we need to change our
`EntitiesEMFExample` class accordingly as follows:

```
Attribute attribute = factory.createAttribute();
attribute.setName("myattribute");
AttributeType attributeType = factory.createAttributeType();
attributeType.setArray(false);
attributeType.setLength(10);
EntityType entityType = factory.createEntityType();
entityType.setEntity(superEntity);
attributeType.setElementType(entityType);
attribute.setType(attributeType);
```

If you reopen the generated **Entities.ecore**, you can see the current metamodel for
the AST of our DSL (note the inheritance relations — `BasicType` and `EntityType`
inherit from `ElementType`). Refer to the following screenshot:shot:

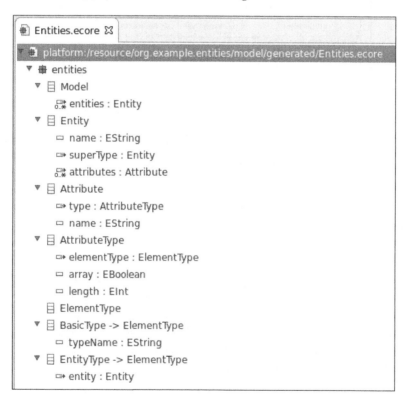

The preceding EMF metamodel can also be represented with a graphical notation following UML-like conventions. Refer to the following diagram:

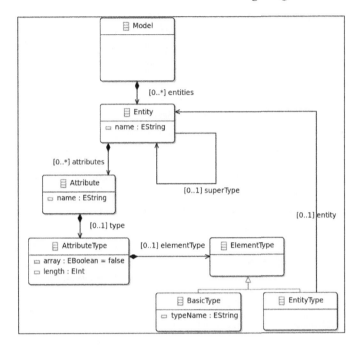

We now have enough features in the Entities DSL to start dealing with additional tasks typical of language implementation. We will be using this example DSL in the upcoming chapters.

Summary

In this chapter, you learned how to implement a simple DSL with Xtext and you saw that, starting from a grammar definition, Xtext automatically generates many artifacts for the DSL, including IDE tooling.

You also started to learn the EMF API that allows you to programmatically manipulate a model representing a program AST. Being able to programmatically access models is crucial to perform additional checks on a program that has been parsed and also to perform code generation, as we will see in the rest of the book.

In the next chapter, we will introduce the programming language Xtend, which is shipped with Xtext and is implemented in Xtext itself. Xtend is a Java-like general purpose programming language, completely inter-operable with Java that allows you to write much simpler and much cleaner programs. We will use Xtend in the rest of the book to implement all the aspects of Xtext languages.

3
Working with the Xtend Programming Language

In this chapter, we will introduce the Xtend programming language, a fully featured general purpose Java-like language that is completely interoperable with Java. Xtend has a more concise syntax than Java and provides powerful features such as type inference, extension methods, dispatch methods, and lambda expressions, not to mention multiline template expressions, which are useful when writing code generators. All the aspects of a DSL implemented in Xtext can be implemented in Xtend instead of Java, since it is easier to use and allows you to write better readable code. Since Xtend is completely interoperable with Java, you can reuse all the Java libraries. Moreover, all the Eclipse **JDT** (**Java Development Tools**) will work with Xtend seamlessly.

This chapter will cover the following topics:

* An introduction to the Xtend programming language
* A description of the main features of Xtend, which we will use throughout the book

An introduction to Xtend

The Xtend programming language comes with very nice documentation, which can be found on its website, https://www.eclipse.org/xtend/documentation/. We will give an overview of Xtend in this chapter, but we strongly suggest that you then go through the Xtend documentation thoroughly. Xtend itself is implemented in Xtext and it is a proof of concept of how involved a language implemented in Xtext can be.

We will use Xtend throughout this book to write all parts of a DSL implementation. Namely, we will use it to customize UI features, to write tests, to implement constraint checks, and to write code generators or interpreters for all the example DSLs we will develop in this book. In particular, all the stub classes generated by Xtext for your DSL projects are Xtend classes.

You can still generate Java stub classes by customizing the MWE2 workflow, but in this book, we will always use Xtend classes. Xtend, besides providing useful mechanisms for writing code generators, for example, multiline template expressions, also provides powerful features that make model visiting and traversing really easy, straightforward, and natural to read and maintain. Indeed, besides the grammar definition, for the rest of the time when implementing a DSL, you will have to visit the AST model. Xtend programs are translated into Java, and Xtend code can access all the Java libraries; thus Xtend and Java can cooperate seamlessly.

> Xtend is a general-purpose programming language, which can be used independently from Xtext language development. In particular, Xtend can be used as an alternative to Java or together with Java for any kind of Java application development, including web applications and Android applications.

Using Xtend in your projects

All the Eclipse projects generated by the Xtext wizard are already setup to use Xtend. However, in this chapter, in order to give an introduction to the language, we will use Xtend independently from Xtext language development.

You can use Xtend in your Eclipse Java projects (both plain Java and plugin projects). Let's now create an Eclipse plugin project where we will write a few Xtend examples. Perform the following steps:

1. Start Eclipse, navigate to **File | New | Project...**, and select **Plug-in Project**.

2. In the next dialog, you should specify the following **Project name:** `org.example.xtend.examples`.

3. Press **Next**, and unselect the checkboxes **Generate an Activator** and **This plugin will make contributions to the UI**.

4. Press **Finish**. If asked to switch to the **Plug-in Development perspective**, choose **Yes**.

In order to create a new Xtend file, for example, an **Xtend Class**, right-click on your source folder and select **New | Xtend Class**. You will see that this wizard is similar to the standard New Java Class wizard, so you can choose the **Package**, the class **Name**, **Superclass**, and **Interfaces**. Refer to the following screenshot:

As soon as the class is created, you will get an error marker with the message `Couldn't find the mandatory library org.eclipse.xtext.xbase.lib 2.8.0 or higher on the project's classpath`. You just need to use the quickfix `Add Xtend libs to classpath` and the required Xtend bundles will be added to your project's dependencies. The quickfix can be accessed by clicking on the error marker in the editor's left ruler.

A new source folder will be created in your plugin project, xtend-gen, where the Java code corresponding to your Xtend code will be automatically generated as soon as you save an .xtend file. Just like src-gen created by the Xtext generator (as seen in the previous chapter), the files in xtend-gen must not be modified by the programmer, since they will be overwritten by the Xtend compiler.

> The folder xtend-gen is not automatically added to the build source folders of your plug-in project, and therefore you should add it manually in your build.properties file. The file has a warning marker and the editor will provide you with a quickfix to add that folder. This is required only for plug-in projects.

You can use the same steps to create an Xtend class in a plain Java project. Also in this case, you will have to use the quickfix to add the Xtend libraries to the classpath. Of course, in this case, there is no build.properties to adjust in plain Java projects.

Xtend – a better Java with less "noise"

Xtend is a statically typed language and it uses the Java type system, including Java generics and Java annotations. Thus, Xtend and Java are completely interoperable.

Most of the linguistic concepts of Xtend are very similar to Java, that is, classes, interfaces, and methods. One of the goals of Xtend is to have a less "*noisy*" version of Java. Indeed, in Java, some linguistic features are redundant and only make programs more verbose.

The Xtend Eclipse editor supports the typical features of the Eclipse Java editor, including templates. Thus, we can create a main method inside the previously created Xtend class as shown in the following screenshot, using the content assist template proposal:

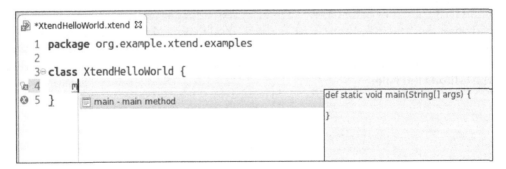

Let's write the "Hello World" print statement in Xtend:

```
package org.example.xtend.examples

class XtendHelloWorld {
  def static void main(String[] args) {
    println("Hello World")
  }
}
```

You can see that it is similar to Java, though the removal of *syntactic noise* is already evident by the fact that terminating semicolons (;) are optional in Xtend. All method declarations start with either `def` or `override` (explained later in the chapter). Methods are `public` by default.

Note that the editor works almost the same as the one provided by JDT. You may also want to take a look at the generated Java class in the `xtend-gen` folder corresponding to the Xtend class.

Although it is usually not required to see the generated Java code, it might be helpful, especially when starting to use Xtend, to see what is generated in order to learn Xtend's new constructs. Instead of manually opening the generated Java file, you can open the Xtend **Generated Code** view. The contents of this view will show the generated Java code, in particular, the code corresponding to the section of the Xtend file you are editing. This view will be updated when the Xtend file is saved.

Since the Xtend class we have just written contains a `main` method, we can execute it. Instead of running the generated Java class, we can directly execute the generated Java class by right-clicking on the Xtend file and navigate to **Run As | Java Application**. The output will be shown, as usual, in the **Console** view.

Types

Class and interface declarations in Xtend are similar to Java syntax, but all Xtend types are `public` by default. Moreover, in Xtend, you can declare multiple public top-level types per file, and they will be compiled into separate Java files. **Inheritance** and **interface implementation** are just the same as in Java. All Xtend classes implicitly extend `java.lang.Object`.

Package declarations in Xtend work as in Java.

In an Xtend class you can define any number of constructors, using the keyword `new`, without repeating the name of the class. Constructors support the same accessibility modifiers as in Java, but they are `public` by default:

```
class MyFirstXtendClass {
  new () {
    ...
  }
  new (String s) {
    ...
  }
}
```

Xtend supports also static **nested classes** and **anonymous inner classes**. Moreover, it supports **annotation** (see `https://eclipse.org/xtend/documentation/204_activeannotations.html`) and **enum** declarations. We will not use such declarations in this book though.

Methods

Method declarations start with either `def` or `override` and are `public` by default. The usual method Java modifiers are available in Xtend.

Xtend is stricter concerning method overriding: if a subclass overrides a method, it must explicitly define that method with `override` instead of `def`, otherwise a compilation error is raised. This will avoid accidental method overrides; that is, you did not intend to provide an overridden version of a method of a superclass. Even more importantly, if the method that is being overridden later is removed.

For example, the following method definition will raise a compiler error, since we should have used `override` instead of `def`:

```
class MyFirstXtendClass {
  def String toString() { // toString() is defined in java.lang.Object
    return ""
  }
}
```

In Xtend there are no statements, since **everything is an expression**. In a method body, the last expression is the **return expression**, and an explicit `return` statement is optional.

The `return` type of a method can be omitted if it can be inferred from the method body. Of course, if the `return` type is specified, then the method body `return` expression must be compliant with the specified `return` type.

For example, all the following method definitions are valid in Xtend:

```
class MyFirstXtendClass {
  def m1() {
    ""
  }
  def String m2() {
    ""
  }
  def m3() {
    return ""
  }
  def String m4() {
    return ""
  }
}
```

> If your Xtend code is meant to be used as API, it is advisable to always specify the return type of the public methods explicitly. This will make your intentions clearer to your users and will avoid inadvertently breaking the API if you change the method body.

The type of method parameters must always be specified, since it cannot be inferred automatically.

Method parameters are always implicitly final in Xtend, and there is no way of specifying a method parameter as non-final.

Fields and Variables

Fields and local variables are declared using val (for **final** fields and variables) and var (for **non-final** fields and variables). Fields are **private** by default. Standard Java accessibility modifiers are available for fields. The type of fields and variables can be omitted and it is inferred from the context, not only from the initialization expression. Of course, final fields and variables must be initialized in the declaration. The standard Java syntax for field definition is also supported, but in this case the type must be declared explicitly.

Here are some examples of Xtend variable declarations:

```
val s = 'my variable' // final variable
var myList = new LinkedList<Integer> // non final variable, type
inferred
val aList = newArrayList
aList += "" // now the type of aList is inferred as ArrayList<String>
```

Note that, in the preceding example, `aList` is inferred as `ArrayList<String>` from its usage, not from the initialization expression.

> Text hovering the Xtend elements in the editor will give you information about the inferred types.

Operators

The semantics of Xtend operators differ slightly from Java. In particular `==` actually compares the values of the objects by mapping the operator to the method `equals`. To achieve the Java semantics of object identifier equality, you must use the triple equality operator: `===`.

Standard arithmetic operators are extended to lists with the expected meaning. For example, when executing the following code:

```
val l1 = newArrayList("a")
l1 += "b"
val l2 = newArrayList("c")
val l3 = l1 + l2
println(l3)
```

The string `[a, b, c]` will be printed.

Syntactic sugar

Xtend provides some *syntactic sugar*, that is, syntax that is designed to write code which is easier to read, for `getter` and `setter` methods. For example, instead of writing, `o.getName()`, you can simply write `o.name`. Similarly, instead of writing `o.setName("...")`, you can simply write `o.name = "..."`. The same convention applies for boolean fields according to JavaBeans conventions, where the `getter` method starts with `is` instead of `get`. Similar syntactic sugar is available for method invocations so that, when a method has no parameter, the parenthesis can be avoided.

Static members and inner types

Access to static members (fields and methods) of types is specified in Xtend, just like in Java, using the dot (.). Refer to the following code snippet:

import java.util.Collections

```
class StaticMethods {
  def static void main(String[] args) {
    val list = Collections.emptyList
    System.out.println(list)
  }
}
```

The same holds for `inner` types (classes and interfaces). For example, given this Xtend class, with an `inner` interface:

```
class MyXtendClass {
  interface MyInnerInterface {
    public static String s = "s";
  }
}
```

We can access the `inner` interface in Xtend using the following syntax:

```
MyXtendClass.MyInnerInterface
```

> In older versions of Xtend, access to `static` members had to be specified using the operator `::`, for example, `System::out.println()`. Access to inner types had to be specified using the operator `$`, for example, `MyXtendClass$MyInnerInterface`. Since this syntax is still valid in Xtend, you may happen to see that in old Xtend programs.

Literals

Literals are specified in Xtend as in Java but for a few exceptions.

References to a type, that is, a **type literal**, is expressed in Xtend simply with the type name (instead, in Java, you need to use the class name followed by `.class`). Type literals can also be specified using the keyword `typeof`, with the type name as an argument, for example, `typeof(String)`. For references to array types, you must use the latter syntax, for example, `typeof(String[])`.

In Xtend (and in general, by default, in any DSL implemented with Xtext using the default terminals grammar), strings can be specified both with single and double quotes. This allows the programmer to choose the preferred format depending on the string contents so that quotes inside the string do not have to be escaped, for example:

```
val s1 = "my 'string'"
val s2 = 'my "string"'
```

Escaping is still possible using the backslash character \ as in Java.

Xtend supports **collection literals** to create immutable collections and arrays. List or array literals are specified using the syntax #[...]. Whether a list or an array is created depends on the target type:

```
val aList = #["a", "b"] // creates a list of strings
val String[] anArray = #["a", "b"] // creates an array of strings
```

Immutable sets are created with the syntax #{...}. Finally, an immutable map is created like this:

```
val aMap = #{"a" -> 0, "b" -> 1} // creates a Map<String, Integer>
```

Extension methods

Extension methods is a syntactic sugar mechanism that allows you to add new methods to existing types without modifying them. Instead of passing the first argument inside the parentheses of a method invocation, the method can be called with the first argument as its receiver. It is as if the method was one of the argument type's members.

For example, if m(Entity) is an extension method, and e is of type Entity, you can write e.m() instead of m(e), even though m is not a method defined in Entity.

Using extension methods often results in a more readable code, since method calls are chained; for example, o.foo().bar() rather than nested, for example, bar(foo(o)).

Xtend provides several ways to make methods available as extension methods, as described in this section.

Xtend provides a rich runtime library with several utility classes and static methods. These static methods are automatically available in Xtend code so that you can use all of them as extension methods. They aim at enhancing the functionality of standard types and collections.

Of course, the editor also provides code completion for `extension` methods so that you can experiment with the code assistant. These utility classes aim at enhancing the functionality of standard types and collections.

 Extension methods are highlighted in orange in the Xtend editor.

```
"my string".toFirstUpper
```

For example, the above code is equivalent to this code:

```
StringExtensions.toFirstUpper("my string")
```

Similarly, you can use some utility methods for collections, for example, `head` and `last` as in the following code:

```
val list =
newArrayList("a", "b", "c")
println(list.head) // prints a
println(list.last) // prints b
```

You can also use `static` methods from existing Java utility classes (for example, `java.util.Collections`) as extension methods using a **static extension import** in an Xtend source file, for example:

```
import static extension java.util.Collections.*
```

In that Xtend file, all the static methods of `java.util.Collections` will then be available as extension methods.

Methods defined in an Xtend class can automatically be used as `extension` methods in that class, for example:

```
class ExtensionMethods {
  def myListMethod(List<?> list) {
    // some implementation
  }

  def m() {
    val list = new ArrayList<String>
    list.myListMethod
  }
}
```

Finally, by adding the extension keyword to a field, a local variable, or a parameter declaration, its instance methods become extension methods in that class, code block, or method body, respectively. For example, assume you have this class:

```
class MyListExtensions {

  def aListMethod(List<?> list) {
    // some implementation
  }

  def anotherListMethod(List<?> list) {
    // some implementation
  }
}
```

Here you want to use its methods as extension methods in another class, C. Then, in C, you can declare an extension field (that is, a field declaration with the extension keyword) of type MyListExtensions, and in the methods of C, you can use the methods declared in MyListExtensions as extension methods:

```
class C {

  extension MyListExtensions e = new MyListExtensions

  def m() {
    val list = new ArrayList<String>
    list.aListMethod // equivalent to e.aListMethod(list)
    list.anotherListMethod // equivalent to e.anotherListMethod(list)
  }
```

As mentioned earlier, you can achieve the same goal by adding the keyword extension to a local variable:

```
def m() {
  val extension MyListExtensions e = new MyListExtensions
  val list = new ArrayList<String>
  list.aListMethod
  list.anotherListMethod
}
```

Alternatively, you can add it to a parameter declaration:

```
def m(extension MyListExtensions e) {
  val list = new ArrayList<String>
  list.aListMethod
  list.anotherListMethod
}
```

When declaring a field with the keyword `extension`, the name of the field is optional. The same holds true when declaring a local variable with the keyword `extension`.

The implicit variable – it

You know that, in Java, the special variable `this` is implicitly bound in a method to the object on which the method was invoked. The same holds true in Xtend. However, Xtend introduces another special variable `it`. While you cannot declare a variable or parameter with name `this`, you are allowed to do so using the name `it`. If in the current program context a declaration for `it` is available, then all the members of that variable are implicitly available, just like all the members of this are implicitly available in an instance method, for example:

```
class ItExamples {
  def trans1(String it) {
    toLowerCase // it.toLowerCase
  }

  def trans2(String s) {
    var it = s
    toLowerCase // it.toLowerCase
  }
}
```

This allows you to write a much more compact code.

Lambda expressions

A **lambda expression** (or **lambda** for short) defines an anonymous function. Lambda expressions are first class objects that can be passed to methods or stored in a variable for later evaluation.

Lambda expressions are typical of functional languages that existed long before object-oriented languages were designed. Therefore, as a linguistic mechanism, they are so old that it is quite strange that Java has provided them only since version 8. Java 8 has been available for some time now, so we assume that you are familiar with Java 8 lambdas. Xtend has been supporting lambda expressions since the very beginning, and Xtend lambdas have a more compact form as we will show in the rest of this section.

When using Java 8, Xtend translates its lambda expressions into Java lambda expressions. When using previous versions of Java, Xtend translates its lambda expressions into Java anonymous inner classes. This is all transparent for the end user.

Xtend lambda expressions are declared using square brackets []; parameters and the actual body are separated by a pipe symbol, |. The body of the lambda is executed by calling its `apply` method and passing the needed arguments.

The following code defines a lambda expression that is assigned to a local variable, taking a string and an integer as parameters and returning the string concatenation of the two. It then evaluates the lambda expression passing the two arguments:

```
val l = [ String s, int i | s + i ]
println(l.apply("s", 10))
```

Xtend also introduces types for lambda expressions (**function types**). Parameter types (enclosed in parentheses) are separated from the `return` type by the symbol =>. Generic types can be fully exploited when defining function types. For example, the preceding declaration could have been written with an explicit type as follows:

```
val (String, int)=>String l = [ String s, int i | s + i ]
```

Recall that Xtend has powerful type inference mechanisms—variable type declarations can be omitted when the context provides enough information. In the preceding declaration, we made the type of the lambda expression explicit, thus the types of parameters of the lambda expression are redundant since they can be inferred:

```
val (String, int)=>String l = [ s, i | s + i ]
```

Function types are useful when declaring methods that take a lambda expression as a parameter (remember that the types of parameters must always be specified), for example:

```
def execute((String, int)=>String f) {
  f.apply("s", 10)
}
```

We can then pass a lambda expression as an argument to this method. When we pass a lambda as an argument to this method, there is enough information to fully infer the types of its parameters, which allows us to omit these declarations:

```
execute([s, i | s + i])
```

A lambda expression also captures the local variables and parameters defined in the current program context. All such variables and parameters can be used within the lambda expression's body. Recall that in Xtend all method parameters are automatically `final`.

Thus, when evaluated, a lambda expression is *closed* over the environment in which it was defined: the referenced variables and parameters of the enclosing context are captured by the lambda expression. For this reason, lambda expressions are often referred to as **closures**.

For example, consider the following code:

```
package org.example.xtend.examples
class LambdaExamples {
  def static execute((String,int)=>String f) {
    f.apply("s", 10)
  }
  def static void main(String[] args) {
    val c = "aaa"
    println(execute([ s, i | s + i + c ])) // prints s10aaa
  }
}
```

You can see that the lambda expression uses the local variable c when it is defined, but the value of that variable is available even when it is evaluated.

> Formally, lambda expressions are a linguistic construct, while closures are an implementation technique. From another point of view, a lambda expression is a function literal definition while a closure is a function value. However, in most programming languages and in the literature, the two terms are often used interchangeably.

Although function types are not available in Java, Xtend can automatically perform the required conversions in the presence of Java **SAM (Single Abstract Method)** types, also known as Java **functional interfaces**. If a Java or Xtend method expects an instance of a SAM type, in Xtend, you can call that method by passing a lambda. Xtend will perform all the type checking and conversions.

For example, `java.util.Collections.sort` expects a `List<T>` and a `Comparator<T>`, which is a functional interface in Java 8, with the abstract method `int compare(T o1, T o2)`. In Xtend, we can pass a lambda that is compliant with such method, just like in Java:

```
val list = newArrayList("Second", "First", "Third")
Collections.sort(list,
  [ arg0, arg1 | arg0.compareToIgnoreCase(arg1) ])
```

Xtend infers the types of the parameters of the lambda automatically.

Xtend provides some additional syntactic sugar for lambdas to make code even more readable.

First of all, when a lambda is the last argument of a method invocation, it can be put outside the (...) parentheses (and if the invocation only requires one argument, the () can be omitted):

```
Collections.sort(list)[arg0, arg1 |
   arg0.compareToIgnoreCase(arg1)]
strings.findFirst[ s | s.startsWith("F") ]
```

Furthermore, the special symbol it we introduced earlier is also the default parameter name in a lambda expression. Thus, if the lambda has only one parameter, you can avoid specifying it and instead use it as the implicit parameter:

```
strings.findFirst[ it.startsWith("F") ]
```

Since all the members of it are implicitly available without using ".", you can simply write the following:

```
strings.findFirst[startsWith("F")]
```

This is even more readable.

If the parameters of a lambda can be inferred from the context, you can avoid specifying the parameter names. In that case, the lambda parameters are automatically available in the shape of $0, $1, and so on. For example, the code invoking Collections.sort can also be written as follows:

```
Collections.sort(list)[ $0.compareToIgnoreCase($1)]
```

Sophisticated data processing queries are easier to express in Xtend than in Java, since there is no need to use Java 8 **Streams**. For example, suppose you have the following list of Person (where Person is a class with string fields firstname, surname, and an integer field age):

```
personList = newArrayList(
   new Person("James", "Smith", 50),
   new Person("John", "Smith", 40),
   new Person("James", "Anderson", 40),
   new Person("John", "Anderson", 30),
   new Person("Paul", "Anderson", 30))
```

Here, you want to find the first three younger persons whose first name starts with J, and we want to print them as `surname, firstname` on the same line separated by `";  "`, thus, the resulting output should be (note: ; must be a separator):

```
Anderson, John; Smith, John; Anderson, James
```

In Xtend, with lambdas and extension methods, it is as simple as follows:

```
val result = personList.filter[firstname.startsWith("J")].
  sortBy[age].
  take(3).
  map[surname + ", " + firstname].
  join("; ")
println(result)
```

Multi-line template expressions

Besides traversing models, when writing a code generator, most of the time you will write strings that represent the generated code. Unfortunately, in Java, you cannot write multi-line string literals.

This actually results in two main issues: if the string must contain a newline character, you have to use the special character \n; if, for readability, you want to break the string literal in several lines, you have to concatenate the string parts with +. If you want to indent the generated code nicely, then things become even harder.

If you have to generate only a few lines, this might not be a big problem. However, a generator of a DSL usually needs to generate lots of lines.

Xtend provides multi-line template expressions to address all of the preceding issues (indeed, all strings in Xtend are multi-line).

For example, let's assume that you want to write a generator for generating some Java method definitions. The corresponding code generator written in Xtend using multi-line template expressions is shown in the following screenshot:

```
XtendCodeGenerator.xtend ⊠
 1  package org.example.xtend.examples
 2
 3  class XtendCodeGenerator {
 4      def generateBody(String name, String body) '''
 5          /* body of «name» */
 6          «body»
 7      '''
 8
 9      def generateMethod(String name, String body) '''
10          public void «name»() {
11              «generateBody(name, body)»
12          }
13      '''
14
15      def static void main(String[] args) {
16          val generator = new XtendCodeGenerator
17          println(generator.generateMethod("m",
18              '''
19                  System.out.println("Hello");
20                  return;
21              '''
22          ))
23      }
24  }
```

Before explaining the code, we must first mention that the final output is nicely formatted as it was meant to be, including indentation:

```
public void m() {
  /* body of m */
  System.out.println("Hello");
  return;
}
```

Template expressions are defined using triple single quotes (' ' '). This allows us to use double quotes directly without escaping them. Template expressions can span multiple lines, and a newline in the expression will correspond to a newline in the final output. Variable parts can be directly inserted in the expression using **guillemets** («», also known as **angle quotes** or **French quotation marks**). Note that between the guillemets, you can specify any expression and even invoke methods. You can also use conditional expressions and loops (we will see an example later in this book; you can refer to the documentation mentioned earlier in the introduction for all the details).

Curly brackets { } are optional for Xtend method bodies that only contain template expressions.

Another important feature of template expressions is that indentation is handled automatically and in a smart way. As you can see from the previous screenshot, the Xtend editor uses a specific syntax coloring strategy for multi-line template strings, in order to give you an idea of what the indentations will look like in the final output.

> To insert the guillemets in the Xtend Eclipse editor, you can use the keyboard shortcuts *Ctrl* + *Shift* + < and *Ctrl* + *Shift* + > for « and » respectively. On a Mac operating system, they are also available with *Alt* + *q* («) and *Alt* + *Q* (»). Alternatively, you can use content assist inside a template expression to insert a pair of them.

The drawback of guillemets is that you will have to have a consistent encoding, especially if you work in a team using different operating systems. You should always use **UTF-8** encoding for all the projects that use Xtend to make sure that the right encoding is stored in your project preferences (which is in turn saved on your versioning system, such as Git). You should right-click on the project and then select **Properties**, and in the **Resource** property, set the encoding explicitly. You must set this property before writing any Xtend code (changing the encoding later will change all the guillemets characters, and you will have to fix them all by hand). Systems such as Windows use a default encoding that is not available in other systems, such as Linux, while **UTF-8** is available everywhere. Refer to the following screenshot:

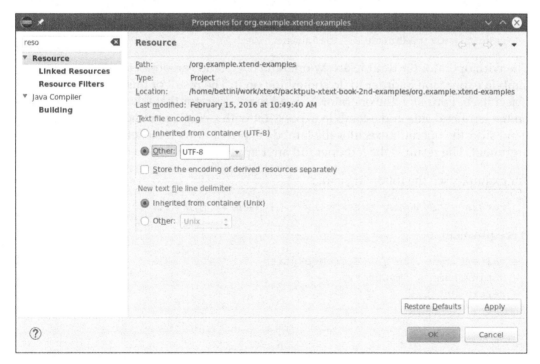

All the projects generated by the Xtext wizard are already created with the UTF-8 encoding. The encoding can also be changed by changing the corresponding property in the MWE2 file.

Additional operators

Besides standard operators, Xtend has additional operators that help to keep the code compact.

Quite often, you will have to check whether an object is not null before invoking a method on it; otherwise, you may want to return `null` or simply perform no operation. As you will see in DSL development, this is quite a recurrent situation. Xtend provides the operator "`?.`", which is the **null-safe** version of the standard selection operator (the dot `.`). Writing `o?.m` corresponds to `if (o != null) o.m`. This is particularly useful when you have cascade selections, for example, `o?.f?.m`.

The **Elvis** operator ("`?:`") is another convenient operator for dealing with default values in case of null instances. It has the following semantics: `x ?: y` returns `x` if it is not `null` and `y` otherwise.

Combining the two operators allows you to set up default values easily, for example:

```
// equivalent to: if (o != null) o.toString else 'default'
result = o?.toString ?: 'default'
```

The **with** operator (or **double arrow** operator), `=>`, binds an object to the scope of a lambda expression in order to do something on it. The result of this operator is the object itself. Formally, the operator `=>` is a binary operator that takes an expression on the left-hand side and a lambda expression with a single parameter on the right-hand side: the operator executes the lambda expression with the left-hand side as the argument. The result is the left operand after applying the lambda expression.

For example, see the following code:

```
return eINSTANCE.createEntity => [ name = "MyEntity"]
```

It is equivalent to:

```
val entity = eINSTANCE.createEntity
entity.name = "MyEntity"
return entity
```

This operator is extremely useful in combination with the implicit parameter `it` and the syntactic sugar for `getter` and `setter` methods to initialize a newly created object to be used in a further assignment without using temporary variables. As a demonstration, consider the Java code snippet we saw in *Chapter 2, Creating Your First Xtext Language*, that we used to build an `Entity` with an `Attribute` (with its type) that we will report here for convenience:

```
Entity entity = eINSTANCE.createEntity();
entity.setName("MyEntity");
entity.setSuperType(superEntity);
Attribute attribute = eINSTANCE.createAttribute();
attribute.setName("myattribute");
AttributeType attributeType = eINSTANCE.createAttributeType();
attributeType.setArray(false);
attributeType.setLength (10);
EntityType entityType = eINSTANCE.createEntityType();
entityType.setEntity(superEntity);
attributeType.setElementType(entityType);
attribute.setType(attributeType);
entity.getAttributes().add(attribute);
```

This requires many variables that are a huge distraction (are you able to get a quick idea of what the code does?). In Xtend, we can simply write the following:

```
eINSTANCE.createEntity => [
  name = "MyEntity"
  superType = superEntity
  attributes += eINSTANCE.createAttribute => [
    name = "myattribute"
    type = eINSTANCE.createAttributeType => [
      array = false
      length = 10
      elementType =  eINSTANCE.createEntityType => [
        entity = superEntity
      ]
    ]
  ]
]
```

 If you want to try the preceding code in the Xtend example project, you need to add as dependencies the bundles `org.example.entities` and `org.eclipse.emf.ecore`.

Polymorphic method invocation

Method overloading resolution in Java and in Xtend is a static mechanism, meaning that the selection of the specific method takes place according to the static type of the arguments. When you deal with objects belonging to a class hierarchy, this mechanism soon shows its limitation you will probably write methods that manipulate multiple polymorphic objects through references to their base classes, but since static overloading only uses the static type of those references, having multiple variants of those methods will not suffice. With **polymorphic method invocation** (also known as **multiple dispatch** or **dynamic overloading**), the method selection takes place according to the runtime type of the arguments.

Xtend provides **Dispatch Methods** for polymorphic method invocation; upon invocation, overloaded methods marked as dispatch are selected according to the runtime type of the arguments.

Going back to our Entities DSL of *Chapter 2, Creating Your First Xtext Language*, ElementType is the base class of BasicType and EntityType, and AttributeType has a reference, elementType, to an ElementType. In order to have a string representation for such a reference, we can write two dispatch methods as in the following example:

```
def dispatch typeToString(BasicType type) {
  type.typeName
}
def dispatch typeToString(EntityType type) {
  type.entity.name
}
```

Now, when we invoke typeToString on the reference elementType, the selection will use the runtime type of that reference:

```
def toString(AttributeType attributeType) {
  attributeType.elementType.typeToString
}
```

With this mechanism, you can get rid of all the ugly instanceof cascades and explicit class casts that have cluttered many Java programs.

Note that Xtend will automatically infer an entry point for `dispatch` methods with a parameter representing the base class of all the parameters used in the `dispatch` methods. In the preceding example, it will generate the Java method `typeToString(ElementType)` since `ElementType` is the base class of `BasicType` and `EntityType`. This generated Java method entry point will throw `IllegalArgumentException` if we pass an `ElementType` (that is, an `ElementType` object which is neither a `BasicType` nor an `EntityType`). For this reason, when writing dispatch methods, you may want to provide yourself a `dispatch` method for the base type and handle the base case manually.

Enhanced switch expressions

Xtend provides a more powerful version of Java `switch` statements. First of all, only the selected case is executed, in comparison to Java that falls through from one case to the next. For this reason, you do not have to insert an explicit break instruction to avoid subsequent case block execution. Indeed, Xtend does not support `break` statements at all. Furthermore, a switch can be used with any object reference.

Xtend switch expressions allow you to write involved case expressions, as shown in the following example:

```
def String switchExample(Entity e, Entity specialEntity) {
  switch e {
    case e.name.length > 0 : "has a name"
    case e.superType != null : "has a super type"
    case specialEntity : "special entity"
    default: ""
  }
}
```

If the case expression is a `boolean` expression (like the first two cases in the preceding example), then the case matches if the case expression evaluates to `true`. If the case expression is not of type `boolean`, it is compared to the value of the main expression using the `equals` method (the third case in the preceding example). The expression after the colon of the matched case is then evaluated, and this evaluation is the result of the whole `switch` expression.

Another interesting feature of Xtend switch expressions is **type guards**. With this functionality, you can specify a type as the case condition and the case matches only if the switch value is an instance of that type (formally, if it conforms to that type). In particular, if the switch value is a variable, that variable is automatically casted to the matched type within the case body. This allows you to implement a cleaner version of the typical Java cascades of instanceof and explicit casts. Although we could use dispatch methods to achieve the same goal, switch expressions with type guards can be a valid and more compact alternative.

For example, the code in the previous section using dispatch methods can be rewritten as follows:

```
def toString(AttributeType attributeType) {
  val elementType = attributeType.elementType
  switch elementType {
    BasicType: // elementType is a BasicType here
      elementType.typeName
    EntityType: // elementType is an EntityType here
      elementType.entity.name
  }
}
```

Note how entityType is automatically casted to the matched type in the case body.

Depending on your programming scenario, you may want to choose between dispatch methods and type-based switch expressions. Keep in mind that, while dispatch methods can be overridden and extended (that is, in a derived class, you can provide an additional dispatch method for a combination of parameters that was not handled in the base class), switch expressions are inside a method, and thus they do not allow for the same extensibility features. Moreover, dispatch cases are automatically reordered with respect to type hierarchy (most concrete types first), while switch cases are evaluated in the specified order.

Other Xtend expressions

Xtend also provides all the typical Java constructs such as for loops, if else, synchronized blocks, try, catch, and finally expressions and instanceof expressions. Recall that, although these have the same syntax as in Java, in Xtend these are considered expressions and not statements. Each of the preceding expressions evaluate to the last expression and can be returned just like any other expression.

Moreover, Xtend type inference is used also for the preceding expressions, thus, for instance, the type of the variable in a for loop can be omitted.

Casts in Xtend are specified using the infix operator as. Thus, the Xtend expression e as T corresponds to the Java cast expression (T) e.

When using instanceof as a condition of an if expression, Xtend automatically casts to the matched type within the body of the if branch. This is shown in the following example, where the casts are implicit and are not needed (Xtend will issue a warning about a useless cast if you insert the cast explicitly):

```
def toString(AttributeType attributeType) {
  val elementType = attributeType.elementType
  if (elementType instanceof BasicType)
    elementType.typeName // elementType is a BasicType here
  else if (elementType instanceof EntityType)
    elementType.entity.name // elementType is an EntityType here
}
```

Xtend introduces **Active Annotations**, which is a mechanism allowing the developer to hook in the translation process of Xtend source code to Java code through library. This is useful to have a lot of boilerplate automatically generated. We will not use active annotations in this book, but we invite you to have a look at the Xtend documentation about that.

The Xtend library provides some ready to use active annotations. For example, annotating an Xtend class with @Data will automatically add in the generated Java class getter methods for the fields, a constructor with parameters and other methods from java.lang.Object, such as equals, hashCode, and toString.

The `Person` class we used in Section *Lambda expressions*, can be implemented in Xtend as follows:

```
import org.eclipse.xtend.lib.annotations.Data

@Data class Person {
    String firstname
    String surname
    int age
}
```

Xtend IDE

Xtend is obviously implemented with Xtext, thus its integration into Eclipse provides rich tooling features. In particular, Xtend provides the same IDE tooling of the Eclipse JDT. Here, we just mention a few features, and we encourage you to experiment further:

- Rich content assist for all the existing Java libraries types and methods
- Automatic import statement insertion during the content assistant
- **Organize Imports** menu and keyboard shortcut (*Ctrl + Shift + O*)
- **Call Hierarchy** view
- Refactoring mechanisms, including **Rename**, **Extract Variable**, and **Extract Method** refactoring

Finally, you can debug Xtend code directly, as we will show in the next section.

Debugging Xtend code

The Java code generated by Xtend is clean and easy to debug. However, it is also possible to debug Xtend code directly (instead of the generated Java), thanks to the complete integration of Xtend with the Eclipse JDT debugger.

This means that you can debug Java code that has been generated by Xtend and, stepping through that, automatically brings you to debugging the original Xtend source. You can also debug an Xtend file containing a `main` method directly, since all the **Run** and **Debug** configuration launches are available for Xtend files as well. Breakpoints can be inserted in an Xtend file by double-clicking on the breakpoint ruler in the editor. The **Debug** context menu is available for Xtend files as well.

The next screenshot shows a debugging session of Xtend code. We have set a breakpoint on the Xtend file, which is also shown in the **Breakpoints** view. Note that all the JDT debugger views are available. Implicit variables such as `it` can be inspected in the **Variables** view:

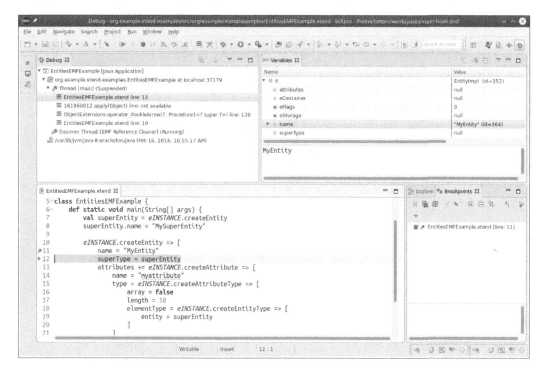

If, for any reason, while debugging Xtend code you need to debug the generated Java code, you can do so by right-clicking on the **Debug** view on an element corresponding to an Xtend file line and selecting **Show Source**. Refer to the following screenshot:

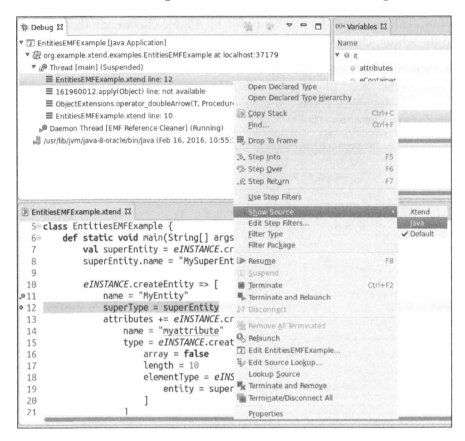

Xtend expressions are indeed Xbase expressions. We will describe Xbase in *Chapter 12, Xbase*.

Summary

Xtend provides many features that allow you to write clean and more readable code. Since it is completely interoperable with Java, all the Java libraries are accessible from within Xtend. Moreover, the IDE tooling of Xtend itself is basically the same as the ones of JDT. For all of the aforementioned reasons, Xtext fosters the use of Xtend to develop all the aspects of a DSL implementation.

In the next chapter, we will show you how to implement constraint checks for a DSL using the EMF Validator mechanism and the Xtext enhanced API.

4
Validation

In this chapter, we will introduce the concept of validation, and in particular, the Xtext mechanism to implement validation: the validator. With validation, you can implement additional constraint checks of a DSL, which cannot be done at parsing time. Xtext allows you to implement such constraint checks in an easy and declarative way. You only need to communicate to Xtext the possible errors or warnings, and it will take care of generating the error markers accordingly in the IDE. The validation will take place in the background while the user of the DSL is typing in the editor so that an immediate feedback is provided. We will also show how to implement quickfixes corresponding to the errors and warnings generated during validation, in order to help the user to solve problems due to validation errors.

This chapter will cover the following topics:

- An introduction to validation in Xtext
- The default Xtext validator for checking duplicate names
- Some examples of custom validations
- Some examples of quickfixes

Validation in Xtext

As we anticipated in *Chapter 1, Implementing a DSL*, parsing a program is only the first stage in a programming language implementation. In particular, the overall correctness of a program cannot always be determined during parsing. Trying to embed additional constraint checks in the grammar specification could either make such specification more complex or it could be simply impossible, as some additional static analysis can be performed only when other program parts are already parsed.

Actually, the best practice is to do as little as possible in the grammar and as much as possible in validation (we will use this practice in *Chapter 9*, *Type Checking* and *Chapter 10*, *Scoping*). This is because it is possible to provide far better error messages and to more precisely detect problems that are eligible for quickfixes.

The mechanism of validation will be used extensively in all example DSLs of this book. Typically, even for small DSLs, a validator has to be implemented to perform additional constraint checks.

In Xtext, these constraints checks are implemented using a **validator**, which is a concept inherited from the corresponding EMF API (see the book *Steinberg et al*, 2008). In EMF, you can implement a validator that performs constraint checks on the elements of an EMF model. Since Xtext uses EMF for representing the AST of a parsed program, the mechanism of the validator naturally extends to an Xtext DSL. Xtext enhances the EMF API for validation, by providing a declarative way to specify rules for constraints of your DSL. Moreover, Xtext comes with default validators, some of which are enabled by default, to perform checks which are common to many DSLs (for example, cross-reference checks). Your custom validator can be composed with the default ones of Xtext.

Default validators

Let's go back to the Entities DSL of *Chapter 2*, *Creating Your First Xtext Language*. Since we expressed cross-references in our Entities grammar, we can see the Xtext cross-reference validator in action in the generated editor. If we enter an incorrect reference, for example, the name of a super entity that does not exist, we get the error `Couldn't resolve reference to...`. This check on cross-references is performed by one of the default validators provided by Xtext (cross-reference resolution is the main subject of *Chapter 10*, *Scoping*).

Another standard validator provided by Xtext is the one that checks whether the names are unique within your program. This check validates that names are unique per element type. For example, you can have an attribute named the same as an entity, but not two entities with the same name.

This validator is not enabled by default, but it can be turned on by modifying the MWE2 file as shown in the following code snippet. In our example, it is `GenerateEntities.mwe2`. We need to uncomment the `composedCheck` specification, which concerns `NamesAreUniqueValidator`:

```
language = StandardLanguage {
    name = "org.example.entities.Entities"
    fileExtensions = "entities"
    ...
```

```
        validator = {
            composedCheck =
                "org.eclipse.xtext.validation.NamesAreUniqueValidator"
        }
    }
```

After that, of course, you need to run the MWE2 workflow.

If you now try to declare two entities with the same name in the Entities DSL editor, you will get an error as shown in the following screenshot:

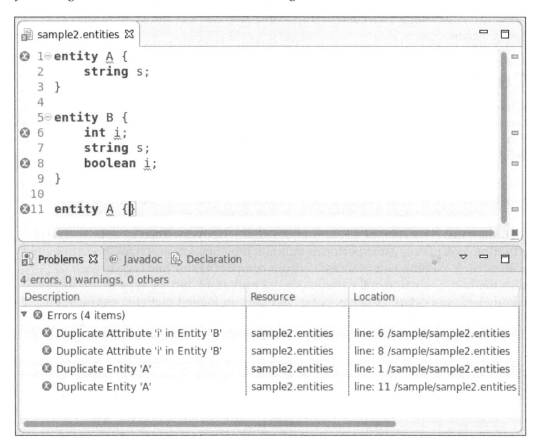

It is interesting to note that, besides the element type, this validator also takes into consideration the containment relations. For example, two attributes declared in two different entities are allowed to have the same name (as you can see from the preceding screenshot, both A and B have the attribute s, and this is allowed).

Technically, everything that can be referenced through name is named in a namespace, implied by the containment relation. This leads to qualified names, which will be explained in *Chapter 10, Scoping*.

The default behavior of this validator should suit most DSLs. If your DSL needs to have more rigid constraints about names, or in general about duplicate elements, you will have to implement a customized `NamesAreUniqueValidator` class or simply disable `NamesAreUniqueValidator` and implement these name checks in your own validator. An example of a custom duplicate name check is shown in *Chapter 9, Type Checking*.

Custom validators

While the default validators can perform some common validation tasks, most of the checks for your DSL will have to be implemented by you, according to the semantics you want your DSL to have. That is why we will usually have to implement a custom validator for a DSL.

These additional checks can be implemented using the Xtend class that Xtext has generated for you in the `validation` subpackage in the `src` folder of the runtime plug-in project. In our example, this class is called `EntitiesValidator`. Remember that, since this class is in the `src` folder, it will not be overwritten by future MWE2 workflow executions. Xtext performs validation by invoking each method annotated with `@Check`, passing all instances having a compatible runtime type to each such method. The name of the method is not important, but the type of the single parameter is important. You can define as many annotated methods as you want for the same type. Xtext will invoke them all. Inside such methods, you implement the semantic checks for that element. If a semantic check fails, you call the `error` method, which will be explained shortly.

For example, we want to make sure that there is no cycle in the hierarchy of an entity. Thus, we write the following annotated method in our validator:

```
package org.example.entities.validation

import org.eclipse.xtext.validation.Check
import org.example.entities.entities.EntitiesPackage
import org.example.entities.entities.Entity

class EntitiesValidator extends AbstractEntitiesValidator {

    @Check
```

```
def checkNoCycleInEntityHierarchy(Entity entity) {
  if (entity.superType == null)
    return // nothing to check

  val visitedEntities = newHashSet(entity)

  var current = entity.superType
  while (current != null) {
    if (visitedEntities.contains(current)) {
      error("cycle in hierarchy of entity '"+current.name+"'",
        EntitiesPackage.eINSTANCE.entity_SuperType)
      return
    }
    visitedEntities.add(current)
    current = current.superType
  }
}
```

In the preceding method, we traverse the hierarchy of an entity by recording all the entities we are visiting. Of course, if an entity has no superType, there is nothing to check. If during this visit we find an entity that we have already visited, it means that the hierarchy contains a cycle and we issue an error. It is crucial to leave the while loop in that case; otherwise, the loop will never end (after all, we found a cycle and we would traverse the hierarchy endlessly).

The error method has many overloaded versions (we refer to Xtext documentation for further details). In this example, we use the version that requires the following:

- A message for the error. It is up to you to provide meaningful information.
- The EMF feature of the examined EObject, which the error should be reported against, that is, which should be marked with error. In this case, the feature containing the error is the superType feature.

 Usually, if in doubt, the feature to place the error on should be the feature name of the erroneous element.

Access to classes and features are obtained from the `EPackage` class that is generated for our DSL's metamodel. In our example, it is `EntitiesPackage`. Using this `EPackage`, EMF features can be obtained in two ways:

- Using the static instance of the package and then the method corresponding to the feature, as we did in the preceding code:

  ```
  EntitiesPackage.eINSTANCE.entity_SuperType.
  ```

- Using the static fields of the inner interface `Literals`:

  ```
  EntitiesPackage.Literals.ENTITY__SUPER_TYPE.
  ```

In both cases, in your Xtend programs, you can rely on the content assist to select the feature easily.

We can now try the preceding validation check in the Entities DSL editor by defining entities which contain a cycle in the hierarchy, as shown in the following screenshot:

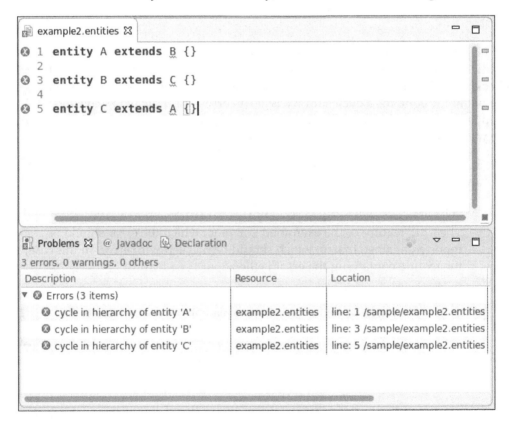

You can see that the elements marked with an error in the editor are the entity names after the keyword `extends`, since they correspond to the `superType` feature.

The three error markers also show that Xtext calls our `@Check` annotated method for all the elements of type `Entity` in the program.

Calling the `error` method with the appropriate information will let Xtext manage the markers for Xtext-based resources, clearing them before reparsing, keeping track of dirty versus saved state, and so on. Markers will appear wherever they are supported in the IDE: in the right and left editor ruler, in the **Problems** view, and in the package explorer.

Errors are considered to mean that the model is invalid. If you want to issue warnings instead of errors, simply call the `warning` method that has the same signature as the `error` method. A program with only warnings and no errors is considered valid anyway.

For example, in our Entities DSL, we follow a standard convention about names — the name of an `entity` should start with a capital letter, while the name of an `attribute` should be lowercase. If the user does not follow this convention, we issue a warning. The program is considered valid anyway. To implement this, we write the following methods in the `EntitiesValidator` class (note the use of imported `static` methods as `extension` methods from the class `Character`):

```
import org.example.entities.entities.Attribute
import static extension java.lang.Character.*
...

class EntitiesValidator extends AbstractEntitiesValidator {

  ...
  @Check
  def checkEntityNameStartsWithCapital(Entity entity) {
    if (entity.name.charAt(0).lowerCase)
      warning("Entity name should start with a capital",
        EntitiesPackage.eINSTANCE.entity_Name)
  }

  @Check
  def checkAttributeNameStartsWithLowercase(Attribute attr) {
    if (attr.name.charAt(0).upperCase)
      warning("Attribute name should start with a lowercase",
        EntitiesPackage.eINSTANCE.attribute_Name)
  }
}
```

The following screenshot shows how warning markers are created instead of error markers:

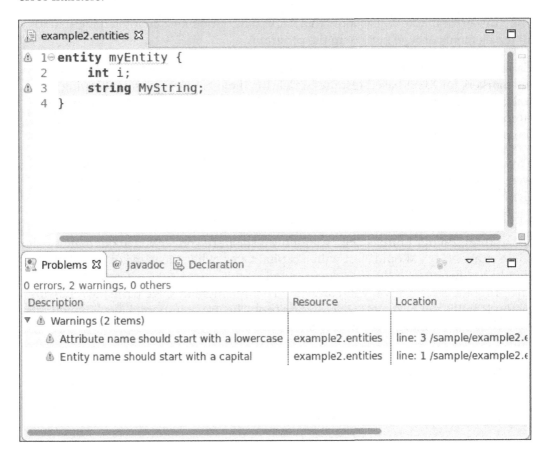

An *info* severity level is also available, and the corresponding method to call is `info`. In this case, an information marker is shown only in the editor's ruler, while the corresponding file is not marked.

This is just an example of a simple validator implementation. In the rest of the book, we will see many other implementations that perform more complex constraint checks (among which, type checking, as shown in *Chapter 8, An Expression Language* and in *Chapter 9, Type Checking*).

Quickfixes

As we said in *Chapter 1, Implementing a DSL*, a quickfix is a proposal to solve a problem in a program. Quickfixes are typically implemented by a context menu available from the error marker, and they are available both in the editor ruler and in the **Problems** view.

 Since quickfixes are tightly connected to validation, we describe them in this chapter. Moreover, they allow us to get familiar with the manipulation of the EMF model representing the AST of a program.

In our Entities DSL, we can provide a quickfix for each warning and error issued by our validator. As we will see later, we can also provide quickfixes for errors issued by Xtext default validators.

Xtext provides an easy mechanism to implement a quickfix connected to an error or warning issued by a validator. The Xtext generator generates an Xtend stub class for quickfixes into the UI plug-in project. In our Entities DSL example, this class is `org.example.entities.ui.quickfix.EntitiesQuickfixProvider`.

A quickfix is triggered by an issue code associated with an error or warning marker. An issue code is simply a string that uniquely identifies the issue. Thus, when invoking the `error` or `warning` method, we must provide an additional argument which represents the issue code. In the validator, this is typically done by defining a public `String` constant, whose value is prefixed with the package name of the DSL and ends with a sensible name for the issue. It might also make sense to pass additional issue data that can be reused by the quickfix provider to show a more meaningful description of the quickfix and to actually fix the program. The issue data is very useful when validation needs to compute something that is costly — the quickfix then avoids having to compute it again. Thus, we use another version of the method `error` and `warning`, which takes four arguments; we modify our validator as follows (only the modified parts are shown):

```
class EntitiesValidator extends AbstractEntitiesValidator {

    protected static val ISSUE_CODE_PREFIX = "org.example.entities.";

    public static val HIERARCHY_CYCLE =
        ISSUE_CODE_PREFIX + "HierarchyCycle";

    public static val INVALID_ENTITY_NAME =
        ISSUE_CODE_PREFIX + "InvalidEntityName";
```

```
    public static val INVALID_ATTRIBUTE_NAME =
        ISSUE_CODE_PREFIX + "InvalidAttributeName";

    @Check
    def checkNoCycleInEntityHierarchy(Entity entity) {
      ...
      error("cycle in hierarchy of entity '"+current.name+"'",
          EntitiesPackage.eINSTANCE.entity_SuperType,
          HIERARCHY_CYCLE, // issue code
          current.superType.name) // issue data
      ...
    }

    @Check
    def checkEntityNameStartsWithCapital(Entity entity) {
      if (entity.name.charAt(0).lowerCase)
        warning("Entity name should start with a capital letter",
          EntitiesPackage.eINSTANCE.entity_Name,
          INVALID_ENTITY_NAME,
          entity.name)
    }

    @Check
    def checkAttributeNameStartsWithLowercase(Attribute attr) {
      if (attr.name.charAt(0).upperCase)
        warning("Attribute name should start with a lowercase",
          EntitiesPackage.eINSTANCE.attribute_Name,
          INVALID_ATTRIBUTE_NAME,
          attr.name)
    }
  }
```

The issue code string constant is passed as the third argument to the methods
error and warning. Issue data is optional, and you can pass a variable number
of issue data arguments. To implement a quickfix, we define a method in
EntitiesQuickfixProvider annotated with @Fix and a reference to the issue code
this quickfix applies to. The name of the method is not important, but the parameter
types are fixed.

For example, for the warning concerning the first letter of an entity name, which
must be capital, we implement a quickfix that automatically capitalizes the first letter
of that entity:

```
package org.example.entities.ui.quickfix

import org.eclipse.xtext.ui.editor.quickfix.DefaultQuickfixProvider
import org.eclipse.xtext.ui.editor.quickfix.Fix
import org.eclipse.xtext.ui.editor.quickfix.IssueResolutionAcceptor
import org.eclipse.xtext.validation.Issue
import org.example.entities.validation.EntitiesValidator

class EntitiesQuickfixProvider extends DefaultQuickfixProvider {

  @Fix(EntitiesValidator.INVALID_ENTITY_NAME)
  def void capitalizeEntityNameFirstLetter(Issue issue,
                          IssueResolutionAcceptor acceptor) {
    acceptor.accept(issue,
      "Capitalize first letter", // label
      "Capitalize first letter of '"
        + issue.data.get(0) + "'", // description
      "Entity.gif", // icon
      [
        context |
        val xtextDocument = context.xtextDocument
        val firstLetter = xtextDocument.get(issue.offset, 1);
        xtextDocument.replace(issue.offset, 1,
                          firstLetter.toFirstUpper);
      ]
    )
  }
}
```

Let's analyze what this code does. The first parameter of a quickfix provider method is the `Issue` object that represents the error information. This is built internally by Xtext using the information passed to `error` or `warning` in your validator. The second parameter is an acceptor. Acceptor is a pattern, and you will see different types of acceptors used in many places in Xtext. You usually only have to invoke the method `accept` on an acceptor, passing some arguments. An acceptor is used when an operation can return any number of results, instead of returning a `List`.

The first three arguments passed to the `accept` method of the acceptor are the label (shown in the quickfix pop-up for this fix), a description (which should show what the effect of selecting this quick fix would mean or something that makes the user confident it is a fix they want to apply), and an icon (if you do not want an icon, you can pass an empty string; how to use custom icons in your DSL UI will be explained in *Chapter 6, Customizing Xtext Components*). Note that, for the description, we use the first element of the issue data (an array) since we know that in the validator we passed the name of the supertype as the single issue data. When implementing the quickfix, you must be consistent with the information passed by the validator.

The fourth argument is the lambda that actually implements the modification code of the quickfix when selected by the user. Quickfixes can perform the correction based on the source text (textual modification) or on the model (semantic modification). These are explained in the next two sections.

Textual modification

You can specify a lambda that takes a single parameter of the type IModificationContext. Due to the type inference mechanisms of Xtend, it is enough to just specify the name of the parameter. In our example, the name of the parameter was explicitly stated for clarity.

In the preceding code, we use the IDocument argument, which is passed in the given modification context, to get access to the text we want to modify in our quickfix. We have been given the offset and length of where the error/warning is marked in the Issue object. We can now use the document methods get(offset, length) and replace(offset, length, text) to perform the capitalization of the first letter.

This quickfix is shown in the following screenshot:

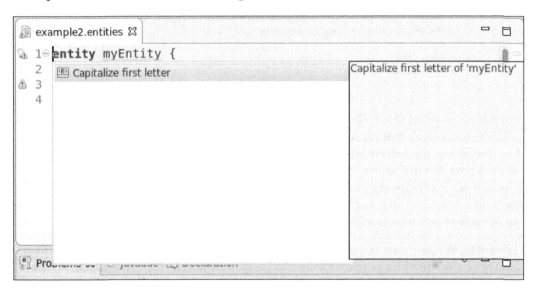

Using this strategy for implementing quickfixes has the drawback that we need to deal with the actual text of the editor.

Model modification

The alternative strategy relies on the fact that the program is also available in memory as an EMF model. If we modify the model, the Xtext editor will automatically update its contents. For this reason, we can specify a lambda, which takes two parameters: the `EObject` that contains the error and the modification context.

For instance, to uncapitalize the first letter of an `attribute`, we write the quickfix using the following strategy (remember to import the `Attribute` type):

```
@Fix(EntitiesValidator.INVALID_ATTRIBUTE_NAME)
def void uncapitalizeAttributeNameFirstLetter(Issue issue,
                              IssueResolutionAcceptor acceptor) {
  acceptor.accept(issue,
    "Uncapitalize first letter", // label
    "Uncapitalize first letter of '"
       + issue.data.get(0) + "'", // description
    "Attribute.gif", // icon
    [
      element, context |
      (element as Attribute).name = issue.data.get(0).toFirstLower
    ]
  )
}
```

In this case, the element is the `Attribute` object against which the warning was reported. Therefore, we simply assign the fixed name to the name of the attribute. Note that, with this strategy, we only manipulate the EMF model, without having to deal with the contents of the editor. Xtext will then take care of updating the editor's contents.

The ability to directly modify the EMF model of the program makes more complex quickfixes easier to implement. For example, if we want to implement the quickfix to remove the `supertype` of the `entity` which contains a cycle in the hierarchy, we just need to set the `superType` feature to `null`, as shown in the following code snippet, where you also have to import the `Entity` type. You can see the quickfix in the following screenshot:

```
@Fix(EntitiesValidator.HIERARCHY_CYCLE)
def void removeSuperType(Issue issue,
                         IssueResolutionAcceptor acceptor) {
  acceptor.accept(issue,
    "Remove supertype",
    '''Remove supertype '«issue.data.get(0)»' ''',
    "delete_obj.gif",
```

```
    [ element, context |
      (element as Entity).superType = null;
    ]
  )
}
```

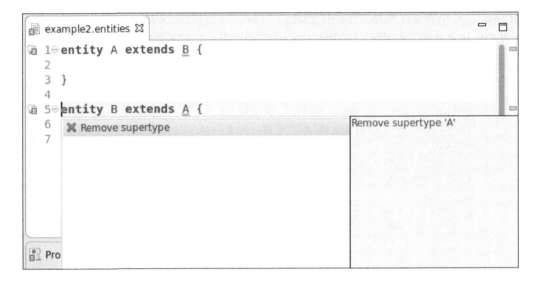

Note that the semantic change results in there not being any supertype in the model element and thus the source text extends is also removed. Implementing the same quickfix by modifying the text of the program would require more effort and would be more error-prone. On the other hand, textual modifications allow you to fix things that are not present in the semantic model. Also, semantic changes always include formatting, and this may have other unwanted side effects (we will deal with formatting in *Chapter 6, Customizing Xtext Components*).

Quickfixes for default validators

We can also provide quickfixes for errors issued by default Xtext validators. You might have noted that, if you refer to a missing entity in the Entities DSL editor, Xtext already proposes some quickfixes: if there are other entities in the source file, it proposes to change the reference to one of the existing entities. We can provide an additional quickfix that proposes to automatically add the missing entity. In order to do this, we must define a method in our quickfix provider for the issue org. eclipse.xtext.diagnostics.Diagnostic.LINKING_DIAGNOSTIC. We want to add the missing entity to the current model. To make things more interesting, the quickfix should add the missing entity after the entity, which refers to the missing entity. For example, consider the following source file:

```
entity MyFirstEntity {
  FooBar s;
  int[] a;
}

entity MyOtherEntity {
}
```

The referred `FooBar` entity in the attribute definition is not defined in the program, and we would like to add it after the definition of `MyFirstEntity` and before `MyOtherEntity`, since that is the entity that contains the attribute definition referring to the missing entity.

Let's first present the code for this quickfix (we will use Xtend features for `getters`, `setters`, template strings, and the **with operator** to make our logic more compact):

```
import static extension org.eclipse.xtext.EcoreUtil2.*


@Fix(Diagnostic.LINKING_DIAGNOSTIC)
def void createMissingEntity(Issue issue,
                             IssueResolutionAcceptor acceptor) {
  acceptor.accept(issue,
    "Create missing entity",
    "Create missing entity",
    "Entity.gif",
    [ element, context |
      val currentEntity =
          element.getContainerOfType(Entity)
      val model = currentEntity.eContainer as Model
      model.entities.add(
          model.entities.indexOf(currentEntity)+1,
          EntitiesFactory.eINSTANCE.createEntity() => [
              name = context.xtextDocument.get(issue.offset,
                                               issue.length)
          ]
      )
    ]
  )
}
```

Consider that the `EObject` element passed to the lambda is the program element which refers to the missing `entity`, thus, it is not necessarily an `Entity`. For instance, if the missing `entity` is in a type specification of an `attribute`, as in the preceding `Entities` program snippet, then the `EObject` element is an `AttributeType`. To get the containing `entity`, we could walk up the containment relation of the EMF model till we get to an `Entity` element. Alternatively, we use one of the many static utility methods, here imported as `extension` methods, provided by Xtext in the class `EcoreUtil2` (this complements the standard `EcoreUtil` class of EMF). In particular, we use `getContainerOfType`, which does this walking up in the containment relation for us, until it finds an element of the specified type. For retrieving the root `Model` element, we can simply cast the container of the found entity because, in our `Entities` DSL, an `Entity` can only be contained in a `Model`. Then, we insert the newly created `entity` in the desired position, that is, right after the position of the current entity.

> Spend some time to take a look at the classes `EcoreUtil` and `EcoreUtil2`, since they provide many useful methods you will need when dealing with an EMF model.

To create the missing entity, we must know its name. For this issue, which is not generated by our own validator, the issue data does not contain any information about the missing element name. However, the issue offset tells us in which position in the document the missing element name is referred. Thus, the name of the missing element can be retrieved using this offset from the editor's document (the length is also contained in the issue).

You can now check what this quickfix does, Refer to the following screenshot; this also shows the default quickfixes provided by Xtext, which propose to change the name of the referred `entity` to one available in the current source:

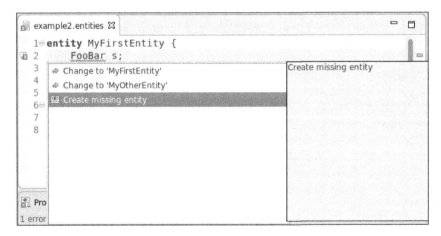

Summary

In this chapter, you learned how to implement constraint checks, using the Xtext validator mechanism based on @Check annotated methods. Just by implementing a custom validator and calling the method error or warning with the appropriate information, Xtext produces error and warning markers that result in marking the text regions as well as showing the markers in the various views in Eclipse.

We also showed how to implement quickfixes. We can implement a quickfix by directly modifying the text of the current program. Alternatively, since Xtext automatically synchronizes the DSL editor's contents with the EMF model of the AST, we can simply modify such model without dealing with the textual representation of the program.

In the next chapter, we will write a code generator for the Entities DSL implemented in Xtend, using its advanced features for code generation. Starting from a program written in our Entities DSL, we will generate the corresponding Java code. You will see that Xtext automatically integrates your code generator into the building infrastructure of Eclipse.

5
Code Generation

In this chapter, you will learn how to write a code generator for your Xtext DSL using the Xtend programming language. Using the Entities DSL that we developed in the previous chapters, we will write a code generator which, for each entity declaration, will generate a Java class. We will also see how the code generator is automatically integrated by Xtext into the Eclipse builder infrastructure. Finally, the DSL implementation can be exported as a Java standalone command-line compiler.

This chapter will cover the following topics:

- How to write a code generator with Xtend
- The integration of your code generator in the Eclipse building mechanisms
- How to export a standalone command-line compiler of your DSL

Introduction to code generation

After a program written in your DSL has been parsed and validated, you might want to do something with the parsed EMF model, that is, the AST of that program. Typically, you may want to generate code in another language, for example, Java code, a configuration file, XML, a text file, and so on. In all of these cases, you will need to write a code generator.

Since the parsed program is an EMF model, you can use any EMF framework which somehow deals with code generation. Of course, you might also use plain Java to generate code, after all, as we saw in the previous chapters, you have all the Java APIs to access the EMF model.

However, in this book, we will use Xtend (introduced in *Chapter 3, Working with the Xtend Programming Language*) to write code generators, since it is very well suited for the task.

Xtext automatically integrates your code generator into the Eclipse build infrastructure. All we have to deal with is producing the desired output, for example, Java source, XML, and so on.

Writing a code generator in Xtend

A generator stub is automatically created by Xtext. In our example, the stub is created in the org.example.entities.generator package:

```
class EntitiesGenerator extends AbstractGenerator {
  override void doGenerate(Resource res,
                           IFileSystemAccess2 fsa, IGeneratorContext
context) {
    // TODO implement me
  }
}
```

Before writing the actual code, let's recall that Xtext is a framework; thus, the overall flow of control is dictated by the framework, not by the programmer. This is also known as the **Hollywood Principle**: *Don't call us, we'll call you*. This means that you do not have to manually run the generator. Your DSL Xtext editor is already integrated in the automatic building infrastructure of Eclipse, and the generator will be automatically called when a source written in your DSL changes. Indeed, it will be called also if one of its dependencies changes, as we will see in later chapters.

Note that the method you have to implement just accepts an EMF Resource, which contains the EMF model representation of the program. If this generation method is invoked, the corresponding source program has already been parsed and validated. The generator will only be called when the source program does not have any validation errors. You do not even have to worry about the physical base path location where your code will be generated; that is hidden in the passed IFileSystemAccess2 argument. You only need to specify the relative path where the generated file will be created and its contents as java.lang.CharSequence (typically, an Xtend template expression). Finally, the third parameter is an IGeneratorContext instance. This interface contains the CancelIndicator getCancelIndicator() method. By calling the method isCanceled() on the CancelIndicator object, you get to know if the Eclipse build has been canceled. This is useful if your generator performs many operations and it generates lots of output files—during the generation you can periodically query the CancelIndicator object; and if the build has been canceled you should interrupt your generation as well. For the example DSLs, we will implement in this book, the generator will not take much computing time, neither it will generate many output files, so we will never use the IGeneratorContext.

First of all, we need to decide what we want to generate from our DSL programs. For the Entities DSL, it might make sense to generate a Java class for each `Entity`. In such a generated Java file, we will generate a field for each `Attribute`, together with a `getter` and a `setter` method. Thus, we need to retrieve all the `Entity` objects in the passed `Resource`. Here is how to do this with Xtend:

```
resource.allContents.toIterable.filter(Entity)
```

Then, we iterate over these entities and generate a Java file for each of them using the entity's name for the filename. Since we do not have explicit packages in our DSL, we choose to generate all the Java classes in the package `entities`. Thus, the Java file path will be as follows:

```
"entities/" + entity.name + ".java"
```

Remember that we do not have to care about the base path since it will be configured into the passed `IFileSystemAccess2` argument.

If you summarize it, we get the following:

```
override void doGenerate(Resource res,
                              IFileSystemAccess2 fsa, IGeneratorContext
context ) {
  for (e : res.allContents.toIterable.filter(Entity)){
    fsa.generateFile(
      "entities/" + e.name + ".java",
      e.compile)
  }
}
```

Now, we have to implement the `compile` method, which must return a string with the contents that will be stored in the generated file. We use Xtend multi-line template expressions to implement such a method. The method is illustrated in the following screenshot:

```
def compile(Entity entity) {
    '''
    package entities;

    public class «entity.name» «IF entity.superType != null»extends «entity.superType.name» «ENDIF»{
        «FOR attribute : entity.attributes»
        private «attribute.type.compile» «attribute.name»;
        «ENDFOR»

        «FOR attribute : entity.attributes»
        public «attribute.type.compile» get«attribute.name.toFirstUpper»() {
            return «attribute.name»;
        }

        public void set«attribute.name.toFirstUpper»(«attribute.type.compile» _arg) {
            this.«attribute.name» = _arg;
        }

        «ENDFOR»
    }
    '''
}
```

Remember that the Xtend editor also shows the tab indentations of the final resulting string. Xtend smartly ignores indentations of the loop constructs, which are there only to make Xtend code more readable: these indentations and newline characters will not be a part of the resulting string.

We basically write a template for a Java class using the information stored in the `Entity` object. We generate the `extends` part only if the entity has a supertype. This is achieved using the `IF` conditional inside the template. Then, we iterate over the entity's attributes twice using the template `FOR` loop construct; the first time to generate Java fields and the second time to generate `getter` and `setter` methods. Doing that in two separate iterations allows us to generate all the fields at the beginning of the Java class. We use the `toFirstUpper` extension method to correctly generate the names of the `getter` and `setter` methods.

 Notice that `IF` and `FOR` (with capital letters) are used to specify conditions and loops, respectively, within a template expression.

We delegate the compilation of attribute types to other methods:

```
def compile(AttributeType attributeType) {
  attributeType.elementType.typeToString +
    if (attributeType.array) "[]"
    else ""
}

def dispatch typeToString(BasicType type) {
  if (type.typeName == "string") "String"
  else type.typeName
}

def dispatch typeToString(EntityType type) {
  type.entity.name
}
```

Observe that the `BasicType` literals of our DSL already correspond to Java primitive types. The only exception is `string`, which in Java corresponds to `String`. To keep the example simple, we do not consider the `length` feature of `AttributeType` during the code generation.

 To generate Java code that corresponds to the JavaBeans convention, the `getter` method for a boolean field should start with `is`, instead of `get`. This is left to the reader as an exercise.

Integration with the Eclipse build mechanism

It is time to see our generator in action: launch Eclipse, create a **Java Project** in the workspace, and in the `src` folder, create a new `.entities` file (remember to accept to convert the project to an Xtext project, otherwise the generator will not run). Continue by adding one or more entities with some attributes. Note that a `src-gen` folder is automatically created as soon as you save the file. At this point, you should also add this generated folder to the projects source folders by navigating to **Build Path | Use as Source Folder**. Exploring the content of the `src-gen` folder, you will find a generated Java class for each entity in your `.entities` file. You can see an example in the following screenshot:

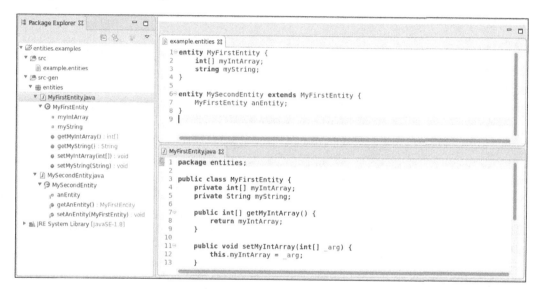

 Observe that a code generator just creates text. Other components have to make sense of that, for example, a Java compiler. That is why we need to add the `src-gen` folder to the project source folders: this way, the Eclipse Java compiler automatically compiles the generated Java sources.

Xtext also generates a context menu for your DSL editor **Open Generated File**. If from the contents of your DSL editor only one output file is generated, that context menu will open the single generated file. If multiple files are generated, like in the previous screenshot, then a dialog will let you select the generated file to open.

Make some changes and observe that the Java files are regenerated as you save the changes. Remove an entity and observe that the corresponding Java file is removed. Your DSL generator is completely integrated in the Eclipse build system.

For instance, in the following screenshot, we can see how the generated Java file is changed after removing a field from MyFirstEntity and how the previously generated Java file for MySecondEntity is automatically deleted after we removed the corresponding entity definition in the input file:

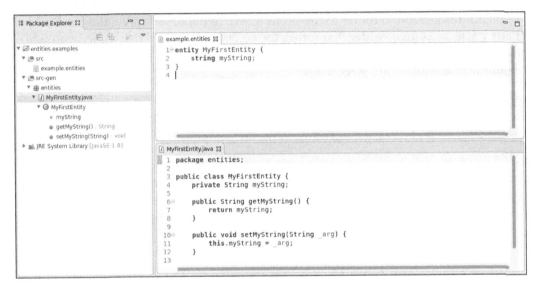

The generator is automatically invoked by Xtext when the input file changes, provided that the file contains no validation error. Xtext also automatically keeps track of the association between the generated files and the original input file. As in this example, from an input file, we can generate several output files. When a DSL source file is found to be invalid, that is, having validation errors, everything that was generated from that file is automatically removed, independent of the input program's element that contains the error.

For instance, in the following screenshot, we show what happens if we modify the `example.entities` file introducing an error and we save the file: even if the error does not concern `MyFirstEntity`, its corresponding generated Java file is still deleted:

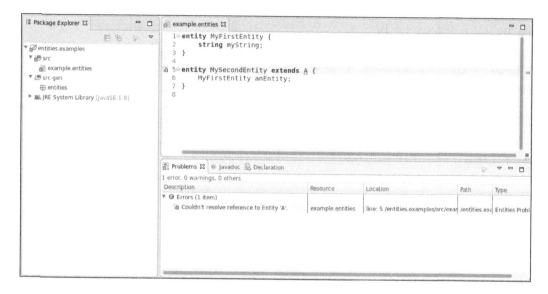

 The integration with the Eclipse build infrastructure is customizable, but the default behavior, including the automatic removal of generated files corresponding to an invalid source file, should fit most cases. In fact, code generators tend to be written for complete and valid models and often throw exceptions for incomplete models or produce complete garbage.

When running the MWE2 workflow, Xtext also creates preference pages for your DSL. One of these preference pages concerns code generation. In the new Eclipse instance, you can check what Xtext created (navigate to **Window | Preferences**). There is a dedicated section for the Entities DSL with typical configurations (for example, syntax highlighting colors and fonts and code generation preferences), see the following screenshot:

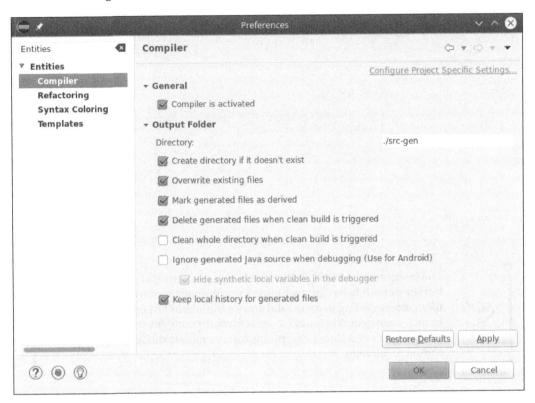

Standalone command-line compiler

We already know that the Xtext project wizard created the projects for our DSL separating the features related to the user interface in separate projects, the `.ide` project and the `.ui` project. The runtime project does not depend on the Eclipse user interface. Thus, we can create a command-line application consisting of a simple class with a `main` method. Xtext can generate such a class for you. We need to add the `generator` specification in the `StandardLanguage` block in the MWE2 workflow file:

```
language = StandardLanguage {
    name = "org.example.entities.Entities"
    fileExtensions = "entities"
    ...
    generator = {
        generateXtendMain = true
    }
}
```

If you now run the workflow, you will find an Xtend `Main` class in the `src` folder of your project in the `org.example.entities.generator` package. As you may recall from *Chapter 2, Creating Your First Xtext Language*, files generated into the `src` folder are only generated once, and thus you can safely add/modify the logic of the `Main` class. This is not required at this point. We will use the class as it was generated. You do not have to worry about not understanding everything that is done by the `Main` class at this point; this will be revealed in later chapters. For now, it is enough to know that the generated `main` method of the `Main` class accepts a command-line argument for the file to parse, validate, and generate code for.

Finally, you can also export a JAR file for the standalone Entities compiler. In Eclipse, an easy way to do that is given in the following steps:

1. Run the `Main.xtend` file as a Java application (right-click and navigate to **Run As | Java Application**). In the **Console** view, you can see that the application terminates with the `Aborting: no path to EMF resource provided!` error, since you did not specify any command-line argument (but that is not the reason why we are creating this launch configuration).

2. From the **File** menu, select **Export... | Java | Runnable JAR File**, then click on **Next**.

3. Select the launch configuration you created in step 1, specify the path of the exported JAR file (for example, `entities-compiler.jar`), and in the **Library handling** section, select **Package required libraries into generated JAR** and click on **Finish**. See the following screenshot:

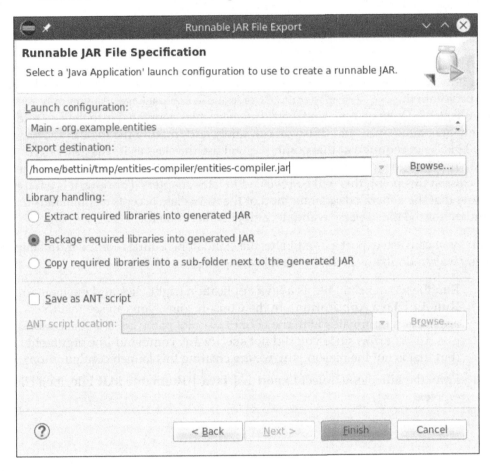

The generated JAR file is found in the directory denoted by the output path. Note that this JAR file is quite big (almost 30 MB) because besides the class files of your projects, it also contains all the required JARs (for example, the Xtext and EMF JAR files). This means that your JAR file is self-contained and does not need any further library. You can now try your standalone compiler from the command line, just go in the directory where the JAR file has been created and run it with Java, giving the path of an `.entities` file as an argument, as shown in the following:

```
java -jar entities-compiler.jar <path to an .entities file>
```

If the given file contains errors, you will see the errors reported as result; otherwise, you should see the `Code generation finished` message. In the latter case, you will find all the generated Java files in the `src-gen` folder.

 This was a demonstration that Xtext can generate a standalone command-line-based compiler that does not require a full Eclipse infrastructure. In the sources of this example you will find a `pom.xml` file that generates such a jar file without using the Eclipse export wizard. This file must be used with Maven, which will be described In *Chapter 11, Continuous Integration*.

Summary

Generating code from your DSL sources is a typical task when developing a DSL. Xtend provides many interesting features that make writing a code generator really easy.

Xtext automatically integrates your code generator into the Eclipse building infrastructure so that building takes place incrementally on file saving, just like in the Eclipse JDT. You can also get a command-line standalone compiler so that your DSL programs can be compiled without Eclipse.

In the next chapter, you will learn about the Dependency Injection framework Google Guice, on which Xtext heavily relies for customizing all of its features. In particular, you will also see how to customize the runtime and the IDE concepts for your DSL.

6
Customizing Xtext Components

In this chapter, we describe the main mechanism for customizing Xtext components—Google Guice, a Dependency Injection framework. With Google Guice, we can easily and consistently inject custom implementations of specific components into Xtext. In the first section, we will briefly show some Java examples that use Google Guice. Then, we will show how Xtext uses this dependency injection framework. In particular, you will learn how to customize both the runtime and the UI aspects.

This chapter will cover the following topics:

- An introduction to Google Guice dependency injection framework
- How Xtext uses Google Guice
- How to customize several aspects of an Xtext DSL

Dependency injection

The **Dependency Injection pattern** (see the article *Fowler*, 2004) allows you to inject implementation objects into a class hierarchy in a consistent way. This is useful when classes delegate specific tasks to objects referenced in fields. These fields have abstract types (that is, interfaces or abstract classes) so that the dependency on actual implementation classes is removed.

In this first section, we will briefly show some Java examples that use Google Guice. Of course, all the injection principles naturally apply to Xtend as well.

 If you want to try the following examples yourself, you need to create a new **Plug-in Project**, for example, org.example. guice and add com.google.inject and javax.inject as dependencies in the MANIFEST.MF.

Let's consider a possible scenario: a Service class that abstracts from the actual implementation of a Processor class and a Logger class. The following is a possible implementation:

```java
public class Service {
  private Logger logger;
  private Processor processor;

  public void execute(String command) {
    logger.log("executing " + command);
    processor.process(command);
    logger.log("executed " + command);
  }
}

public class Logger {
  public void log(String message) {
    System.out.println("LOG: " + message);
  }
}

public interface Processor {
  public void process(Object o);
}

public class ProcessorImpl implements Processor {
  private Logger logger;

  public void process(Object o) {
    logger.log("processing");
    System.out.println("processing " + o + "...");
  }
}
```

These classes correctly abstract from the implementation details, but the problem of initializing the fields correctly still persists. If we initialize the fields in the constructor, then the user still needs to hardcode the actual implementation classnames. Also, note that Logger is used in two independent classes; thus, if we have a custom logger, we must make sure that all the instances use the correct one.

These issues can be dealt with using dependency injection. With dependency injection, hardcoded dependencies will be removed. Moreover, we will be able to easily and consistently switch the implementation classes throughout the code. Although the same goal can be achieved manually by implementing **factory method** or **abstract factory** patterns (see the book *Gamma et al*, 1995), with dependency injection framework it is easier to keep the desired consistency and the programmer needs to write less code. Xtext uses the dependency injection framework **Google Guice**, https://github.com/google/guice. We refer to the Google Guice documentation for all the features provided by this framework. In this section, we just briefly describe its main features.

You annotate the fields you want Guice to inject with the @Inject annotation (com.google.inject.Inject):

```
public class Service {
  @Inject private Logger logger;
  @Inject private Processor processor;

  public void execute(String command) {
    logger.log("executing " + command);
    processor.process(command);
    logger.log("executed " + command);
  }
}

public class ProcessorImpl implements Processor {
  @Inject private Logger logger;

  public void process(Object o) {
    logger.log("processing");
    System.out.println("processing " + o + "...");
  }
}
```

The mapping from injection requests to instances is specified in a Guice Module, a class that is derived from com.google.inject.AbstractModule. The method configure is implemented to specify the bindings using a simple and intuitive API.

You only need to specify the bindings for interfaces, abstract classes, and for custom classes. This means that you do not need to specify a binding for Logger since it is a concrete class. On the contrary, you need to specify a binding for the interface Processor. The following is an example of a Guice module for our scenario:

```
public class StandardModule extends AbstractModule {
  @Override
  protected void configure() {
    bind(Processor.class).to(ProcessorImpl.class);
  }
}
```

You create an Injector using the static method Guice.createInjector by passing a module. You then use the injector to create instances:

```
Injector injector = Guice.createInjector(new StandardModule());
Service service = injector.getInstance(Service.class);
service.execute("First command");
```

The initialization of injected fields will be done automatically by Google Guice. It is worth noting that the framework is also able to initialize (inject) private fields, like in our example. Instances of classes that use dependency injection must be created only through an injector. Creating instances with new will not trigger injection, thus all the fields annotated with @Inject will be null.

When implementing a DSL with Xtext you will never have to create a new injector manually. In fact, Xtext generates utility classes to easily obtain an injector, for example, when testing your DSL with JUnit, as we will see in *Chapter 7, Testing*. We also refer to the article *Köhnlein*, 2012 for more details. The example shown in this section only aims at presenting the main features of Google Guice.

If we need a different configuration of the bindings, all we need to do is define another module. For example, let's assume that we defined additional derived implementations for logging and processing. Here is an example where Logger and Processor are bound to custom implementations:

```
public class CustomModule extends AbstractModule {
  @Override
  protected void configure() {
    bind(Logger.class).to(CustomLogger.class);
    bind(Processor.class).to(AdvancedProcessor.class);
  }
}
```

Creating instances with an injector obtained using this module will ensure that the right classes are used consistently. For example, the `CustomLogger` class will be used both by `Service` and `Processor`.

You can create instances from different injectors in the same application, for example:

```
executeService(Guice.createInjector(new StandardModule()));
executeService(Guice.createInjector(new CustomModule()));

void executeService(Injector injector) {
  Service service = injector.getInstance(Service.class);
  service.execute("First command");
  service.execute("Second command");
}
```

> It is possible to request injection in many different ways, such as injection of parameters to constructors, using named instances, specification of default implementation of an interface, `setter` methods, and much more. In this book, we will mainly use injected fields.

Injected fields are instantiated only once when the class is instantiated. Each injection will create a new instance, unless the type to inject is marked as `@Singleton` (com. google.inject.Singleton). The annotation `@Singleton` indicates that only one instance per injector will be used. We will see an example of `Singleton` injection in *Chapter 10, Scoping*.

If you want to decide when you need an element to be instantiated from within method bodies, you can use a **provider**. Instead of injecting an instance of the wanted type `C`, you inject a `com.google.inject.Provider<C>` instance, which has a `get` method that produces an instance of `C`.

For example:

```
public class Logger {
  @Inject
  private Provider<Utility> utilityProvider;

  public void log(String message) {
    System.out.println("LOG: " + message + " - " +
      utilityProvider.get().m());
  }
}
```

Each time we create a new instance of Utility using the injected Provider class. Even in this case, if the type of the created instance is annotated with @Singleton, then the same instance will always be returned for the same injector. The nice thing is that to inject a custom implementation of Utility, you do not need to provide a custom Provider: you just bind the Utility class in the Guice module and everything will work as expected:

```
public class CustomModule extends AbstractModule {
  @Override
  protected void configure() {
    bind(Logger.class).to(CustomLogger.class);
    bind(Processor.class).to(AdvancedProcessor.class);
    bind(Utility.class).to(CustomUtility.class);
  }
}
```

> It is crucial to keep in mind that once classes rely on injection, their instances must be created only through an injector; otherwise, all the injected elements will be null. In general, once dependency injection is used in a framework, all classes of the framework must rely on injection.

Google Guice in Xtext

All Xtext components rely on Google Guice dependency injection, even the classes that Xtext generates for your DSL. This means that in your classes, if you need to use a class from Xtext, you just have to declare a field of such type with the @Inject annotation.

The injection mechanism allows a DSL developer to customize basically every component of the Xtext framework. This boils down to another property of dependency injection, which, in fact, inverts dependencies. The Xtext runtime can use your classes without having a dependency to its implementer. Instead, the implementer has a dependency on the interface defined by the Xtext runtime. For this reason, dependency injection is said to implement **inversion of control** and **the dependency inversion principle**.

When running the MWE2 workflow, Xtext generates both a fully configured module and an empty module that inherits from the generated one. This allows you to override generated or default bindings. Customizations are added to the empty stub module. The generated module should not be touched. Xtext generates one runtime module that defines the non-user interface-related parts of the configuration and one specific for usage in the Eclipse IDE. Guice provides a mechanism for composing modules that is used by Xtext—the module in the UI project uses the module in the runtime project and overrides some bindings.

Let's consider the Entities DSL example. You can find in the src directory of the runtime project the Xtend class EntitiesRuntimeModule, which inherits from AbstractEntitiesRuntimeModule in the src-gen directory. Similarly, in the UI project, you can find in the src directory the Xtend class EntitiesUiModule, which inherits from AbstractEntitiesUiModule in the src-gen directory.

The Guice modules in src-gen are already configured with the bindings for the stub classes generated during the MWE2 workflow. Thus, if you want to customize an aspect using a stub class, then you do not have to specify any specific binding. The generated stub classes concern typical aspects that the programmer usually wants to customize, for example, validation and generation in the runtime project (as we saw in the previous chapters), and labels, and outline in the UI project (as we will see in the next sections). If you need to customize an aspect which is not covered by any of the generated stub classes, then you will need to write a class yourself and then specify the binding for your class in the Guice module in the src folder. We will see an example of this scenario in the *Other customizations* section.

Bindings in these Guice module classes can be specified as we saw in the previous section, by implementing the configure method. However, Xtext provides an enhanced API for defining bindings; Xtext reflectively searches for methods with a specific signature in order to find Guice bindings. Thus, assuming you want to bind a BaseClass class to your derived CustomClass, you can simply define a method in your module with a specific signature, as follows:

```
def Class<? extends BaseClass> bindBaseClass() {
  return CustomClass
}
```

> Remember that in Xtend, you must explicitly specify that you are overriding a method of the base class; thus, in case the bind method is already defined in the base class, you need to use override instead of def.

These methods are invoked reflectively, thus their signature must follow the expected convention. We refer to the official Xtext documentation for the complete description of the module API. Typically, the binding methods that you will see in this book will have the preceding shape, in particular, the name of the method must start with `bind` followed by the name of the class or interface we want to provide a binding for.

It is important to understand that these `bind` methods do not necessarily have to override a method in the module base class. You can also make your own classes, which are not related to Xtext framework classes at all, participants of this injection mechanism, as long as you follow the preceding convention on method signatures.

In the rest of this chapter, we will show examples of customizations of both IDE and runtime concepts. For most of these customizations, we will modify the corresponding Xtend stub class that Xtext generated when running the MWE2 workflow. As hinted before, in these cases, we will not need to write a custom Guice binding. We will also show an example of a customization, which does not have an automatically generated stub class.

Xtext uses injection to inject services and not to inject state (apart from EMF Singleton registries). Thus, the things that are injected are interfaces consisting of functions that take state as arguments (for example, the document, the resource, and so on.). This leads to a service-oriented architecture, which is different from an object-oriented architecture where state is encapsulated with operations. An advantage of this approach is that there are far less problems with synchronization of multiple threads.

Customizations of IDE concepts

In this section, we show typical concepts of the IDE for your DSL that you may want to customize. Xtext shows its usability in this context as well, since, as you will see, it reduces the customization effort.

Labels

Xtext UI classes make use of an `ILabelProvider` interface to obtain textual labels and icons through its methods `getText` and `getImage`, respectively. `ILabelProvider` is a standard component of Eclipse JFace-based viewers. You can see the label provider in action in the **Outline** view and in content assist proposal popups (as well as in various other places).

Xtext provides a default implementation of a label provider for all DSLs, which does its best to produce a sensible representation of the EMF model objects using the `name` feature, if it is found in the corresponding object class, and a default image. You can see that in the **Outline** view when editing an `entities` file, refer to the following screenshot:

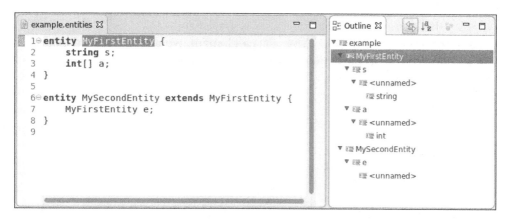

However, you surely want to customize the representation of some elements of your DSL.

The label provider Xtend stub class for your DSL can be found in the UI plug-in project in the subpackage `ui.labeling`. This stub class extends the base class `DefaultEObjectLabelProvider`. In the Entities DSL, the class is called `EntitiesLabelProvider`.

This class employs a **Polymorphic Dispatcher** mechanism (similar to the dispatch methods of Xtend described in *Chapter 3, Working with the Xtend Programming Language*), which is also used in many other places in Xtext. Thus, instead of implementing the `getText` and `getImage` methods, you can simply define several versions of methods `text` and `image` taking as parameter an `EObject` object of the type you want to provide a representation for. Xtext will then search for such methods according to the runtime type of the elements to represent.

For example, for our Entities DSL, we can change the textual representation of attributes in order to show their names and a better representation of types (for example, `name : type`). We then define a method `text` taking `Attribute` as a parameter and returning a string:

```
class EntitiesLabelProvider extends ... {

    @Inject extension TypeRepresentation
```

```
    def text(Attribute a) {
        a.name +
            if (a.type != null)
                " : " + a.type.representation
            else ""
    }
}
```

To get a representation of the `AttributeType` element, we use an injected extension, `TypeRepresentation`, in particular its method `representation`:

```
class TypeRepresentation {
    def representation(AttributeType t) {
        val elementType = t.elementType
        val elementTypeRepr =
            switch (elementType) {
                BasicType : elementType.typeName
                EntityType : elementType?.entity.name
            }
        elementTypeRepr + if (t.array) "[]" else ""
    }
}
```

> Remember that the label provider is used, for example, for the **Outline** view, which is refreshed when the editor contents change, and its contents might contain errors. Thus, you must be ready to deal with an incomplete model, and some features might still be null. That is why you should always check that the features are not null before accessing them.

Note that we inject an extension field of type `TypeRepresentation` instead of creating an instance with new in the field declaration. Although it is not necessary to use injection for this class, we decided to rely on that because in the future we might want to be able to provide a different implementation for that class. Another point for using injection instead of new is that the other class may rely on injection in the future. Using injection leaves the door open for future and unanticipated customizations.

The **Outline** view now shows as in the following screenshot:

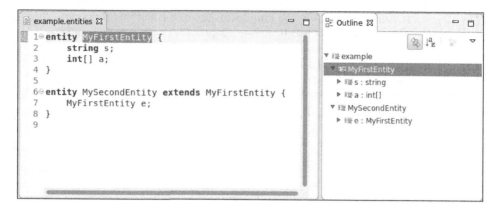

We can further enrich the labels for entities and attributes using images for them. To do this, we create a directory in the `org.example.entities.ui` project where we place the image files of the icons we want to use. In order to benefit from Xtext's default handling of images, we call the directory `icons`, and we place two gif images there, `Entity.gif` and `Attribute.gif` (for entities and attributes, respectively). You fill find the icon files in the accompanying source code in the `org.example.entities.ui/icons` folder. We then define two `image` methods in `EntitiesLabelProvider` where we only need to return the name of the image files and Xtext will do the rest for us:

```
class EntitiesLabelProvider extends DefaultEObjectLabelProvider {
    ... as before
    def image(Entity e) { "Entity.gif" }

    def image(Attribute a) { "Attribute.gif" }
}
```

You can see the result by relaunching Eclipse, as seen in the following screenshot:

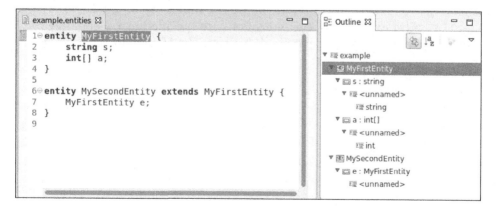

Now, the entities and attributes labels look nicer.

> If you plan to export the plugins for your DSL so that others can install them in their Eclipse (see *Chapter 11, Continuous Integration*), you must make sure that the icons directory is added to the build.properties file, otherwise that directory will not be exported. The bin.includes section of the build.properties file of your UI plugin should look like the following:
>
> ```
> bin.includes = META-INF/,\
>                .,\
>                plugin.xml,\
>                icons/
> ```

The Outline view

The default **Outline** view comes with nice features. In particular, it provides toolbar buttons to keep the **Outline** view selection synchronized with the element currently selected in the editor. Moreover, it provides a button to sort the elements of the tree alphabetically.

By default, the tree structure is built using the containment relations of the metamodel of the DSL. This strategy is not optimal in some cases. For example, an Attribute definition also contains the AttributeType element, which is a structured definition with children (for example, elementType, array, and length). This is reflected in the **Outline** view (refer to the previous screenshot) if you expand the Attribute elements.

This shows unnecessary elements, such as BasicType names, which are now redundant since they are shown in the label of the attribute, and additional elements which are not representable with a name, such as the array feature.

We can influence the structure of the **Outline** tree using the generated stub class EntitiesOutlineTreeProvider in the src folder org.example.entities. ui.outline. Also in this class, customizations are specified in a declarative way using the polymorphic dispatch mechanism. The official documentation, https://www.eclipse.org/Xtext/documentation/, details all the features that can be customized.

In our example, we just want to make sure that the nodes for attributes are leaf nodes, that is, they cannot be further expanded and they have no children. In order to achieve this, we just need to define a method named _isLeaf (note the underscore) with a parameter of the type of the element, returning true. Thus, in our case we write the following code:

```
class EntitiesOutlineTreeProvider extends
        DefaultOutlineTreeProvider {
    def _isLeaf(Attribute a) { true }
}
```

Let's relaunch Eclipse, and now see that the attribute nodes do not expose children anymore.

Besides defining leaf nodes, you can also specify the children in the tree for a specific node by defining a _createChildren method taking as parameters the type of outline node and the type of the model element. This can be useful to define the actual root elements of the **Outline** tree. By default, the tree is rooted with a single node for the source file. In this example, it might be better to have a tree with many root nodes, each one representing an entity. The root of the **Outline** tree is always represented by a node of type DefaultRootNode. The root node is actually not visible, it is just the container of all nodes that will be displayed as roots in the tree.

Thus, we define the following method (our Entities model is rooted by a Model element):

```
public class EntitiesOutlineTreeProvider ... {
    ... as before
    def void _createChildren(DocumentRootNode outlineNode,
                             Model model) {
        model.entities.forEach[
            entity |
            createNode(outlineNode, entity);
        ]
    }
}
```

This way, when the **Outline** tree is built, we create a root node for each `entity` instead of having a single root for the source file. The `createNode` method is part of the Xtext base class. The result can be seen in the following screenshot:

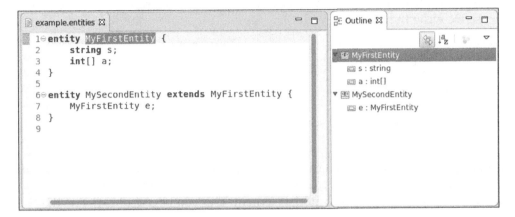

Customizing other aspects

In *Chapter 8, An Expression Language*, we will show how to customize the content assistant. There is no need to do this for the simple Entities DSL since the default implementation already does a fine job.

Custom formatting

An editor for a DSL should provide a mechanism for rearranging the text of the program in order to improve its readability, without changing its semantics. For example, nested regions inside blocks should be indented, and the user should be able to achieve that with a menu.

Besides that, implementing a custom formatter has also other benefits, since the formatter is automatically used by Xtext when you change the EMF model of the AST. If you tried to apply the quickfixes we implemented in *Chapter 4, Validation*, you might have noticed that after the EMF model has changed, the editor immediately reflects this change. However, the resulting textual representation is not well formatted, especially for the quickfix that adds the missing referred entity.

In fact, the EMF model representing the AST does not contain any information about the textual representation, that is, all white space characters are not part of the EMF model (after all, the AST is an abstraction of the actual program).

Xtext keeps track of such information in another in-memory model called the **node model**. The node model carries the syntactical information, that is, offset and length in the textual document. However, when we manually change the EMF model, we do not provide any formatting directives, and Xtext uses the default formatter to get a textual representation of the modified or added model parts.

Xtext already generates the menu for formatting your DSL source programs in the Eclipse editor. As it is standard in Eclipse editors (for example, the JDT editor), you can access the **Format** menu from the context menu of the editor or using the *Ctrl + Shift + F* key combination.

The default formatter is OneWhitespaceFormatter and you can test this in the Entities DSL editor; this formatter simply separates all tokens of your program with a space. Typically, you will want to change this default behavior.

If you provide a custom formatter, this will be used not only when the **Format** menu is invoked, but also when Xtext needs to update the editor contents after a manual modification of the AST model, for example, a quickfix performing a semantic modification.

The easiest way to customize the formatting is to have the Xtext generator create a stub class. To achieve this, you need to add the following formatter specification in the StandardLanguage block in the MWE2 workflow file, requesting to generate an Xtend stub class:

```
language = StandardLanguage {
    name = "org.example.entities.Entities"
    fileExtensions = "entities"
    ...
    formatter = {
        generateStub = true
        generateXtendStub = true
    }
}
```

If you now run the workflow, you will find the formatter Xtend stub class in the main plugin project in the formatting2 package. For our Entities DSL, the class is org.example.entities.formatting2.EntitiesFormatter. This stub class extends the Xtext class AbstractFormatter2.

Note that the name of the package ends with 2. That is because Xtext recently completely changed the customization of the formatter to enhance its mechanisms. The old formatter is still available, though deprecated, so the new formatter classes have the 2 in the package in order not to be mixed with the old formatter classes.

In the generated stub class, you will get lots of warnings of the shape `Discouraged access: the type AbstractFormatter2 is not accessible due to restriction on required project org.example. entities.` That is because the new formatting API is still provisional, and it may change in future releases in a non-backward compatible way. Once you are aware of that, you can decide to ignore the warnings. In order to make the warnings disappear from the Eclipse project, you configure the specific project settings to ignore such warnings, as shown in the following screenshot:

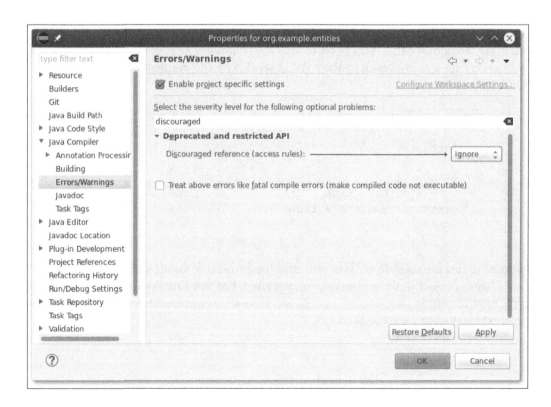

The Xtend stub class already implements a few dispatch methods, taking as parameters the AST element to format and an IFormattableDocument object. The latter is used to specify the formatting requests. A **formatting request** will result in a **textual replacement** in the program text. Since it is an extension parameter, you can use its methods as extension methods (for more details on extension methods, refer to *Chapter 3, Working with the Xtend Programming Language*, Section *Extension methods*). The IFormattableDocument interface provides a Java API for specifying formatting requests. Xtend features such as extension methods and lambdas will allow you to specify formatting request in an easy and readable way.

The typical formatting requests are line wraps, indentations, space addition and removal, and so on. These will be applied on the textual regions of AST elements. As we will show in this section, the textual regions can be specified by the EObject of AST or by its keywords and features.

For our Entities DSL, we decide to perform formatting as follows:

1. Insert two newlines after each entity so that entities will be separated by an empty line; after the last entity, we want a single empty line.

2. Indent attributes between entities curly brackets.

3. Insert one line-wrap after each attribute declaration.

4. Make sure that entity name, super entity, and the extends keyword are surrounded by a single space.

5. Remove possible white spaces around the ; of an attribute declaration.

To achieve the empty lines among entities, we modify the stub method for the Entities Model element:

```
def dispatch void format(Model model,
                            extension IFormattableDocument
document) {
  val lastEntity = model.entities.last
  for (entity : model.entities) {
    entity.format
    if (entity === lastEntity)
      entity.append[setNewLines(1)]
    else
      entity.append[setNewLines(2)]
  }
}
```

We append two newlines after each entity. This way, each entity will be separated by an empty line, since each entity, except for the first one, will start on the second added newline. We append only one newline after the last entity.

Now start a new Eclipse instance and manually test the formatter with some entities, by pressing *Ctrl + Shift + F*. We modify the `format` stub method for the `Entity` elements. In order to separate each `attribute`, we follow a logic similar to the previous format method. For the sake of the example, we use a different version of `setNewLines`, that is `setNewLines(int minNewLines, int defaultNewLines, int maxNewLines)`, whose signature is self-explanatory:

```
for (attribute : entity.attributes) {
  attribute.append[setNewLines(1, 1, 2)]
}
```

Up to now, we referred to a textual region of the AST by specifying the `EObject`. Now, we need to specify the textual regions of keywords and features of a given AST element.

In order to specify that the `"extends"` keyword is surrounded by one single space we write the following:

```
entity.regionFor.keyword("extends").surround[oneSpace]
```

We also want to have no space around the terminating semicolon of attributes, so we write the following:

```
attribute.regionFor.keyword(";").surround[noSpace]
```

In order to specify that the the entity's name and the super entity are surrounded by one single space we write the following:

```
entity.regionFor.feature(ENTITY__NAME).surround[oneSpace]
entity.regionFor.feature(ENTITY__SUPER_TYPE).surround[oneSpace]
```

After having imported statically all the `EntitiesPackage.Literals` members, as follows:

```
import static org.example.entities.entities.EntitiesPackage.Literals.*
```

Finally, we want to handle the indentation inside the curly brackets of an entity and to have a newline after the opening curly bracket. This is achieved with the following lines:

```
val open = entity.regionFor.keyword("{")
val close = entity.regionFor.keyword("}")
open.append[newLine]
interior(open, close)[indent]
```

Summarizing, the `format` method for an `Entity` is the following one:

```
def dispatch void format(Entity entity,
                         extension IFormattableDocument document) {
  entity.regionFor.keyword("extends").surround[oneSpace]
  entity.regionFor.feature(ENTITY__NAME).surround[oneSpace]
  entity.regionFor.feature(ENTITY__SUPER_TYPE).surround[oneSpace]

  val open = entity.regionFor.keyword("{")
  val close = entity.regionFor.keyword("}")
  open.append[newLine]
  interior(open, close)[indent]

  for (attribute : entity.attributes) {
    attribute.regionFor.keyword(";").surround[noSpace]
    attribute.append[setNewLines(1, 1, 2)]
  }
}
```

Now, start a new Eclipse instance and manually test the formatter with some attributes and entities, by pressing *Ctrl + Shift + F*.

In the generated Xtend stub class, you also find an injected extension for accessing programmatically the elements of your grammar. In this DSL it is the following:

```
@Inject extension EntitiesGrammarAccess
```

For example, to specify the left curly bracket of an entity, we could have written this alternative line:

```
val open = entity.regionFor.keyword(entityAccess.
leftCurlyBracketKeyword_3)
```

Similarly, to specify the terminating semicolon of an attribute, we could have written this alternative line:

```
attribute.regionFor.keyword(attributeAccess.semicolonKeyword_2)
  .surround[noSpace]
```

Eclipse content assist will help you in selecting the right method to use.

Note that the method names are suffixed with numbers that relate to the position of the keyword in the grammar's rule. Changing a rule in the DSL's grammar with additional elements or by removing some parts will make such method invocations invalid since the method names will change. On the other hand, if you change a keyword in your grammar, for example, you use square brackets instead of curly brackets, then referring to keywords with string literals as we did in the original implementation of the format methods will issue no compilation errors, but the formatting will not work anymore as expected. Thus, you need to choose your preferred strategy according to the likeliness of your DSL's grammar evolution.

You can also try and apply our quickfixes for missing entities and you will see that the added entity is nicely formatted, according to the logic we implemented.

What is left to be done is to format the attribute type nicely, including the array specification. This is left as an exercise. The `EntitiesFormatter` you find in the accompanying sources of this example DSL contains also this formatting logic for attribute types.

You should specify formatting requests avoiding conflicting requests on the same textual region. In case of conflicts, the formatter will throw an exception with the details of the conflict.

Other customizations

All the customizations you have seen so far were based on modification of a generated stub class with accompanying generated Guice bindings in the module under the `src-gen` directory.

However, since Xtext relies on injection everywhere, it is possible to inject a custom implementation for any mechanism, even if no stub class has been generated.

If you installed Xtext SDK in your Eclipse, the sources of Xtext are available for you to inspect. You should learn to inspect these sources by navigating to them and see what gets injected and how it is used. Then, you are ready to provide a custom implementation and inject it. You can use the Eclipse **Navigate** menu. In particular, to quickly open a Java file (even from a library if it comes with sources), use *Ctrl + Shift + T* (**Open Type...**). This works both for Java classes and Xtend classes. If you want to quickly open another source file (for example, an Xtext grammar file) use *Ctrl + Shift + R* (**Open Resource...**). Both dialogs have a text field where, if you start typing, the available elements soon show up. Eclipse supports **CamelCase** everywhere, so you can just type the capital letters of a compound name to quickly get to the desired element. For example, to open the `EntitiesRuntimeModule` Java class, use the **Open Type...** menu and just digit `ERM` to see the filtered results.

As an example, we show how to customize the output directory where the generated files will be stored (as we saw in *Chapter 5, Code Generation*, the default is `src-gen`). Of course, this output directory can be modified by the user using the **Properties** dialog that Xtext generated for your DSL (see *Chapter 5, Code Generation*), but we want to customize the default output directory for Entities DSL so that it becomes `entities-gen`.

The default output directory is retrieved internally by Xtext using an injected `IOutputConfigurationProvider` instance. If you take a look at this class (see the preceding tip), you will see the following:

```
import com.google.inject.ImplementedBy;

@ImplementedBy(OutputConfigurationProvider.class)
public interface IOutputConfigurationProvider {
  Set<OutputConfiguration> getOutputConfigurations();
  ...
```

The `@ImplementedBy` Guice annotation tells the injection mechanism the default implementation of the interface. Thus, what we need to do is create a subclass of the default implementation (that is, `OutputConfigurationProvider`) and provide a custom binding for the `IOutputConfigurationProvider` interface.

The method we need to override is `getOutputConfigurations`; if we take a look at its default implementation, we see the following:

```
public Set<OutputConfiguration> getOutputConfigurations() {
  OutputConfiguration defaultOutput = new
    OutputConfiguration(IFileSystemAccess.DEFAULT_OUTPUT);
  defaultOutput.setDescription("Output Folder");
  defaultOutput.setOutputDirectory("./src-gen");
  defaultOutput.setOverrideExistingResources(true);
  defaultOutput.setCreateOutputDirectory(true);
  defaultOutput.setCleanUpDerivedResources(true);
  defaultOutput.setSetDerivedProperty(true);
  defaultOutput.setKeepLocalHistory(true);
  return newHashSet(defaultOutput);
}
```

Of course, the interesting part is the call to `setOutputDirectory`.

We define an Xtend subclass as follows:

```
class EntitiesOutputConfigurationProvider extends
        OutputConfigurationProvider {

  public static val ENTITIES_GEN = "./entities-gen"

  override getOutputConfigurations() {
    super.getOutputConfigurations() => [
      head.outputDirectory = ENTITIES_GEN
    ]
  }
}
```

Note that we use a public constant for the output directory since we might need it later in other classes. We use several Xtend features: the `with` operator, the implicit static extension method `head`, which returns the first element of a collection, and the syntactic sugar for `setter` method.

We create this class in the main plug-in project, since this concept is not just an UI concept and it is used also in other parts of the framework. Since it deals with generation, we create it in the `generator` subpackage.

Now, we must bind our implementation in the `EntitiesRuntimeModule` class:

```
class EntitiesRuntimeModule extends
    AbstractEntitiesRuntimeModule {

  def Class<? extends IOutputConfigurationProvider>
        bindIOutputConfigurationProvider() {
    return EntitiesOutputConfigurationProvider
  }
}
```

If we now relaunch Eclipse, we can verify that the Java code is generated into `entities-gen` instead of `src-gen`. If you previously used the same project, the `src-gen` directory might still be there from previous generations; you need to manually remove it and set the new `entities-gen` as a source folder.

Summary

In this chapter, we introduced the Google Guice dependency injection framework on which Xtext relies. You should now be aware of how easy it is to inject custom implementations consistently throughout the framework. You also learned how to customize some basic runtime and IDE concepts for a DSL.

The next chapter shows how to perform unit testing for languages implemented in Xtext. Test-driven development is an important programming technique, which will make your implementations more reliable, resilient to changes of the libraries, and will allow you to program quickly.

7
Testing

In this chapter, you will learn how to test a DSL implementation using the JUnit framework and the additional utility classes provided by Xtext. This way, your DSL implementation will have a suite of tests that can be run automatically. We will use the Entities DSL developed in the previous chapters for showing the typical techniques for testing both the runtime and the UI features of a DSL implemented in Xtext.

This chapter will cover the following topics:

- A small introduction to automated testing with JUnit
- How to test the runtime and the UI aspects of an Xtext DSL
- Some hints on how to keep the code clean and modular

Introduction to testing

Writing automated tests is a fundamental technology/methodology when developing software. It will help you write quality software where most aspects (possibly all aspects) are somehow verified in an automatic and continuous way. Although successful tests do not guarantee that the software is bug free, automated tests are a necessary condition for professional programming (see the books *Beck* 2002, *Martin* 2002, 2008, 2011 for some insightful reading about this subject).

Tests are a form of documentation that does not risk getting stale with respect to the implementation itself. Javadoc comments will likely not be kept in synchronization with the code they document; manuals will tend to become obsolete if not updated consistently, while tests will fail if they are not up to date.

The **Test Driven Development** (TDD) methodology fosters the writing of tests even before writing production code. When developing a DSL, one can relax this methodology by not necessarily writing the tests first. However, one should write tests as soon as a new functionality is added to the DSL implementation. This must be taken into consideration right from the beginning, thus, you should not try to write the complete grammar of a DSL, but proceed gradually; write a few rules to parse a minimal program, and immediately write tests for parsing some test input programs. Only when these tests pass, you should go on to implementing other parts of the grammar.

Moreover, if some validation rules can already be implemented with the current version of the DSL, you should write tests for the current validator checks as well.

Ideally, one does not have to run Eclipse to manually check whether the current implementation of the DSL works as expected. Using tests will then make the development much faster.

The number of tests will grow as the implementation grows, and tests should be executed each time you add a new feature or modify an existing one. You will see that since tests will run automatically, executing them over and over again will require no additional effort besides triggering their execution (think instead if you should manually check what you added or modified did not break something).

This also means that you will not be scared to touch something in your implementation; after you made some changes, just run the whole test suite and check whether you broke something. If some tests fail, you will just need to check whether the failure is actually expected (and in case, fix the test) or whether your modifications have to be fixed.

 It is worth noting that using a version control system (such as Git) is essential to easily get back to a known state. Just experimenting with your code and finding errors using tests does not mean you can easily backtrack.

You will not even be scared to port your implementation to a new version of the used frameworks. Even if your sources still compile using the new version of a framework, it will be your test suite to tell you whether the behavior of your program is still the same. In particular, if some of the tests fail, you can get an immediate idea of which parts need to be changed.

If your implementation relies on a solid test suite, it will be easier for contributors to provide patches and enhancements for your DSL; they can run the test suite themselves or they can add further tests for a specific bugfix or for a new feature. It will also be easy for the main developers to decide whether to accept the contributions by running the tests.

Last but not the least, you will discover that writing tests right from the beginning will force you to write modular code; otherwise you will not be able to easily test it, and it will make programming much more fun.

Xtext and Xtend themselves are developed with a lot of tests.

JUnit 4

JUnit is the most popular unit test framework for Java, and it is shipped with Eclipse **Java Development Tools (JDT)**. In particular, the examples in this book are based on JUnit version 4.

To implement JUnit tests, you just need to write a class with methods annotated with `@org.junit.Test`. We will call such methods simply **test methods**. Such Java or Xtend classes can then be executed in Eclipse using the *JUnit test* launch configuration. All methods annotated with `@Test` will be then executed by JUnit. In test methods you can use **assert** methods provided by the `org.junit.Assert` class. For example, `assertEquals(expected, actual)` checks whether the two arguments are equal; `assertTrue(expression)` checks whether the passed expression evaluates to `true`. If an assertion fails, JUnit will record such failure. In Eclipse, the **JUnit** view will provide you with a report about tests that failed. Ideally, no test should fail, and you should see the green bar in the **JUnit** view.

> All test methods can be executed by JUnit in any order; thus, you should never write a test method that depends on the outcome of another one. All test methods should be executable independently from each other.

If you annotate a method with `@Before`, that method will be executed before each test method in that class, thus, it can be used to prepare a common setup for all the test methods in that class. Similarly, a method annotated with `@After` will be executed after each test method, even if it fails, thus, it can be used to clean up the environment. A static method annotated with `@BeforeClass` will be executed only once before the start of all test methods (`@AfterClass` has the complementary intuitive functionality). All these methods must be void methods.

The ISetup interface

Running tests means that we somehow need to bootstrap the environment to make it support EMF and Xtext in addition to the implementation of our DSL. This is done with a suitable implementation of ISetup. We need to configure things differently depending on how we want to run tests; with or without Eclipse and with or without Eclipse UI being present. The way to set up the environment is quite different when Eclipse is present, since many services are shared and already part of the Eclipse environment. When setting up the environment for non-Eclipse use (also referred to as **standalone**) there are a few things that must be configured, such as creating a Guice injector and registering information required by EMF. The method createInjectorAndDoEMFRegistration in the ISetup interface is there to do exactly this.

Besides the creation of an Injector, this method also performs the initialization of EMF global registries so that after the invocation of that method, the EMF API to load and store models of your language can be fully used, even without a running Eclipse. Xtext generates an implementation of this interface, named after your DSL, which can be found in the runtime plug-in project. For our Entities DSL, it is called EntitiesStandaloneSetup.

 The name *standalone* expresses the fact that this class has to be used when running outside Eclipse. Thus, the preceding method **must never be called** when running inside Eclipse; otherwise, the EMF registries will become inconsistent.

In a plain Java application, the typical steps to set up the DSL (for example, our Entities DSL) can be sketched as follows:

```
Injector injector = new
  EntitiesStandaloneSetup().createInjectorAndDoEMFRegistration();
XtextResourceSet resourceSet =
  injector.getInstance(XtextResourceSet.class);
resourceSet.addLoadOption
  (XtextResource.OPTION_RESOLVE_ALL, Boolean.TRUE);
Resource resource = resourceSet.getResource
  (URI.createURI("/path/to/my.entities"), true);
IResourceValidator validator =
  injector.getInstance(IResourceValidator.class);
List<Issue> issues = validator.validate(resource, CheckMode.ALL,
  CancelIndicator.NullImpl);
// check possible validation issues (omitted)
Model model = (Model) resource.getContents().get(0);
```

This standalone setup class is especially useful also for JUnit tests that can then be run without an Eclipse instance. This will speed up the execution of tests. Of course, in such tests, you will not be able to test UI features.

As we will see in this chapter, Xtext provides many utility classes for testing, which do not require us to set up the runtime environment explicitly. However, it is important to know about the existence of the setup class in case you either need to tweak the generated standalone compiler (see *Chapter 5, Code Generation*, section *Standalone command-line compiler*) or you need to set up the environment in a specific way for unit tests.

Implementing tests for your DSL

Xtext highly fosters using unit tests, and this is reflected by the fact that, by default, the MWE2 workflow generates specific plug-in projects for testing your DSL. In fact, usually tests should reside in a separate project, since they should not be deployed as part of your DSL implementation. Xtext generates two test projects. One that ends with the .tests suffix, for tests that do not depend on the UI, and one that ends with the .ui.tests suffix, for tests that depend on the UI. For our Entities DSL, these two projects are org.example.entities.tests and org.example.entities.ui.tests. The test plug-in projects have the needed dependencies on the required Xtext utility bundles for testing.

We will use Xtend to write JUnit tests; thanks to all its features, tests will be easier to write and easier to read.

In the src-gen directory of the test projects, you will find the injector providers for headless and UI tests respectively. You can use these providers to easily write JUnit test classes without having to worry about the injection mechanisms setup. The JUnit tests that use the injector provider will typically have the following shape (using the Entities DSL as an example):

```
@RunWith(XtextRunner)
@InjectWith(EntitiesInjectorProvider)
class MyTest {
  @Inject MyClass
  ...
```

As hinted in the preceding code, in this class you can rely on injection. We used @InjectWith and declared that EntitiesInjectorProvider has to be used to create the injector. EntitiesInjectorProvider will transparently provide the correct configuration for a standalone environment. As we will see later in this chapter, when we want to test UI features, we will use EntitiesUiInjectorProvider(note the "Ui" in the name). The injector provider for the UI is generated in the ui.tests project.

Testing the parser

The first tests you might want to write are the ones which concern parsing.

This reflects the fact that the grammar is the first thing you must write when implementing a DSL. You should not try to write the complete grammar before starting testing: you should write only a few rules and soon write tests to check if those rules actually parse an input test program as you expect.

The nice thing is that you do not have to store the test input in a file (though you could do that); the input to pass to the parser can be a string, and since we use Xtend, we can use multiline strings.

The Xtext test framework provides the class ParseHelper to easily parse a string. The injection mechanism will automatically tell this class to parse the input string with the parser of your DSL. To parse a string, we inject an instance of ParseHelper<T>, where T is the type of the root class in our DSL's model—in our Entities example, this class is called Model. The ParseHelper.parse method will return an instance of T after parsing the input string given to it.

By injecting the ParseHelper class as an extension, we can directly use its methods on the strings we want to parse.

The Xtext generator already generates a stub class in the .tests project for testing the parser. In the Entities DSL, this Xtend class is called EntitiesParsingTest. This stub class is generated for the initial "hello" grammar, so if you run it as it is, the test will fail.

Thus, we modify the stub class as follows:

```
@RunWith(XtextRunner)
@InjectWith(EntitiesInjectorProvider)
class EntitiesParsingTest {

  @Inject extension ParseHelper<Model>

  @Test
  def void testParsing() {
    val model = '''
      entity MyEntity {
          MyEntity attribute;
      }
    '''.parse

    val entity = model.entities.get(0)
```

```
   Assert.assertEquals("MyEntity", entity.name)

   val attribute = entity.attributes.get(0)
   Assert.assertEquals("attribute", attribute.name);
   Assert.assertEquals("MyEntity",
      (attribute.type.elementType as EntityType).
         entity.name);
}
...
```

In this test, we parse the input and test that the AST of the parsed program has the expected structure. These tests do not add much value in the Entities DSL, but in a more complex DSL you do want to test that the structure of the parsed EMF model is as you expect (we will see an example of that in *Chapter 8, An Expression Language*).

You can now run the test; right-click on the Xtend file and navigate to **Run As | JUnit Test**. The test should pass, and you should see the green bar in the **JUnit** view.

Note that the parse method returns an EMF model even if the input string contains syntax errors since it tries to parse as much as it can. Thus, if you want to make sure that the input string is parsed without any syntax error, you have to check that explicitly. To do that, you can use another utility class, ValidationTestHelper. This class provides many assert methods that take an EObject argument. You can use an extension field and simply call assertNoErrors on the parsed EMF object. Alternatively, if you do not need the EMF object, but you just need to check that there are no parsing errors, you can simply call it on the result of parse, for example:

```
class EntitiesParsingTest {

   @Inject extension ParseHelper<Model>
   @Inject extension ValidationTestHelper
...
   @Test
   def void testCorrectParsing() {
      '''
         entity MyEntity {
            MyEntity attribute
         }
      '''.parse.assertNoErrors
}
```

If you try to run the tests again, you will get a failure for this new test:

```
java.lang.AssertionError: Expected no errors, but got :
ERROR (org.eclipse.xtext.diagnostics.Diagnostic.Syntax)
'missing ';' at '}'' on Entity, offset 41, length 1
```

The reported error should be clear enough: we forgot to add the terminating ' ; ' in our input program; thus, we can fix it and run the test again. This time, the green bar should be back.

You can now write other @Test methods for testing the various features of the DSL (see the sources of the examples). Depending on the complexity of your DSL, you may have to write many of them.

 Tests should test one specific thing at a time; lumping things together (to reduce the overhead of having to write many test methods) usually makes it harder later.

Remember that you should follow this methodology while implementing your DSL, not after having implemented all of it. If you follow this strictly, you will not have to launch Eclipse to manually check that you implemented a feature correctly, and you will note that this methodology will let you program really fast.

Testing the validator

Earlier, we used the ValidationTestHelper class to test that it was possible to parse without errors. Of course, we also need to test that errors and warnings are detected. In particular, we should test any error situation handled by our own validator. The ValidationTestHelper class contains utility methods, besides assertNoErrors, that allow us to test whether the expected errors are correctly issued.

For instance, for our Entities DSL, we wrote a custom validator method that checks that the entity hierarchy is acyclic (*Chapter 4, Validation*). Thus, we should write a test that, given an input program with a cycle in the hierarchy, checks that such an error is indeed raised during validation.

It is better to separate JUnit test classes according to the tested features; thus, we write another JUnit class, EntitiesValidatorTest, which contains tests related to validation. The start of this new JUnit test class should look familiar:

```
@RunWith(XtextRunner)
@InjectWith(EntitiesInjectorProvider)
class EntitiesValidatorTest {

  @Inject extension ParseHelper<Model>
  @Inject extension ValidationTestHelper
  ...
```

We are now going to use the `assertError` method from `ValidationTestHelper`, which, besides the EMF model element to validate, requires the following arguments:

- The `EClass` of the object which contains the error. This is usually retrieved through the EMF `EPackage` class generated when running the MWE2 workflow.
- The expected issue code.
- An optional string describing the expected error message.

Thus, we parse input containing an entity extending itself, and we pass the arguments to `assertError` according to the error generated by `checkNoCycleInEntityHierarchy` in `EntitiesValidator` (see *Chapter 4, Validation*):

```
@Test
def void testEntityExtendsItself() {
  '''
    entity MyEntity extends MyEntity {

    }
  '''.parse.assertCycleInHierarchy("MyEntity")
}

def private assertCycleInHierarchy(Model m, String entityName) {
  m.assertError(
    EntitiesPackage.eINSTANCE.entity,
    EntitiesValidator.HIERARCHY_CYCLE,
    "cycle in hierarchy of entity '" + entityName + "'"
  )

}
```

Note that the `EObject` argument is the one returned by the `parse` method (we use `assertError` as an extension method). Since the error concerns an `Entity` object, we specify the corresponding `EClass` (retrieved using `EntitiesPackage`), the expected issue code, and finally, the expected error message. This test should pass.

We can now write another test, which tests the same validation error on a more complex input with a cycle in the hierarchy involving more than one entity. In this test, we make sure that our validator issues an error for each of the entities involved in the hierarchy cycle:

```
@Test
def void testCycleInEntityHierarchy() {
  '''
```

```
        entity A extends B {}
        entity B extends C {}
        entity C extends A {}
    '''.parse => [
        assertCycleInHierarchy("A")
        assertCycleInHierarchy("B")
        assertCycleInHierarchy("C")
  ]
}
```

You can also check that the error marker generated by the validator is created on the right element in the source file. In order to do that, you use the version of assertError that also takes the expected offset and the expected length of the text region marked with error. For example, the EntitiesValidator should generate the error for a cycle in the hierarchy on the superType feature. We write the following test to check this:

```
@Test
def void testCycleInHierarchyErrorPosition() {
  val testInput =
  '''
    entity MyEntity extends MyEntity {
    }
  '''
  testInput.parse.assertError(
    EntitiesPackage.eINSTANCE.entity,
    EntitiesValidator.HIERARCHY_CYCLE,
    testInput.lastIndexOf("MyEntity"), // offset
    "MyEntity".length // length
  )
}
```

We check that the offset and the length of the text region marked with error corresponds to the entity named after "extends", that is, the last occurrence of "MyEntity" in the input.

You can also assert warnings, using assertWarning, which has the same signatures as the assertError used in the previous code snippet. Similarly, you can use assertNoWarnings, which corresponds to assertNoErrors, but with respect to warnings. The assertIssue and assertNoIssues methods perform similar assertions without considering the severity level.

You should keep in mind that a broken implementation of a validation rule could always mark entities with errors. For this reason, you should always write a test for positive cases as well:

```
@Test
def void testValidHierarchy() {
  '''
    entity FirstEntity {}
    entity SecondEntity extends FirstEntity {}
  '''.parse.assertNoErrors
}
```

> Do not worry if it seems tricky to get the arguments for assertError right the first time; writing a test that fails the first time it is executed is expected in Test Driven Development. The error of the failing test should put you on the right track to specify the arguments correctly. However, by inspecting the error of the failing test, you must first make sure that the actual output is what you expected, otherwise something is wrong either with your test or with the implementation of the component that you are testing.

Testing the formatter

As we said in the previous chapter, the formatter is also used in a non-UI environment, thus, we can test the formatter for our DSL with plain JUnit tests. To test the formatter, we create a new Xtend class, and we inject as extension the FormatterTester class:

```
@RunWith(XtextRunner)
@InjectWith(EntitiesInjectorProvider)
class EntitiesFormatterTest {

    @Inject extension FormatterTester

...
```

> Just like it happened in *Chapter 6, Customizing Xtext Components*, when we used the new formatter API, we get a lot of *Discouraged Access* warnings when using FormatterTester. Refer to that chapter for the reasons of the warnings and how to disable them.

To test the formatter, we use the `assertFormatted` method that takes a lambda where we specify the input to be formatted and the expected formatted program:

```
@Test
def void testEntitiesFormatter() {
    assertFormatted[
        toBeFormatted = '''
                entity E1 { int i ; string s; boolean b    ;}
                entity  E2  extends  E1{}
        '''
        expectation = '''
                ...
        '''
    ]
}
```

Why did we specify ... as the expected formatted output? Why did we not try to specify what we really expect as the formatted output? Well, we could have written the expected output and probably we would have gotten it right on the first try, but why not simply make the test fail and see the actual output? We can then copy that in our test once we are convinced that it is correct. So let's run the test, and when it fails, the **JUnit** view tells us what the actual result is, as shown in the following screenshot:

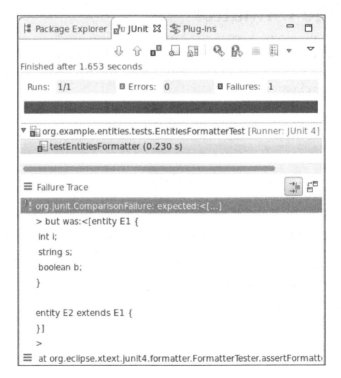

If you now double-click on the line showing the comparison failure in the **JUnit** view, you will get a dialog showing a line-by-line comparison, as shown in the following screenshot:

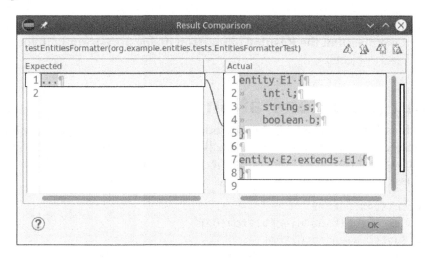

You can verify that the actual output is correct, copy that, and paste it into your test as the expected output. The test will now succeed:

```
@Test
def void testEntitiesFormatter() {
    assertFormatted[
        toBeFormatted = '''

            entity E1 { int i ; string s; boolean b    ;}
            entity  E2  extends  E1{}
        '''
        expectation = '''
            entity E1 {
                    int i;
                    string s;
                    boolean b;
            }

            entity E2 extends E1 {
            }
        '''
    ]
}
```

Note that the Xtend editor will automatically indent the pasted contents.

Using this technique, you can easily write JUnit tests that deal with comparisons. However, remember that the **Result Comparison** dialog appears only if you compare String objects.

Testing code generation

Xtext provides a helper class to test your code generator, CompilationTestHelper, which we inject as an extension field in the JUnit test class. This helper class parses an input string and runs the code generator, thus we do not need the parser helper in this test class:

```
@RunWith(XtextRunner)
@InjectWith(EntitiesInjectorProvider)
class EntitiesGeneratorTest {

    @Inject extension CompilationTestHelper
```

 The CompilationTestHelper requires the Eclipse JDT compiler, so you must add org.eclipse.jdt.core as dependency of the .tests project.

This helper class provides the method assertCompilesTo, which takes a char sequence representing an input program and a char sequence representing the expected generated output. Using that as an extension method, we can then write the following test method, which tests that the generated Java code is as we expect (we use the technique of the **JUnit** view to get the actual output as illustrated in the previous section):

```
@Test
def void testGeneratedCode() {
  '''
  entity MyEntity {
    string myAttribute;
  }
  '''.assertCompilesTo(
  '''
  package entities;

  public class MyEntity {
```

```
    private String myAttribute;

    public String getMyAttribute() {
      return myAttribute;
    }

    public void setMyAttribute(String _arg) {
      this.myAttribute = _arg;
    }

  }
  ''')
}
```

Testing that the generated output corresponds to what we expect is already a good testing technique. However, when the generated code is Java code, it might be good to also test that it is valid Java code, that is, the Java compiler compiles the generated code without errors.

To test that the generated code is valid Java code, we use the `CompilationTestHelper.compile` method, which takes an input string and a lambda. The parameter of the lambda is a `Result` object (an inner class). In the lambda, we can use the `Result` object to perform additional checks. To test the validity of the generated Java code, we can call the `Result.getCompiledClass` method. This method compiles the generated code with the Eclipse Java compiler. If the Java compiler issues an error, then our test will fail and the **JUnit** view will show the compilation errors.

We write the following test (remember that if no parameter is explicitly declared in the lambda, the special implicit variable `it` is used):

```
@Test
def void testGeneratedJavaCodeIsValid() {
  '''
  entity MyEntity {
    string myAttribute;
  }
  '''.compile[getCompiledClass]
  // check that it is valid Java code
}
```

If the `getCompiledClass` class terminates successfully, it also returns a Java `Class` object, which can be used to instantiate the compiled Java class by reflection. This allows us to test the generated Java class' runtime behavior. We can easily invoke the created instance's methods through the reflection support provided by the Xtext class `ReflectExtensions`. For example (`Assert`'s static methods are imported statically):

```
@Inject extension ReflectExtensions

@Test
def void testGeneratedJavaCode() {
  '''
  entity E {
    string myAttribute;
  }
  '''.compile[
    getCompiledClass.newInstance => [
      assertNull(it.invoke("getMyAttribute"))
      it.invoke("setMyAttribute", "value")
      assertEquals("value",
        it.invoke("getMyAttribute"))
    ]
  ]
}
```

This method tests (through the `getter` method) that the attributes are initialized to `null` and that the `setter` method sets the corresponding attribute.

You can test situations when the generator generates several files originating from a single input. In the Entities DSL, a Java class is generated for each entity, thus, we can perform checks on each generated Java file by using the `Result.getGeneratedCode(String)` method that takes the name of the generated Java class as an argument and returns its contents. Since the generator for our Entities DSL should generate the Java class `entities.E` for an entity named "E", you must specify the fully qualified name to retrieve the generated code for an entity.

Similarly, we can check that the several generated Java files compile correctly. We can perform reflective Java operations on all the compiled Java classes using `Result.getCompiledClass(String)` specifying the fully qualified name of the generated Java class:

```
@Test def void testGeneratedJavaCodeWithTwoClasses() {
  '''
  entity FirstEntity {
    SecondEntity myAttribute;
  }
```

```
entity SecondEntity {
  string s;
}
'''.compile[
  val FirstEntity =
    getCompiledClass("entities.FirstEntity").newInstance
  val SecondEntity =
    getCompiledClass("entities.SecondEntity").newInstance
  SecondEntity.invoke("setS", "testvalue")
  FirstEntity.invoke("setMyAttribute", SecondEntity)
  SecondEntity.assertSame(FirstEntity.invoke("getMyAttribute"))
  "testvalue".assertEquals
    (FirstEntity.invoke("getMyAttribute").invoke("getS"))
  ]
}
```

In particular, in this last example, the first generated Java class depends on the second generated Java class.

These tests might not be valuable in this DSL, but in more complex DSLs, having tests which automatically check the runtime behavior of the generated code enhances productivity.

> The getGeneratedCode method assumes that the requested generated artifact is a Java file. If your DSL generates other artifacts, such as XML or textual files, you must use getAllGeneratedResources, which returns a java.util. Map where the key is the file path of the generated artifact and the value is its content.

The CompilationTestHelper class runs your DSL validator, but it will call the generator even if the parsed model is not valid. The output of the generator might be meaningless in such cases. If you want to make sure that's what you pass to CompilationTestHelper is a valid input for your DSL, you need to manually check whether the Result contains validation errors. This is an example of how to do that:

```
def void testInputWithValidationError() {
    '''
        entity MyEntity {
                // missing ;
                string myAttribute
        }
    '''.compile [
        val allErrors = getErrorsAndWarnings.filter[severity ==
Severity.ERROR]
```

```
        if (!allErrors.empty) {
                throw new IllegalStateException(
                        "One or more resources contained errors : " +
                        allErrors.map[toString].join(", ")
                );
        }
    ]
}
```

If you run this test it will fail, since the input contains a parser error.

Test suite

When you write several JUnit classes, it becomes uncomfortable to run them individually. You can run all the Xtend tests in a package by right-clicking on the corresponding package in the xtend-gen folder and select **Run As | JUnit Test**.

If you need more control over the tests that must be run or you want to group some tests, you can write a JUnit **Test Suite**. For example, you can write a suite for tests which are not related to generation as shown in the following Java class:

```java
import org.junit.runner.RunWith;
import org.junit.runners.Suite;

@RunWith(Suite.class)
@Suite.SuiteClasses({
    EntitiesParsingTest.class,
    EntitiesFormatterTest.class,
    EntitiesValidatorTest.class
})
public class EntitiesNotGeneratorRelatedTests {
}
```

You can run such suite as a standard JUnit test, and it will run all the test methods in all the test classes specified in the test suite.

Testing the UI

Most of the mechanisms of a DSL implemented in Xtext can be tested with plain Java JUnit tests without a UI environment. However, when testing UI features, tests need a running Eclipse.

Eclipse provides a specific launch configuration, "JUnit Plug-in Test", which executes JUnit tests with a running Eclipse.

Implementing tests for the UI concepts might be tricky, since usually you will need to write code to set up Eclipse workbench infrastructures such as projects, files, and so on. Xtext provides some base classes for testing UI concepts, which do most of the job for you so that you can simply test specific features without having to worry about the setup steps.

All the UI tests we implement in this section are created in the project `org.example.entities.ui.tests`.

 The examples in this section do not necessarily represent valuable tests; they should be seen as starting points for more complex tests of more complex DSLs.

Testing the content assist

In the Entities DSL, we did not customize the content assist, thus we do not really need to test it. For more complex DSLs, you want to test that the custom content assist works as expected, and you want to avoid having to manually check that. Thus, it is better to learn how to test it right now. To test the content assist, we use the base class `AbstractContentAssistTest`.

 This class requires `org.eclipse.xtext.common.types.ui` and `org.eclipse.jdt.core`, so you must add them as dependencies in the `MANIFEST.MF` of the `.ui.tests` project. You will then have to configure the project setting to get rid of the *Discouraged Access* warnings as we did when using `FormatterTester`.

We use the `@RunWith` and `@InjectWith` annotations, as we did in the previous sections but we use the generated UI injector provider `EntitiesUiInjectorProvider` (note the "Ui" in the name):

```
@RunWith(XtextRunner)
@InjectWith(EntitiesUiInjectorProvider)
class EntitiesContentAssistTest extends
    AbstractContentAssistTest {
```

Then, in the test methods, we can simply use the API of the `AbstractContentAssistTest` base class:

- `newBuilder` creates an object to test the content assist
- `append` appends some input text
- `assertText` declares the expected content assist proposals as strings (there are other assert methods, but this is the only one we will use)

Thus, our test class looks like as follows:

```
@RunWith(typeof(XtextRunner))
@InjectWith(typeof(EntitiesUiInjectorProvider))
class EntitiesContentAssistTest extends
      AbstractContentAssistTest {
  @Test def void testEmptyProgram() {
    newBuilder.assertText("entity")
  }

  @Test def void testSuperEntity() {
    newBuilder.append
      ("entity E extends ").assertText("E")
  }
  @Test def void testSuperEntity2() {
    newBuilder.append("entity A{} entity E extends ").
      assertText("A", "E")
  }

  @Test def void testAttributeTypes() {
    newBuilder.append("entity E { ").
      assertText
      ("E", "boolean", "int", "string", "}")
  }
}
```

Remember that you must run this class as a "JUnit Plug-in Test".

Let's examine what the preceding tests do:

- When the input is empty, we should get "entity" as the only proposal
- After an "extends", we should get as proposals the names of the available entities (with a single entity, we get its own name as the only proposal)
- If there are two entities, we get both names as proposals.
- After the entity opening curly bracket, we get as proposals all the types available, but also the closing curly bracket, since an entity can be defined without attributes.

Testing workbench integration

Sometimes you may want to test whether your DSL implementation "integrates" correctly with the Eclipse workbench. Usually, in these tests you also need a project in the running Eclipse.

 These kinds of tests are called **integration tests**, since they test the integration of several software components. In our case, they test the integration of our DSL implementation with the Eclipse workbench. Integration tests are expected to be long running.

In the following example, we want to test whether a project with Entities DSL files builds correctly without errors.

Xtext provides the base class `AbstractWorkbenchTest` for testing Eclipse workbench related operations. In particular, this base class implements `@Before` and `@After` methods so that each `@Test` method is executed in a clean environment (that is, with an empty workbench), and the workbench is cleaned after each test (that is, all test projects are closed and deleted).

Besides that, Xtext provides the classes `IResourcesSetupUtil` and `JavaProjectSetupUtil` with many static utility methods to programmatically create workspace projects. We will import these static methods as static extension methods in the Xtend test class.

In our case, before each test we want to create a Java workspace project and add the **Xtext nature** to that project (this corresponds to the dialog you get when you first add an `entities` file into a project, asking you to convert that project to an Xtext project); moreover, we also add `entities-gen` as a source folder. The ID of Xtext nature is retrieved using the `XtextProjectHelper` class.

We then write a reusable method which:

- Creates an `entities` file in the workspace project with the specified contents
- Waits for Eclipse to build the project
- Checks whether there are error markers related to the entities file.

All these operations use the utility methods of the two preceding mentioned classes (the error markers are retrieved using the standard Eclipse API):

```
import static org.junit.Assert.*
import static extension org.eclipse.xtext.junit4.ui.util.
JavaProjectSetupUtil.*
```

```
import static extension org.eclipse.xtext.junit4.ui.util.
IResourcesSetupUtil.*

class EntitiesWorkbenchTest extends AbstractWorkbenchTest {

  val TEST_PROJECT = "mytestproject"

  @Before
  override void setUp() {
    super.setUp
    createJavaProjectWithXtextNature
  }

  def void createJavaProjectWithXtextNature() {
    createJavaProject(TEST_PROJECT) => [
      getProject().addNature
        (XtextProjectHelper.NATURE_ID)
      addSourceFolder("entities-gen")
    ]
  }

  def void checkEntityProgram(String contents,
      int expectedErrors) {
    val file = createFile(TEST_PROJECT +
      "/src/test.entities", contents)
    waitForBuild();
    assertEquals(expectedErrors,
      file.findMarkers(EValidator.MARKER, true,
        IResource.DEPTH_INFINITE).size);
  }
```

Now, we can write two test methods to check that for a valid entities file there is no error marker and that for a non-valid entities file we get an error marker:

```
  @Test
  def void testValidProgram() {
    checkEntityProgram("entity E {}", 0)
  }

  @Test
  def void testNotValidProgram() {
    checkEntityProgram("foo", 1)
  }
```

We did not use any injection mechanisms in the test. Indeed, we only manipulate Eclipse concepts (such as projects, files, and so on); thus, we do not need direct access to classes of our DSL implementation. Xtext is executing in the background while we programmatically create projects and files in the Eclipse test workbench.

Testing the editor

There are situations where you may want to perform specific test operations with the editor of your DSL. The test class in this case should derive from `AbstractEditorTest` (which in turn derives from `AbstractWorkbenchTest`). This base class provides utility methods to programmatically open an Eclipse editor on a file in the workbench (represented by `IFile`). The base class `AbstractEditorTest` requires us to implement the method `getEditorId` to return the ID of the editor of the DSL we want to test; the setup methods are similar to `EntitiesWorkbenchTest`, so we omit them here:

```
class EntitiesEditorTest extends AbstractEditorTest {

  ... as in EntitiesWorkbenchTest

  override protected getEditorId() {
    "org.example.entities.Entities"
  }

  def createTestFile(String contents) {
    createFile(TEST_PROJECT +
      "/src/test.entities", contents)
  }

  @Test
  def void testEntitiesEditor() {
    createTestFile("entity E {}").openEditor
  }
```

The code also shows a first test, which checks that we can open an editor for our DSL. Note that `openEditor` returns an instance of `XtextEditor`, which can be used to access (and possibly to modify) the editor contents, as shown in the next section.

Learning Tests

When developing your DSL, you may want to add further features in the IDE which are not covered by the Xtext framework itself; for example, you may want to add context menus for the editor of your DSL that perform some actions on the contents of the editor and possibly change the contents. As we saw in *Chapter 6, Customizing Xtext Components*, Xtext already adds menus such as "Format" and mechanisms such as quickfixes. In order to do that, you must learn the API of Eclipse editors and, in particular, of XtextEditor, which specializes the standard Eclipse text editor.

A nice way of learning a new API is to write **Learning Tests** (see the book *Beck* 2002); these tests basically verify that the API works as expected. Thus, in the rest of this section, we write some tests which allow us to learn how to use the XtextEditor API. Note that, besides making you learn how to use this API, these tests will also guarantee that if that API changes in a non-backward compatible way in the future, we will realize that since these tests will fail.

The actual text edited by an Eclipse editor is stored in an IDocument instance and can be retrieved as a String using the get method (we have already used this in *Chapter 4, Validation*, when implementing quickfixes). This works also with XtextEditor, as shown by following test, which only checks that the editor's text is exactly the same as stored in the test file:

```
@Test
def void testEntitiesEditorContents() {
  "entity E {}".assertEquals(
    createTestFile("entity E {}").
      openEditor.document.get)
}
```

Usually, you will not need the string text, you will need the parsed EMF model. The class XtextEditor uses a specialization of IDocument, IXtextDocument, which provides access to the underlying parsed EMF model. However, in an Eclipse workbench, the access to the EMF model underlying an edited program must be performed in a "synchronized" way, since there are concurrent components running in different threads accessing such model (both UI components, like the editor itself, and non UI components, such as the parser and validator). Thus, for example, if you open an Xtext editor and you need the parsed EMF model, you will have to wait for the editor's text to be parsed. Similarly, if you want to modify the underlying model, you will have to wait until there are no other threads that are using it. This is also due to the fact that EMF has no support for concurrent threads.

The EMF model of an Xtext editor's document can be accessed using the method `readOnly`; this method takes as an argument a lambda with a parameter of type `XtextResource` (a specialized EMF resource). We can retrieve the model from the passed `XtextResource`. When the body of the lambda is executed, there will be no other concurrent threads accessing the EMF resource. Thus, within the body of the lambda, the access to the model is guaranteed to be synchronized. This learning test reads the EMF model corresponding to the editor contents, retrieves the entity, and checks that its name is as expected:

```
@Test
def void testEntitiesEditorContentsAsModel() {
  "E".assertEquals(
    createTestFile("entity E {}").
      openEditor.document.readOnly [
        // 'it' is an XtextResource
        contents.get(0) as Model
      ].entities.get(0).name
  )
}
```

The lambda passed to `readOnly` can return any type (Xtend will infer it). In the preceding test, the return type of the lambda is `Model`.

 The `.tests.ui` project of a DSL does not have the runtime project as dependency. If you need to use the EMF model types of your DSL, you need to explicitly add such dependency. In this example, you need to add `org.example.entities` as dependency of the project `org.example.entities.ui.tests`.

Similarly, we can access and modify the EMF model using the method `modify` and passing a lambda. The synchronization, in case of a modification, will also ensure that after the underlying model is modified, all the other components (such as the parser and validator) will be notified.

The following test creates a test file with a single entity, `E`, and then modifies the EMF model by adding another entity, `Added`, which extends `E`; it then checks that the editor string contents have been updated accordingly:

```
@Test
def void testChangeContents() {
  val editor = createTestFile("entity E {}").openEditor

  editor.document.modify [
    val model = (contents.get(0) as Model)
    val currentEntity = model.entities.get(0)
```

```
        model.entities +=
        EntitiesFactory.eINSTANCE.createEntity => [
          name = "Added"
          superType = currentEntity
        ]
    ]
    '''
    entity E {}

    entity Added extends E {
    }
    '''.toString.assertEquals(editor.document.get)
}
```

Note that the resulting editor's text corresponding to the entity we added programmatically is formatted according to the formatter we implemented in *Chapter 6, Customizing Xtext Components*. In that chapter, we also saw that the formatter is automatically triggered when selecting the quickfix provider based on semantic modification. Indeed, quickfix provider implementations are also automatically executed in a synchronous way.

Although the tests for the editor shown in this section are learning tests, they should give you an idea of how the Xtext editor API works.

Both `readOnly` and `modify` take a `IUnitOfWork` as an argument. This interface defines a single method `exec` with a single generic parameter. Since this is a **Single Abstract Method (SAM)** type (introduced in *Chapter 3, Working with the Xtend Programming Language*), you can pass a lambda as argument. There is a specialization of `IUnitOfWork` called `CancelableUnitOfWork` whose `exec` abstract method also takes a `CancelIndicator` as argument. We have already seen the `CancelIndicator` class in *Chapter 5, Code Generation*. This is useful if the unit of work performs many operations: you can periodically query the `CancelIndicator` object, and if other Xtext components has requested a cancel operation you should interrupt your operations as well. For example, you may want to implement a modify operation that has to perform several changes on the model. While performing such modification, the user can type something in the editor and this invalidates the model and you will be notified that the modification operation should be canceled.

Testing the outline

In the Entities DSL, we customized the **Outline** view. To test the Outline, we use the
base class `AbstractOutlineTest`. This class extends `AbstractEditorTest`, so we
must implement the method `getEditorId` to return the `ID` of our editor as we did
in the previous sections. We then use the `assertAllLabels` method that takes two
arguments: the input program and the expected string representation of the outline.
This method creates a string representation of the outline tree, indenting the children
and then compares that with the passed expected representation. This also allows
us to test that the label provider works as expected, since the the label provider is
implicitly used for representing the labels of the outline tree. We can then test the
outline simply as follows:

```
@RunWith(XtextRunner)
@InjectWith(EntitiesUiInjectorProvider)
class EntitiesOutlineTest extends AbstractOutlineTest {

    override protected getEditorId() {
        "org.example.entities.Entities"
    }

    @Test
    def void testOutline() {
        '''
        entity E1 {
                string s;
                int i;
        }

        entity E2 {}
        '''.assertAllLabels(
        '''
        E1
            s : string
            i : int
        E2
        '''
        )
    }
}
```

Other testing frameworks

In this section, we briefly describe some other testing frameworks that you can use to test several aspects of an Xtext DSL. The treatment of these frameworks is out of the scope of this book.

An interesting framework for testing XtextDSLs is Xpect (`http://www.xpect-tests.org`). Xpect aims at reducing the effort of writing the tests, by stating assertions in a more expressive way.

The UI tests, we saw in the previous sections, do not test the actual operations that a user can perform in the IDE, like, for example, selecting a menu, right-clicking on an item and selecting a context menu, interacting with a dialog, and so on. The tests that confirm that a system does what the users are expecting it to are called **Functional Tests**.

The most known functional testing frameworks in the Eclipse context are **SWTBot** (`http://www.eclipse.org/swtbot`), **Jubula** (`http://www.eclipse.org/jubula`), and **RCP Testing Tool** (`http://www.eclipse.org/rcptt`). Other frameworks (free, open source, or commercial) are briefly described at this URL — `http://wiki.eclipse.org/Eclipse/Testing`.

Testing and modularity

One of the nice advantages of TDD is that it forces you to write modular code; it is not easy to test code that is not modular. Thus, either you give up on testing (an option, which I hope you will never consider) or you decouple modules to easily test them. If you did not adopt this methodology from the beginning, remember that it is always possible to refactor the code to make it more modular and more testable. Thus, TDD and modular/decoupled design go hand in hand and drive quality; well designed modular code is easier to test and well-tested code has a known quality.

When evaluating whether to accept this programming methodology, you should also take into consideration that testing UI aspects is usually harder. Thus, you should try to isolate the code that does not depend on a running Eclipse. Fortunately, in a DSL implementation this is easy.

Let's consider the quickfix provider we implemented in *Chapter 4, Validation*, which adds the missing referred `entity`; we show that here again for convenience:

```
@Fix(Diagnostic.LINKING_DIAGNOSTIC)
def void createMissingEntity(Issue issue,
                             IssueResolutionAcceptor acceptor) {
  acceptor.accept(issue,
    "Create missing entity",
```

```
      "Create missing entity",
      "Entity.gif",
      [ EObject element, IModificationContext context |
        val currentEntity =
          element.getContainerOfType(Entity)
        val model = currentEntity.eContainer as Model
        model.entities.add(model.entities.indexOf(currentEntity)+1,
          EntitiesFactory.eINSTANCE.createEntity() => [
            name =
              context.xtextDocument.get(issue.offset, issue.length)
          ]
        )
      ]
    );
}
```

Testing the quickfix provider is not straightforward. However, what we would really like to test here is that the desired entity is added in the right place in the model; this has nothing to do with the quickfix provider itself.

The manipulation of the EMF model does not need any IDE feature; thus, we can isolate that in a utility class' static method, for example:

```
class EntitiesModelUtil {
  def static addEntityAfter(Entity entity,
          String nameOfEntityToAdd) {
    val model = entity.eContainer as Model
    EntitiesFactory.eINSTANCE.createEntity() => [
      name = nameOfEntityToAdd
      model.entities.add
        (model.entities.indexOf(entity)+1, it)
    ]
  }
}
```

Manipulating an EMF model is easy using the EMF API, but when the operations to perform on the model are complex, it is crucial to test them. Now that the code that modifies the EMF model is in a method that is independent from the UI, it is easy to test the insertion of an entity in the expected position:

```
class EntitiesModelUtilTest {
  val factory = EntitiesFactory.eINSTANCE

  @Test
  def void testAddEntityAfter() {
    val e1 = factory.createEntity => [name = "First"]
```

```
    val e2 = factory.createEntity => [name = "Second"]
    val model = factory.createModel => [
      entities += e1
      entities += e2
    ]

    EntitiesModelUtil.addEntityAfter(e1, "Added").
      assertNotNull
    3.assertEquals(model.entities.size)
    "First".assertEquals(model.entities.get(0).name)
    "Added".assertEquals(model.entities.get(1).name)
    "Second".assertEquals(model.entities.get(2).name)
  }
}
```

This checks that the new entity is inserted right after the desired existing entity, that is, between First and Second.

Now, we can also test that this code can be executed with an EMF model underlying an Xtext editor:

```
class EntitiesEditorTest extends AbstractEditorTest {
  … as in the preceding code
@Test
def void testAddEntity() {
  val editor = createTestFile(
  '''
  entity E1 {}

  entity E2 {}
  ''').openEditor

  editor.document.modify [
    EntitiesModelUtil.addEntityAfter(
      (contents.get(0) as Model).entities.get(0),
      "Added")
  ]
  '''
  entity E1 {}

  entity Added {
  }

  entity E2 {}
  '''.toString.assertEquals(editor.document.get)
}
```

This shows that our method for adding an entity works also in the context of an Xtext editor and that its contents get updated consistently.

Now, we can refactor our quickfix provider method as follows:

```
@Fix(Diagnostic.LINKING_DIAGNOSTIC)
def void createMissingEntity(Issue issue,
                             IssueResolutionAcceptor acceptor) {
  acceptor.accept(issue,
    "Create missing entity", // label
    "Create missing entity", // description
    "Entity.gif", // icon
    [ EObject element, IModificationContext context |
      EntitiesModelUtil.addEntityAfter(
        element.getContainerOfType(Entity),
        context.xtextDocument.get(issue.offset, issue.length)
      )
    ]
  )
}
```

We can safely assume that this quickfix provider will work, since it depends on concepts that we have already tested in isolation. We could retrieve the name of the entity to add in the wrong way, but that would be easier to spot in the preceding code than in the original implementation of the quickfix provider.

Clean code

Keeping your code *clean* (see the books *Martin* 2008, 2011) is important for the development of software and this includes modularity, readability, and maintainability. Xtext provides many features to keep your DSL implementation clean and modular, thanks to its decomposition into many customizable aspects. Xtend extremely enhances the ability to write clean code thanks to its syntax and its features such as lambda expressions and extension methods. In this book, we will put much effort into writing clean code when implementing a DSL; in particular, we will try to write small methods and to factor common code into reusable methods.

Tests must be clean as well, since they are part of the development cycle, and they will have to be modified often. Remember that tests also provide documentation, thus they must be easily readable. In this chapter, we tried to write small test methods by relying on reusable utility methods and classes. Note that writing small methods does not necessarily mean writing a few lines of code; for example, when we want to compare generated code, we need to embed the expectation in the test method. However, the number of expressions/statements is kept to the minimum, and the meaning of the test should be easily understood.

Summary

In this chapter, we introduced unit testing for languages implemented with Xtext. Being able to test most of the DSL aspects without having to start an Eclipse environment, really speeds up development.

TDD is an important programming methodology that helps you make your implementations more modular, more reliable, and resilient to changes of the libraries used by your code.

In the next chapter, we will implement a DSL based on expressions. In spite of the apparent simplicity, parsing and checking expressions is not that simple, since arithmetic and boolean expressions are inherently recursive, and dealing with recursion always requires some additional attention and effort. We will also implement a type system to check that expressions are well typed. Finally, we will implement an interpreter for these expressions.

An Expression Language

8

In this chapter, we will implement a DSL for expressions, including arithmetic, boolean, and string expressions. We will do that incrementally and in a test-driven way. Since expressions are by their own nature recursive, writing a grammar for this DSL requires some additional efforts, and this allows us to discover additional features of Xtext grammars.

You will also learn how to implement a type system for a DSL to check that expressions are correct with respect to types, for example, you cannot add an integer and a boolean. We will implement the type system so that it fits the Xtext framework and integrates correctly with the corresponding IDE tooling.

Finally, we will implement an interpreter for these expressions. We will use this interpreter to write a simple code generator that creates a text file with the evaluation of all the expressions of the input file, and also to show the evaluation of an expression in the editor.

This chapter will cover the following topics:

- Additional details on Xtext grammars
- Dealing with left recursion in an Xtext grammar
- Writing a small type system for expressions
- Writing an interpreter
- Some hints on fine tuning a DSL implementation

The Expressions DSL

In the DSL we develop in this chapter, which we call **Expressions DSL**, we want to accept input programs consisting of the following statements: variable declarations with an initialization expression and evaluations of expressions. Variable declarations have the shape var name = exp and evaluation statements have the shape eval exp. Expressions can refer to variables and can perform arithmetic operations, compare expressions, use logical connectors (and and or), and concatenate strings. We will use + both for representing arithmetic addition and for string concatenation. When used with strings, the + will also have to automatically convert integers and Booleans occurring in such expressions into strings.

Here is an example of a program that we want to write with this DSL:

```
var i = 0
var j = (i > 0 && 1 < (i+1))
var k = 1
eval j || true
eval "a" + (2 * (3 + 5)) // string concatenation
eval (12 / (3 * 2))
```

For example, "a" + (2 * (3 + 5)) should evaluate to the string "a16".

Creating the project

First of all, we will use the Xtext project wizard to create the projects for our DSL (following the same procedure explained in *Chapter 2, Creating Your First Xtext Language*).

Start Eclipse and perform the following steps:

1. Navigate to **File | New | Project...**, and in the dialog, navigate to the **Xtext** category and click on **Xtext Project**.

2. In the next dialog, provide the following values:
   - **Project name:** org.example.expressions
   - **Name:** org.example.expressions.Expressions
   - **Extensions:** expressions

3. Press **Finish**.

4. The wizard will create several projects, and it will open the Expressions. xtext file, which is the grammar definition.

Digression on Xtext grammar rules

Before writing the Xtext grammar for the Expressions DSL, it is important to spend some time to understand how the rules in an Xtext grammar and the corresponding EMF model generated for the AST are related.

From the previous chapters, we know that Xtext, while parsing the input program, will create a Java object corresponding to the used grammar rule. Let's go back to our Entities DSL example and consider the rule:

```
Entity:
    'entity' name = ID ('extends' superType=[Entity])? '{'
       attributes += Attribute*
    '}' ;
```

When the parser uses this rule, it will create an instance of the `Entity` class (that class has been generated by Xtext during the MWE2 workflow). However, the actual creation of such an instance will be deferred to the first assignment to a feature of the rule; in this example, no object will be created when the input only contains `entity`; the object will be created as soon as a name is specified, for example, when the input contains `entity A`. This happens because such an ID is assigned to the feature `name` in the rule. This is reflected in the outline view, as shown in the following two screenshots:

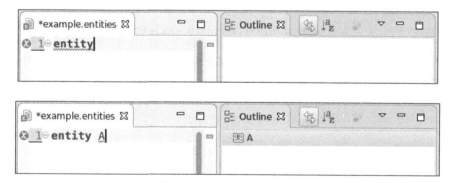

This also means that the created `Entity` object is not "complete" at this stage, that is, when only a part of the rule has been applied. That is why when writing parts of the DSL implementation, for example, the validator, the UI customizations, and so on, you must always take into consideration that the model you are working on may have some features set to `null`.

The actual creation of the object of the AST can be made explicit by the programmer using the notation {type name} inside the rule; for example:

```
Entity:
  'entity' {Entity} name = ID ('extends' superType=[Entity])? '{'
    attributes += Attribute*
  '}' ;
```

If you change the rule as shown, then an Entity object will be created as soon as the entity keyword has been parsed, even if there has not been a feature assignment.

In the examples we have seen so far, the type of the object corresponds to the rule name; however, the type to instantiate can be specified using returns in the rule definition:

```
A returns B:
  ... rule definition ...
;
```

In this example, the parser will create an instance of B. A is simply the name of the rule, and there will be no generated A class. Indeed, the shape of the rule definitions we have used so far is just a shortcut for:

```
A returns A:
  ... rule definition ...
;
```

That is, if no returns is specified, the type corresponds to the name of the rule.

Moreover, the returns statement and the explicit {type name} notation can be combined:

```
A returns B:
  ... {C} ... rule definition ...
;
```

In this example, the parser will create an instance of C (and the class C is generated as a subclass of B). However, the object returned by the rule will have type B. Also in this case, there will be no generated A class.

The Xtext editor highlights rule's name and rule's type differently — the types are in italic font.

> When defining a cross-reference in the grammar, the name enclosed in square brackets refers to a type, not to a rule's name, unless they are the same.

When writing the grammar for the Expressions DSL, we will use these features.

The grammar for the Expressions DSL

The DSL that we want to implement in this chapter should allow us to write lines containing either a variable declaration consisting of the keyword "var", an identifier and an initialization expression (the angle brackets denote non-terminal symbols):

```
var <ID> = <Expression>
```

Or the evaluation of an expression, consisting of the keyword "eval" and the expression to evaluate:

```
eval <Expression>
```

If we write something as follows:

```
ExpressionsModel:
  variables += Variable*
  evaluations += EvalExpression*
;
```

We will not be able to write a program where variables and evaluations can be defined in any order; we can only write variables first and then evaluations.

To achieve the desired flexibility, we introduce an abstract class for both variable declarations and evaluations; then, our model will consist of a (possibly empty) sequence of such abstract elements.

For the moment, we consider a very simple kind of expression—integer constants. These are the first rules (we skip the initial declaration parts of the grammar):

```
ExpressionsModel:
  elements += AbstractElement*;

AbstractElement:
  Variable | EvalExpression ;

Variable:
  'var' name=ID '=' expression=Expression;

EvalExpression:
  'eval' expression=Expression;

Expression:
  value=INT;
```

The generated EMF classes for `Variable` and `EvalExpression` will be subclasses of `AbstractElement`.

 Since both the rule `Variable` and the rule `EvalExpression` have the feature `expression` of the same type (Expression), then the generated class `AbstractElement` will have the corresponding field `Expression expression` inherited by the two generated subclasses.

We are ready to write the first tests for this grammar. This chapter assumes that you fully understood the previous chapter about testing; thus, the code for testing we show here should be clear:

```
import static extension org.junit.Assert.*

@RunWith(XtextRunner)
@InjectWith(ExpressionsInjectorProvider)
class ExpressionsParsingTest {

  @Inject extension ParseHelper<ExpressionsModel>


  @Test def void testEvalExpression() {
    "eval 10".parse.assertNotNull
  }

  @Test def void testVariable() {
    "var i = 10".parse.assertNotNull
  }
}
```

These methods test that both variable declarations and expressions can be parsed.

We now continue adding rules. We want to parse string and boolean constants besides integer constants.

We could write a single rule for all these constant expressions:

```
Expression:
  (intvalue=INT) |
  (stringvalue=STRING) |
  (boolvalue=('true'|'false'));
```

But, this would not be good. It is generally not a good idea to have constructs that result in a single class that represents multiple language elements, since later when we are performing validation and other operations, we cannot differentiate on class alone and instead have to inspect the corresponding fields.

It is much better to write a separate rule for each element as shown in the following code snippet, and this will lead to the generation of separate classes:

```
Expression:
    IntConstant | StringConstant | BoolConstant;

IntConstant: value=INT;
StringConstant: value=STRING;
BoolConstant: value=('true'|'false');
```

Note that, although `IntConstant`, `StringConstant` and `BoolConstant` will all be subclasses of `Expression`, the field `value` will not be part of the `Expression` superclass; for `IntConstant`, the field `value` will be of type integer; while for the other two, it will be of type string. Thus, it cannot be made common.

At this point, you must run the MWE2 workflow, and make sure that the previous tests still run successfully; then, you should add additional tests for parsing a string constant and a boolean constant (this is left as an exercise). We can write the aforementioned rules in a more compact form, using the {type name} notation that we introduced in the previous section, *Digression on Xtext grammar rules*:

```
Expression:
    {IntConstant} value=INT |
    {StringConstant} value=STRING |
    {BoolConstant} value=('true'|'false');
```

Again, run the workflow and make sure the tests still pass.

We add a rule, which accepts a reference to an existing variable as follows:

```
Expression:
    {IntConstant} value=INT |
    {StringConstant} value=STRING |
    {BoolConstant} value=('true'|'false') |
    {VariableRef} variable=[Variable];
```

To test this last modification, we need an input with a variable declaration and an expression that refers to that variable:

```
@Test def void testVariableReference() {
    '''
```

```
var i = 10
eval i
'''.parse => [
  (elements.last.expression as VariableRef).variable.
  assertSame(elements.head)
]
}
```

Note that we also test that the variable reference actually corresponds to the declared variable; `assertSame` comes from `org.junit.Assert`, whose static methods have been imported as extension methods.

Left recursive grammars

When moving on to more complex expressions, such as addition, we need to write a recursive rule since the left and right parts of an addition are expressions themselves. It would be natural to express such a rule as follows:

```
Expression:
  ... as above
  {Plus} left=Expression '+' right=Expression;
```

However, this results in an error from the Xtext editor as shown in the following screenshot:

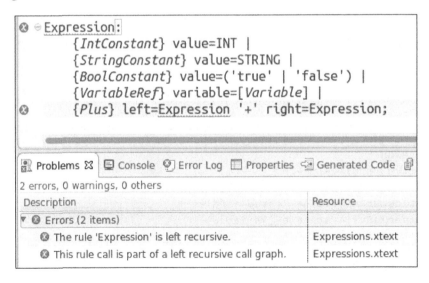

Xtext uses a parser algorithm that is suitable for interactive editing due to its better handling of error recovery. Unfortunately, this parser algorithm does not deal with left recursive rules. A rule is **left recursive** when the first symbol of the rule is non-terminal and refers to the rule itself. The preceding rule for addition is indeed left recursive and is rejected by Xtext. Note that a rule can also be left recursive via multiple rule calls without any token consumption.

> Xtext generates an ANTLR parser (see the book *Parr* 2007), which relies on an LL(*) algorithm; we will not go into detail about parsing algorithms; we refer the interested reader to the book Aho et al, 2007. Such parsers have nice advantages concerning debugging and error recovery, which are essential in an IDE to provide a better feedback to the programmer. However, such parsers cannot deal with left-recursive grammars.

The good news is that we can solve this problem; the bad news is that we have to modify the grammar to remove the left recursion using a transformation referred to as **left factoring**.

The parser generated by ANTLR cannot handle left recursion since it relies on a top-down strategy. Bottom-up parsers do not have this problem, but they would require handling **operator precedence** (which determines which sub-expressions should be evaluated first in a given expression) and **associativity** (which determines how operators of the same precedence are grouped in the absence of parentheses). As we will see in this section, left factoring will allow us to implicitly define operator precedence and associativity.

We remove the left recursion using a standard technique: we introduce a rule for expressions which are **atomic**, and we state that an addition consists of a left part, which is an atomic expression, and an optional right part, which is recursively an expression (note that the right recursion does not disturb the ANTLR parser):

```
Expression:
  {Plus} left=Atomic ('+' right=Expression)?;

Atomic returns Expression:
  {IntConstant} value=INT |
  {StringConstant} value=STRING |
  {BoolConstant} value=('true'|'false') |
  {VariableRef} variable=[Variable];
```

Remember that the rule name is `Atomic`, but objects in the AST created by this rule will be of type `IntConstant`, `StringConstant`, and so on, according to the alternative used (indeed, no `Atomic` class will be generated from the preceding rule). Statically, these objects will be considered of type `Expression`, and thus the `left` and `right` fields in the `Plus` class will be of type `Expression`.

The preceding solution still has a major drawback, that is, additional useless nodes will be created in the AST. For example, consider an atomic expression such as a variable reference; when the atomic expression is parsed using the preceding rule, the AST will consist of a `Plus` object where the `VariableRef` object is stored in the `left` feature:

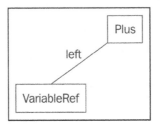

This indirection tends to be quite disturbing. For instance, the previous test method `testVariableReference` will now fail due to a `ClassCastException`.

What we need is a way of telling the parser to:

- Try to parse an expression using the `Atomic` rule
- Search for an optional + followed by another expression
- If the optional part is not found, then the expression is the element parsed with the `Atomic` rule
- Otherwise, instantiate a `Plus` object where `left` is the previously parsed expression with `Atomic` and `right` is the expression parsed after the +

All these operations can be expressed in an Xtext grammar as follows:

```
Expression:
    Atomic ({Plus.left=current} '+' right=Expression)? ;
```

The `{Plus.left=current}` part is an **assigned action** (which is similar to a **tree rewrite action** in Antlr), and it does what we want: if the part `(...)?` can be parsed, then the resulting tree will consist of a `Plus` object where `left` is assigned the subtree previously parsed by the `Atomic` rule and `right` is assigned the subtree recursively parsed by the `Expression` rule.

Now, the test method `testVariableReference` can go back to its original form, since parsing an atomic expression does not result in an additional `Plus` object.

Associativity

Associativity instructs the parser how to build the AST when there are several infix operators with the same precedence in an expression. It will also influence the order in which elements of the AST should be processed in an interpreter or compiler.

What happens if we try to parse something like 10 + 5 + 1? The parsing rule invokes the rule for Expression recursively; the rule is right recursive, and thus we expect the preceding expression to be parsed in a **right-associative** way, that is, 10 + 5 + 1 will be parsed as 10 + (5 + 1). In fact, the optional part (...)? can be used only once; thus, the only way to parse 10 + 5 + 1 is to parse 10 with the Atomic rule and the rest with the optional part:

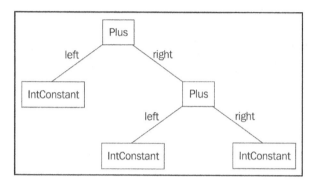

If, on the contrary, we write the rule as follows:

```
Expression:
    Atomic ({Plus.left=current} '+' right=Atomic)* ;
```

We will get **left associativity**, that is, 10 + 5 + 1 will be parsed as (10 + 5) + 1. In fact, the optional part (...)* can be used many times; thus, the only way to parse 10 + 5 + 1 is to apply that part twice (note that right=Atomic and not right=Expression as in the previous section).

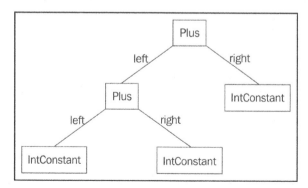

It is important to check that the associativity of the parsed expressions is as expected. A simple way to check the result of associativity is to generate a string representation of the AST where nonatomic expressions are enclosed in parentheses.

```
def private String stringRepr(Expression e) {
  switch (e) {
    Plus:
    '''(«e.left.stringRepr» + «e.right.stringRepr»)'''
    IntConstant: '''«e.value»'''
    StringConstant: '''«e.value»'''
    BoolConstant: '''«e.value»'''
    VariableRef: '''«e.variable.name»'''
  }.toString
}
```

Then, we write a method `assertRepr(input,expected)` that checks that the associativity of the input corresponds to the expected representation:

```
def private assertRepr(CharSequence input, CharSequence expected) {
  ("eval " + input).parse => [
    expected.assertEquals(
      elements.last.expression.stringRepr
    )
  ]
}
```

We will use this method in the rest of the section to test the associativity of expressions. For instance, for testing the associativity of an addition, we write:

```
@Test def void testPlus() {
  "10 + 5 + 1 + 2".assertRepr("(((10 + 5) + 1) + 2)")
}
```

We add a rule for parsing expressions in parentheses:

```
Atomic returns Expression:
  '(' Expression ')' |
  {IntConstant} value=INT |
  ... as above
```

Note that the rule for parentheses does not perform any assignment to features; thus, given the parsed text `(exp)` the AST will contain a node for `exp`, not for `(exp)`. This can be verified by this test:

```
@Test def void testParenthesis() {
  10.assertEquals(
    ("eval (10)".parse.elements.head.expression as IntConstant).value)
}
```

Although parentheses will not be part of the AST, they will influence the structure of the AST:

```
@Test def void testPlusWithParenthesis() {
  "( 10 + 5 ) + ( 1 + 2 )".assertRepr("((10 + 5) + (1 + 2))")
}
```

For the sum operator, left associativity and right associativity are equivalent, since sum is an **associative operation**. The same holds for multiplication (with the possible exception of overflows or loss of precision that depends on the order of evaluation). This does not hold for subtraction and division. In fact, how we parse and then evaluate such operations influences the result: (3 - 2) - 1 is different from 3 - (2 - 1).

In these cases, you can disable associativity using this pattern for writing the grammar rule:

```
Expression:
  Atomic ({Operation.left=current} '-' right=Atomic)? ;
```

In fact the ? operator (instead of *) does not allow to parse an Atomic on the right more than once. This way, the user will be forced to explicitly use grouping expressions for the operations with no associativity when there are more than two operands.

The alternative solution is to choose an associativity strategy for the parser and implement the evaluator accordingly. Typically arithmetic operations are parsed and evaluated in a left-associative way, as, for example, in Java. We prefer this solution since users will get no surprises with this default behavior. Of course, parentheses can always be used for grouping. We modify the grammar for dealing with subtractions; we want to use a dedicated class for a subtraction expression, for example, Minus. We then modify the rule for Expression as follows:

```
Expression:
  Atomic (
    ({Plus.left=current} '+' | {Minus.left=current} '-')
    right=Atomic
  )* ;
```

Note that the assigned action inside the rule is selected according to the parsed operator. Though we are not doing that in this section, you should write a test with a subtraction operation; of course, you must also update the stringRepr utility method for handling the case for Minus.

An example of right associative operator is the **exponentiation** operator, that is, 2**3**4 = 2**(3**4), which is different from (2**3)**4. Another example is the **assignment** operator; as we will see in *Chapter 9, Type Checking*, a nested assignment a = b = c must be parsed as a = (b = c).

Precedence

We can write the case for addition and subtraction in the same rule because they have the same arithmetic operator precedence. If we add a rule for multiplication and division, we must handle their precedence with respect to addition and subtraction.

To define the precedence, we must write the rule for the operator with less precedence in terms of the rule for the operator with higher precedence. This means that in the grammar, the rules for operators with less precedence are defined first. Since multiplication and division have higher precedence than addition and subtraction, we modify the grammar as follows:

```
Expression: PlusOrMinus;

PlusOrMinus returns Expression:
  MulOrDiv (
    ({Plus.left=current} '+' | {Minus.left=current} '-')
    right=MulOrDiv
  )* ;

MulOrDiv returns Expression:
  Atomic (
    ({MulOrDiv.left=current} op=('*'|'/'))
    right=Atomic
  )* ;
```

In the preceding rules, we use `returns` to specify the type of the created objects; thus, the features `left` and `right` in the corresponding generated Java classes will be of type `Expression`.

We added a main rule for `Expression`, which delegates to the first rule to start parsing the expression. Remember that this first rule (at the moment, `PlusOrMinus`) concerns the operators with lowest precedence. There will be no class called `PlusOrMinus` since only objects of class `Plus` and `Minus` will be created by this rule. On the contrary in the rule `MulOrDiv`, we create objects of class `MulOrDiv`. In this rule, we also chose another strategy: we have a single object type, `MulOrDiv`, both for multiplication and division expressions. After parsing, we can tell between the two using the operator, which is saved in the feature `op`. Whether to have a different class for each expression operator or group several expression operators into one single class is up to the developer. Both strategies have their advantages and drawbacks, as we will see in the next sections.

We now test the precedence of these new expressions:

```
@Test def void testPlusMulPrecedence() {
  "10 + 5 * 2 - 5 / 1".assertRepr("((10 + (5 * 2)) - (5 / 1))")
}

def stringRepr(Expression e) {
  switch (e) {
    Plus:
    '''(«e.left.stringRepr» + «e.right.stringRepr»)'''
    Minus:
    '''(«e.left.stringRepr» - «e.right.stringRepr»)'''
    MulOrDiv:
    '''(«e.left.stringRepr» «e.op» «e.right.stringRepr»)'''
... as before
```

Now, we add boolean expressions and comparison expressions to the DSL. Again, we have to deal with their precedence, which is as follows, starting from the ones with less precedence:

1. **boolean or** (operator | |)
2. **boolean and** (operator &&)
3. **equality** and **dis-equality** (operators == and !=, respectively)
4. **comparisons** (operators <, <=, >, and >=)
5. **addition** and **subtraction**
6. **multiplication** and **division**

Following the same strategy for writing the grammar rules, we end up with the following expression grammar:

```
Expression: Or;

Or returns Expression:
  And ({Or.left=current} "||" right=And)* ;

And returns Expression:
  Equality ({And.left=current} "&&" right=Equality)* ;

Equality returns Expression:
  Comparison (
    {Equality.left=current} op=("=="|"!=")
    right=Comparison
  )* ;
```

```
Comparison returns Expression:
  PlusOrMinus (
    {Comparison.left=current} op=(">="|"<="|">"|"<")
    right=PlusOrMinus
  )* ;
```

```
... as before
```

When writing tests for these new expressions, we need to test the correct precedence for the new operators both in isolation and in combination with other expressions (remember to update the `stringRepr` method to handle the new classes). We leave these tests as an exercise; they can be found in the sources of the examples. While adding rules for new expressions, we also added test methods in our parser test class, and we run all these tests each time; this will not only ensure that the new rules work correctly, but also that they do not break existing rules.

As a final step, we add a rule for boolean negation (operator "!"); this operator has the highest precedence among all the operators seen so far. Therefore, we can simply add a case in the `Atomic` rule:

```
Atomic returns Expression:
  '(' Expression ')' |
  {Not} "!" expression=Atomic |
  ... as before
```

We can now write a test with a complex expression and check that the parsing takes place correctly:

```
@Test def void testPrecedences() {
  "!true||false&&1>(1/3+5*2)".
    assertRepr
      ("(((!true) || (false && (1 > ((1 / 3) + (5 * 2)))))")
}
```

Now might be a good time to refactor the rule `Atomic`, since it includes cases that are not effective atomic elements. We introduce the rule `Primary` for expressions with the highest priority the rule `MulOrDiv` is refactored accordingly:

```
MulOrDiv returns Expression:
  Primary (
    {MulOrDiv.left=current} op=('*'|'/')
    right=Primary
  )*
  ;
```

```
Primary returns Expression:
  '(' Expression ')' |
  {Not} "!" expression=Primary |
  Atomic
;

Atomic returns Expression:
  {IntConstant} value=INT |
  {StringConstant} value=STRING |
  {BoolConstant} value=('true'|'false') |
  {VariableRef} variable=[Variable]
;
```

 We also refer the interested reader to the article *Efftinge* 2016, for another example of parsing expressions with Xtext.

The complete grammar

We sum up the section by showing the complete grammar of the Expressions DSL:

```
grammar org.example.expressions.Expressions with
  org.eclipse.xtext.common.Terminals

generate expressions
  "http://www.example.org/expressions/Expressions"

ExpressionsModel:
  elements += AbstractElement*;

AbstractElement:
  Variable | EvalExpression ;

Variable:
  'var' name=ID '=' expression=Expression;

EvalExpression:
  'eval' expression=Expression;

Expression: Or;

Or returns Expression:
```

```
    And ({Or.left=current} "||" right=And)*
;

And returns Expression:
  Equality ({And.left=current} "&&" right=Equality)*
;

Equality returns Expression:
  Comparison (
    {Equality.left=current} op=("=="|"!=")
    right=Comparison
  )*
;

Comparison returns Expression:
  PlusOrMinus (
    {Comparison.left=current} op=(">="|"<="|">"|"<")
    right=PlusOrMinus
  )*
;

PlusOrMinus returns Expression:
  MulOrDiv (
    ({Plus.left=current} '+' | {Minus.left=current} '-')
    right=MulOrDiv
  )*
;

MulOrDiv returns Expression:
  Primary (
    {MulOrDiv.left=current} op=('*'|'/')
    right=Primary
  )*
;

Primary returns Expression:
  '(' Expression ')' |
  {Not} "!" expression=Primary |
  Atomic
;

Atomic returns Expression:
  {IntConstant} value=INT |
  {StringConstant} value=STRING |
  {BoolConstant} value=('true'|'false') |
  {VariableRef} variable=[Variable]
;
```

Forward references

You should know by now that parsing is only the first stage when implementing a DSL and that it cannot detect all the errors from the programs. We need to implement additional checks in a validator.

One important thing we need to check in our Expressions DSL is that an expression does not refer to a variable defined after the very expression. Using an identifier before its declaration is usually called a **forward reference**.

Therefore, this program should not be considered valid:

```
var i = j + 1
var j = 0
```

Since the initialization expression of i refers to j, which is defined after. Of course, this is a design choice. Since we want to interpret the expressions, it makes sense to interpret them in the order they are defined.

This strategy also avoids possible mutual dependency problems:

```
var i = j + 1
var j = i + 1
```

A variable which is initialized referring to itself is a special case of the preceding:

```
var i = i + 1
```

We want to avoid this because our interpreter would enter an endless loop when evaluating expressions.

Restricting the visibility of references can also be implemented with a custom ScopeProvider; the subject of **Scoping** will be detailed in *Chapter 10, Scoping*. However, **visibility** and **validity** are not necessarily the same mechanism. Therefore, it also makes sense to implement this checking in the validator.

We write a @Check method in the ExpressionsValidator class to report such problems.

Given a variable reference inside an expression, we need to:

- Get the list of all the variables defined before the containing expression
- Check that the referred variable is in the list

Note that we need to do that only if the variable is correctly bound; that is, if the cross-reference has already been resolved by Xtext, otherwise an error has already been reported.

This functionality only deals with model traversing, and we isolate it into a utility class, ExpressionsModelUtil (we have already seen this technique in *Chapter 7, Testing*, section *Testing and Modularity*). We will also reuse this utility class when implementing other parts of this DSL.

We implement the method variablesDefinedBefore. Given an expression, we get the AbstractElement containing such expression, let's call it containingElement, using the method org.eclipse.xtext.EcoreUtil2.getContainerOfType. From the root, we get the list of all the elements. Then, we get the sublist of variables up to containingElement. The method isVariableDefinedBefore checks that the referred variable is contained in the set returned by variablesDefinedBefore. This is implemented in Xtend as follows:

```
import static extension org.eclipse.xtext.EcoreUtil2.*

class ExpressionsModelUtil {
  def isVariableDefinedBefore(VariableRef varRef) {
    varRef.variablesDefinedBefore.contains(varRef.variable)
  }

  def variablesDefinedBefore(Expression e) {
    e.getContainerOfType(AbstractElement).variablesDefinedBefore
  }

  def variablesDefinedBefore(AbstractElement containingElement) {
    val allElements =
      (containingElement.eContainer as ExpressionsModel).elements

    allElements.subList(0,
      allElements.indexOf(containingElement)).typeSelect(Variable).
toSet
  }
}
```

 This algorithm is potentially slow when dealing with large models and complex logic, since it always searches from the top element down. Depending on your DSL, you might want to implement other strategies, such as bottom-up search, creating an index upfront, and so on. Once you have a bunch of tests for the simple implementation, you can experiment with optimizations and make sure that the tests still succeed. We will show some examples of optimizations later in this chapter.

We can now test this class in a separate JUnit test class (we show only a snippet) to make sure it does what we expect (testing the method isVariableDefinedBefore is left as an exercise):

```
@Inject extension ParseHelper<ExpressionsModel>
@Inject extension ExpressionsModelUtil

@Test def void variablesBeforeVariable() {
  '''
  eval true    // (0)
  var i = 0    // (1)
  eval i + 10   // (2)
  var j = i    // (3)
  eval i + j   // (4)
  '''.parse => [
    assertVariablesDefinedBefore(0, "")
    assertVariablesDefinedBefore(1, "")
    assertVariablesDefinedBefore(2, "i")
    assertVariablesDefinedBefore(3, "i")
    assertVariablesDefinedBefore(4, "i,j")
  ]
}

def void assertVariablesDefinedBefore(ExpressionsModel model,
    int elemIndex, CharSequence expectedVars) {
  expectedVars.assertEquals(
    model.elements.get(elemIndex).variablesDefinedBefore.
    map[name].join(",")
  )
}
```

Writing the @Check method in the validator is easy now:

```
class ExpressionsValidator extends AbstractExpressionsValidator {
  protected static val ISSUE_CODE_PREFIX = "org.example.expressions."
  public static val FORWARD_REFERENCE =
    ISSUE_CODE_PREFIX + "ForwardReference"

  @Inject extension ExpressionsModelUtil

  @Check
  def void checkForwardReference(VariableRef varRef) {
    val variable = varRef.getVariable()
```

```
    if (!varRef.isVariableDefinedBefore)
      error("variable forward reference not allowed: '"
        + variable.name + "'",
        ExpressionsPackage..eINSTANCE.variableRef_Variable,
        FORWARD_REFERENCE, variable.name)
    }
  }
```

It is also easy to test it (we show only a snippet):

```
@Test
def void testForwardReferenceInExpression() {
  '''var i = j var j = 10'''.parse => [
      assertError(ExpressionsPackage.eINSTANCE.variableRef,
        ExpressionsValidator.FORWARD_REFERENCE,
        "variable forward reference not allowed: 'j'"
      )
      // check that it is the only error
      1.assertEquals(validate.size)
    ]
}

@Test
def void testNoForwardReference() {
  '''var j = 10 var i = j'''.parse.assertNoErrors
}
```

Note that in this test we also make sure that there is only one error. We test this using the list of issues returned by `ValidationTestHelper.validate`. We also write a test where there is no forward reference and we make sure that no error is raised.

Custom Content Assist

We issue an error in case of a forward reference, but we did not customize the way Xtext resolves references; thus, the user of the Expressions DSL can still jump to the actual declaration of the variable, also in case of a forward reference error. This is considered a good thing in the IDE; for example, in Eclipse Java editor if you try to access a private member of a different class, you get an error, but you can still jump to the declaration of that member.

At the same time, though, the content assist of our DSL will also propose variables defined after the context where we are writing in the editor; this should be avoided since it is misleading. We can fix this by customizing the content assist. Xtext already generated an Xtend stub class in the UI plug-in project for customizing this; in this example, it is `org.example.expressions.ui.contentassist.ExpressionsProposalProvider` in the `src` folder. Also, this class relies on a method signature convention as shown in the following code snippet:

```
public void complete{RuleName}_{FeatureName} (
   EObject element, Assignment assignment,
   ContentAssistContext context,
   ICompletionProposalAcceptor acceptor)
public void complete_{RuleName} (
   EObject element, RuleCall ruleCall,
   ContentAssistContext context,
   ICompletionProposalAcceptor acceptor)
```

In the signatures, `RuleName` is the name of the rule in the grammar and `FeatureName` is the name of the feature (with the first letter capitalized) assigned in that rule. The idea is to use the first method signature to customize the proposals for a specific feature of that rule and the second one for customizing the proposals for the rule itself. In our case, we want to customize the proposals for the `variable` feature in the `Atomic` rule (that is, the rule which parses a `VariableRef`); thus, we define a method called `completeAtomic_Variable`. The stub class extends a generated class in the `src-gen` folder, `AbstractExpressionsProposalProvider` that implements all of these `complete` methods. You can inspect the base class to get the signature right. Most of the time, you will only use the first parameter, which is the `EObject` object representing the object corresponding to the rule being used and the acceptor to which you will pass your custom proposals.

In the `completeAtomic_Variable` method, we get the variables defined before the passed `EObject` and create a proposal for each variable:

```
@Inject extension ExpressionsModelUtil

override completeAtomic_Variable(EObject elem,
   Assignment assignment,
   ContentAssistContext context,
   ICompletionProposalAcceptor acceptor) {
   if (elem instanceof Expression)
     elem.variablesDefinedBefore.forEach[
       variable |
       acceptor.accept(
```

```
createCompletionProposal(
  variable.name, variable.name + " - Variable", null, context
)
)
]
}
```

Proposals are created using the `createCompletionProposal` method; you need to pass the string which will be inserted in the editor, the string shown in the content assist menu, a default image, and the context you received as a parameter. Each proposal must be passed to the acceptor.

> Remember that for a given offset in the input program file, there can exist several possible grammar elements. Xtext will dispatch to the method declarations for any valid element, and thus many `complete` methods may be called.

In the previous chapter, we showed you how to test the content assist; we will now test our custom implementation (we only show the relevant parts):

```
@Test def void testVariableReference() {
  newBuilder.append("var i = 10 eval 1+").
  assertText('!', '"Value"', '(', '+', '1', 'false', 'i', 'true')
}

@Test def void testForwardVariableReference() {
  newBuilder.append("var k = 0 var j=1 eval 1+  var i = 10 ").
    assertTextAtCursorPosition("+", 1,
    '!', '"Value"', '(', '+', '1', 'false', 'j', 'k', 'true')
}
```

In the first method, we verify that we did not remove variable proposals that are valid; in the second one, we verify that only the variables that are defined before the current context are proposed. In particular, in the second test, we used an assert method passing the character in the input to set the (virtual) cursor at and an additional offset: we ask for the proposals right after the first + in the input string. We test that j and k are proposed, but not i.

Typing expressions

In the Expressions DSL, types are not written explicitly by the programmer. However, due to the simple nature of our expressions, we can easily deduce the type of an expression by looking at its shape. In this DSL, we have a fixed set of types: string, integer, and boolean. The mechanism of deducing a type for an expression is usually called **type computation** or **type inference**.

The base cases for type computation in the Expressions DSL are constants; trivially, an integer constant has type integer, a string constant has type string, and a boolean constant has type boolean.

As for composed expressions, besides computing a type, we must also check that its sub-expressions are correct with respect to types. This mechanism is usually called **type checking**. For example, consider the expression !e, where e is a generic expression. We can say that it has type boolean, provided that, recursively, the sub-expression e has type boolean; otherwise, the whole expression is not **well-typed**.

All the type mechanisms are part of the **type system** of the language. The type system depends on the semantics, that is, the meaning that we want to give to the elements of the DSL. For the Expressions DSL we design a type system that reflects the natural treatment of arithmetic and boolean expressions, in particular:

- If in a Plus expression one of the sub-expressions has type string, the whole expression is considered to have type string; if they have both type integer, then the whole expression has type integer; two boolean expressions cannot be added

- Equality can only act on sub-expressions with the same type

- Comparison can only act on sub-expressions with the same type, but not on booleans

Of course, a type system should also be consistent with code generation or interpretation; this is typically formally proved, but this is out of the scope of the book (we refer the interested reader to the books *Hindley* 1987 and *Pierce* 2002 and to the article *Cardelli* 1996). For instance, in our DSL, we allow expressions of the shape 1 + "a" and "a" + true: we consider these expressions to have type string, since we use + also for string concatenation and implicit string conversion. If in a Plus expression the two sub-expressions have both type integers then the whole expression will have type integer, since that will be considered as the arithmetic addition. During interpretation, we must interpret such expressions accordingly.

Loose type computation, strict type checking

Typically, type computation and type checking are implemented together and, as just seen, they are recursive. In general, the type of an expression depends on the type of the sub-expressions; the whole expression is not well-typed if any of its sub-expressions are not well-typed. Here are some examples: `j * true` is not well-typed since multiplication is defined only on integers; `true == "abc"` is not well-typed, since we can only compare by equality expressions of the same type; `true < false` is not well-typed since comparison operators do not make sense on booleans, and so on.

When implementing a type system in an Xtext DSL, we must take into consideration a few aspects; Xtext automatically validates each object in the AST, not only on the first level elements. For instance, in our validator, we have these two `@Check` methods:

```
@Check
def checkType(And and)

@Check
def checkType(Not not)
```

And the input expression is `!a && !b`, then Xtext will automatically call the second method on the `Not` objects corresponding to `!a` and `!b` and the first method on the object `And` corresponding to the whole expression. Therefore, it makes no sense to perform recursive invocations ourselves inside the validator's methods. If an expression contains some sub-expressions which are not well-typed, it should be considered not well-typed itself; however, does it make sense to mark the whole expression with an error? For example, consider this expression:

```
(1 + 10) < (2 * (3 + "a"))
```

If we mark the whole expression as not well-typed, we would provide useless information to the programmer. The same holds true if we generate additional errors for the sub-expressions `(2 * (3 + "a"))` and `(3 + "a")`. Indeed, the useful information is that `(3 + "a")` has type string while an integer type was expected by the multiplication expression.

Due to all the aforementioned reasons, we adopt the following strategy:

- Type computation is performed without recurring on sub-expressions unless required in some cases; for example, a `MulOrDiv` object has type integer independently of its sub-expressions. This is implemented by the class `ExpressionsTypeComputer`.

- In the validator, we have a @Check method for each kind of expression, excluding the constant expressions, which are implicitly well-typed; each method checks that the types of the sub-expressions, obtained using ExpressionsTypeComputer, are as expected by that specific expression. For example, for MulOrDiv, we check that its sub-expressions have both type integer, otherwise, we issue an error on the sub-expression that does not have type integer.

As we will see, this strategy avoids checking the same object with the validator several times, since the type computation is delegated to ExpressionsTypeComputer, which is not recursive. It will also allow the validator to generate meaningful error markers only on the problematic sub-expressions.

Type computer

Since we do not have types in the grammar of the Expressions DSL, we need a way of representing them. The types for this DSL are simple; we just need an interface for types, for example, ExpressionsType, and a class implementing it for each type, for example, StringType, IntType, and BoolType. These classes implement a toString method for convenience, but they do not contain any other information.

> We write the classes for types and for the type computer in the new Java sub-package typing. If you want to make its classes visible outside the main plug-in project, for example, for testing, you should add this package to the list of exported packages in the **Runtime** tab of the MANIFEST.MF editor.

In the type computer, we define a static field for each type. Using singletons will allow us to simply compare a computed type with such static instances (remember that triple equal in Xtend, ===, corresponds to Java object reference equality):

```
class ExpressionsTypeComputer {
  public static val STRING_TYPE = new StringType
  public static val INT_TYPE = new IntType
  public static val BOOL_TYPE = new BoolType

  def isStringType(ExpressionsType type) {
    type === STRING_TYPE
  }
... isIntType and isBoolType are similar
```

We now write a method, typeFor, which, given an Expression, returns an ExpressionsType object. We use the dispatch methods for special cases and switch for simple cases. For expressions whose type can be computed directly, we write:

```
def dispatch ExpressionsType typeFor(Expression e) {
  switch (e) {
    StringConstant: STRING_TYPE
    IntConstant: INT_TYPE
    BoolConstant: BOOL_TYPE
    Not: BOOL_TYPE
    MulOrDiv: INT_TYPE
    Minus: INT_TYPE
    Comparison: BOOL_TYPE
    Equality: BOOL_TYPE
    And: BOOL_TYPE
    Or: BOOL_TYPE
  }
}
```

We now write a test class for our type computer with several test methods (we only show some of them):

```
import static extension org.junit.Assert.*
import static org.example.expressions.typing.ExpressionsTypeComputer.*

@RunWith(XtextRunner)
@InjectWith(ExpressionsInjectorProvider)
class ExpressionsTypeComputerTest {
  @Inject extension ParseHelper<ExpressionsModel>
  @Inject extension ExpressionsTypeComputer
  @Test def void intConstant() { "10".assertEvalType(INT_TYPE) }
  @Test def void stringConstant() { "'foo'".assertEvalType(STRING_
TYPE) }
  ...
  @Test def void notExp() { "!true".assertEvalType(BOOL_TYPE) }
  @Test def void multiExp() { "1 * 2".assertEvalType(INT_TYPE) }
  ...
  def assertEvalType(CharSequence input, ExpressionsType expectedType)
{
    ("eval " + input).assertType(expectedType)
  }

  def assertType(CharSequence input, ExpressionsType expectedType) {
    input.parse.elements.last.
```

```
      expression.assertType(expectedType)
  }

  def assertType(Expression e, ExpressionsType expectedType) {
    expectedType.assertSame(e.typeFor)
  }
}
```

We wrote the methods `assertEvalType` and `assertType` that do most of the work.

Then, we can move on to more elaborate type computations, which we implement in a `dispatch` method for better readability.

```
  def dispatch ExpressionsType typeFor(Plus e) {
    val leftType = e.left.typeFor
    val rightType = e.right?.typeFor
    if (leftType.isStringType || rightType.isStringType)
      STRING_TYPE
    else
      INT_TYPE
  }
```

For `Plus`, we need to compute the types of the sub-expressions, since if one of them has type string, the whole expression is considered to be a string concatenation (with implicit conversion to string); thus, we give it a string type. Otherwise, it is considered to be the arithmetic sum and we give it type integer. In this type system, this is the only case where type computation depends on the types of sub-expressions.

Remember that the type computer can also be used on a non-complete model, and thus we use the null-safe operator `?.`, described in *Chapter 3, Working with the Xtend Programming Language*. We do that only on the right sub-expression. In fact, if a `Plus` is parsed, then the left sub-expression must be non-null.

We can now test this case for the type computer:

```
  @Test def void numericPlus() { "1 + 2".assertEvalType(INT_TYPE) }
  @Test def void stringPlus() { "'a' + 'b'".assertEvalType(STRING_TYPE)
  }
  @Test def void numAndStringPlus() { "'a' + 2".assertEvalType(STRING_
  TYPE) }
  @Test def void numAndStringPlus2() { "2 + 'a'".assertEvalType(STRING_
  TYPE) }
  @Test def void boolAndStringPlus(){"'a' + true".assertEvalType(STRING_
  TYPE) }
  @Test def void boolAndStringPlus2(){"false+'a'".assertEvalType(STRING_
  TYPE) }
```

Also, the case for variable reference requires some more work:

```
@Inject extension ExpressionsModelUtil
...
def dispatch ExpressionsType typeFor(VariableRef varRef) {
  if (!varRef.isVariableDefinedBefore)
      return null
  else
      return varRef.variable.expression.typeFor
}
```

We must check that the reference concerns a variable defined before the current expression, otherwise we might enter an infinite loop. We reuse `ExpressionsModelUtil`. In case the referred variable is not defined before the current variable reference we simply return `null`, and we know that an error has already been reported by our validator. Otherwise, the type of a variable reference is the type of the referred variable, which, in turn, is the type of its initialization expression. The tests for this case of the type computer is as follows:

```
@Test def void varRef() { "var i = 0 eval i".assertType(INT_TYPE) }
@Test def void varRefToVarDefinedAfter() {
  "var i = j var j = i".assertType(null)
}
```

Remember that you should follow the **Test Driven Development** strategy illustrated in *Chapter 7, Testing*; first, write the implementation for a single kind of expression, write a test for that case then execute it; then, proceed with the implementation for another kind of expression, write a test for that case and run all the tests, and so on. As an exercise, you should try to re-implement everything seen in this section from scratch yourself following this methodology.

Validator

We are ready to write the `@Check` methods in the `ExpressionsValidator` for checking that the types of expressions are correct.

In the existing validator, we inject an instance of `ExpressionsTypeComputer` and we write some reusable methods, which perform the actual checks. Thanks to these methods, we will be able to write the `@Check` methods in a very compact form.

```
class ExpressionsValidator extends
  AbstractExpressionsValidator {
    ...
```

```
public static val TYPE_MISMATCH =
  ISSUE_CODE_PREFIX + "TypeMismatch"

@Inject extension ExpressionsTypeComputer
...
def private checkExpectedBoolean(Expression exp,
                                 EReference reference) {
  checkExpectedType(exp,
    ExpressionsTypeComputer.BOOL_TYPE, reference)
}

def private checkExpectedInt(Expression exp,
                             EReference reference) {
  checkExpectedType(exp,
    ExpressionsTypeComputer.INT_TYPE, reference)
}

def private checkExpectedType(Expression exp,
    ExpressionsType expectedType, EReference reference) {
  val actualType = getTypeAndCheckNotNull(exp, reference)
  if (actualType != expectedType)
    error("expected " + expectedType +
      " type, but was " + actualType,
      reference, TYPE_MISMATCH)
}

def private ExpressionsType getTypeAndCheckNotNull(
    Expression exp, EReference reference) {
  var type = exp?.typeFor
  if (type == null)
    error("null type", reference, TYPE_MISMATCH)
  return type;
}...
```

 Although we present the reusable methods first, the actual strategy we followed when implementing the type checking in the validator is to first write some @Check methods, and then refactor the common parts. Before refactoring, we wrote some tests; after refactoring, we execute the tests to verify that refactoring did not break anything.

It should be straightforward to understand what the aforementioned methods do. The methods are parametrized over the EMF feature to use when generating an error; remember that this feature will be used to generate the error marker appropriately.

Let's see some @Check methods:

```
@Check def checkType(Not not) {
  checkExpectedBoolean(not.expression,
    ExpressionsPackage.Literals.NOT__EXPRESSION)
}

@Check def checkType(And and) {
  checkExpectedBoolean(and.left,
    ExpressionsPackage.Literals.AND__LEFT)
  checkExpectedBoolean(and.right,
    ExpressionsPackage.Literals.AND__RIGHT)
}
```

For Not, And, and Or, we check that the sub-expressions have type boolean, and we pass the EMF features corresponding to the sub-expressions. (The case for Or is similar to the case of And and it is therefore not shown).

Following the same approach, it is easy to check that the sub-expressions of Minus and MultiOrDiv both have integer types (we leave this as an exercise, but you can look at the sources of the example).

For an Equality expression, we must check that the two sub-expressions have the same type. This holds true also for a Comparison expression, but in this case, we also check that the sub-expressions do not have type boolean, since in our DSL, we do not want to compare two boolean values. The implementation of these @Check methods are as follows, using two additional reusable methods:

```
@Check def checkType(Equality equality) {
  val leftType = getTypeAndCheckNotNull(equality.left,
    ExpressionsPackage.Literals.EQUALITY__LEFT)
  val rightType = getTypeAndCheckNotNull(equality.right,
    ExpressionsPackage.Literals.EQUALITY__RIGHT)
  checkExpectedSame(leftType, rightType)
}

@Check def checkType(Comparison comparison) {
  val leftType = getTypeAndCheckNotNull(comparison.left,
    ExpressionsPackage.Literals.COMPARISON__LEFT)
  val rightType = getTypeAndCheckNotNull(comparison.right,
    ExpressionsPackage.Literals.COMPARISON__RIGHT)
  checkExpectedSame(leftType, rightType)
  checkNotBoolean(leftType,
    ExpressionsPackage.Literals.COMPARISON__LEFT)
  checkNotBoolean(rightType,
```

```
        ExpressionsPackage.Literals.COMPARISON__RIGHT)
    }


    def private checkExpectedSame(ExpressionsType left,
                                   ExpressionsType right) {
      if (right != null && left != null && right != left) {
        error("expected the same type, but was "+left+", "+right,
          ExpressionsPackage.Literals.EQUALITY.getEIDAttribute(),
          TYPE_MISMATCH)
      }
    }


    def private checkNotBoolean(ExpressionsType type,
                                 EReference reference) {
      if (type.isBoolType) {
        error("cannot be boolean", reference, TYPE_MISMATCH)
      }
    }
```

The final check concerns the `Plus` expression; according to our type system, if one of the two sub-expressions has type string, everything is fine and therefore all these combinations are accepted as valid: string+string, int+int, string+boolean, and string+int (and the corresponding specular cases). We cannot add two boolean expressions or an integer and a boolean. Therefore, when one of the two sub-expressions has type integer or when they both have a type different from string, we must check that they do not have type boolean:

```
    @Check def checkType(Plus plus) {
      val leftType = getTypeAndCheckNotNull(plus.left,
        ExpressionsPackage.Literals.PLUS__LEFT)
      val rightType = getTypeAndCheckNotNull(plus.right,
        ExpressionsPackage.Literals.PLUS__RIGHT)
      if (leftType.isIntType          || rightType.isIntType
          || (!leftType.isStringType &&         !rightType.
    isStringType)) {
        checkNotBoolean(leftType,
          ExpressionsPackage.Literals.PLUS__LEFT)
        checkNotBoolean(rightType,
          ExpressionsPackage.Literals.PLUS__RIGHT)
      }
    }
```

Of course, while writing these methods, we also wrote test methods in the `ExpressionsValidatorTest` class. Due to a lack of space, we are not showing these tests, and instead we refer you to the source code of the Expressions DSL.

Let's try the editor and look at the error markers, as shown in the following screenshot:

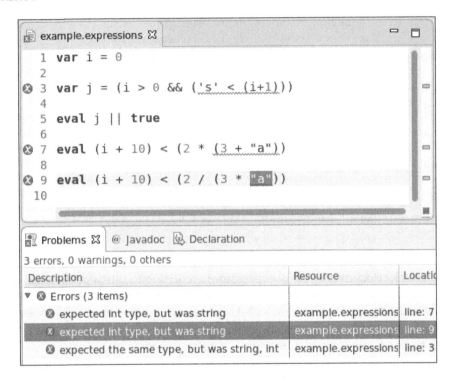

The error markers are only placed on the sub-expression that is not well-typed; it is clear where the problem inside the whole expression is. If we did not follow the preceding strategy for computing and checking types, in a program with some not well-typed expressions, most of the lines would be red, and this would not help. With our implementation, the expression j || true does not have error markers, although the initialization expression of j contains an error; our type computer is able to deduce that j has type boolean anyway. Formally, also j, and in turn j || true, are not well-typed; however, marking j || true with an error would only generate confusion.

Writing an interpreter

We will now write an interpreter for our Expressions DSL. The idea is that this interpreter, given an AbstractElement, returns a Java object, which represents the evaluation of that element. Of course, we want the object with the result of the evaluation to be of the correct Java type; that is, if we evaluate a boolean expression, the corresponding object should be a Java boolean object.

Such an interpreter will be recursive, since to evaluate an expression, we must first evaluate its sub-expressions and then compute the result.

When implementing the interpreter we make the assumption that the passed `AbstractElement` is valid. Therefore, we will not check for null sub-expressions. We will assume that all variable references are resolved, and we will assume that all the sub-expressions are well-typed. For example, if we evaluate an `And` expression, we assume that the objects resulting from the evaluation of its sub-expressions are Java `Boolean` objects.

 We write the classes for the interpreter in the new Java sub-package `interpreter`. If you want to make its classes visible outside the main plug-in project, for example, for testing, you should add this package to the list of exported packages in the **Runtime** tab of the `MANIFEST.MF` editor.

For constants, the implementation of the evaluation is straightforward:

```
class ExpressionsInterpreter {

  def dispatch Object interpret(Expression e) {
    switch (e) {
      IntConstant: e.value
      BoolConstant: Boolean.parseBoolean(e.value)
      StringConstant: e.value
```

Note that the feature `value` for an `IntConstant` object is of Java type `int` and for a `StringConstant` object, it is of Java type `String`, and thus we do not need any conversion. For a `BoolConstant` object the feature `value` is also of Java type `String`, and thus we perform an explicit conversion using the static method of the Java class `Boolean`.

As usual, we immediately start to test our interpreter, and the actual assertions are all delegated to a reusable method:

```
class ExpressionsInterpreterTest {
  @Inject extension ParseHelper<ExpressionsModel>
  @Inject extension ValidationTestHelper
  @Inject extension ExpressionsInterpreter

  @Test def void intConstant() { "eval 1".assertInterpret(1) }
  @Test def void boolConstant() { "eval true".assertInterpret(true) }
  @Test def void stringConstant() {"eval 'abc'".
assertInterpret("abc") }
```

```
def assertInterpret(CharSequence input, Object expected) {
  input.parse => [
    assertNoErrors
    expected.assertEquals(elements.last.expression.interpret)
  ]
}...
```

Note that in order to correctly test the interpreter, we check that there are no errors in the input (since that is the assumption of the interpreter itself) and we compare the actual objects, not their string representation. This way, we are sure that the object returned by the interpreter is of the expected Java type.

Then, we write a case for each expression. We recursively evaluate the sub-expressions and then apply the appropriate Xtend operator to the result of the evaluation of the sub-expressions. For example, for `And`:

```
switch (e) {
...
  And: {
    (e.left.interpret as Boolean) && (e.right.interpret as Boolean)
}
```

Note that the method `interpret` returns an `Object`, and thus we need to cast the result of the invocation on sub-expressions to the right Java type. We do not perform an `instanceof` check because, as hinted previously, the interpreter assumes that the input is well-typed.

With the same strategy, we implement all the other cases. We show here only the most interesting ones. For `MulOrDiv`, we will need to check the actual operator, stored in the feature op:

```
switch (e) {
...
  MulOrDiv: {
    val left = e.left.interpret as Integer
    val right = e.right.interpret as Integer
    if (e.op == '*')
      left * right
    else
      left / right
}
```

For `Plus`, we need to perform some additional operations; since we use + both as the arithmetic sum and as string concatenation, we must know the type of the sub-expressions. We use the type computer and write the following:

```
class ExpressionsInterpreter {
  @Inject extension ExpressionsTypeComputer

  def dispatch Object interpret(Expression e) {
    switch (e) {
    ...
    Plus: {
      if (e.left.typeFor.isStringType || e.right.typeFor.isStringType)
        e.left.interpret.toString + e.right.interpret.toString
      else
        (e.left.interpret as Integer) +
            (e.right.interpret as Integer)
    }...
```

Finally, we deal with the case of variable reference, variable declaration and evaluation statement. We handle variable declaration and evaluation statement in a single method, using their common superclass `AbstractElement`:

```
def dispatch Object interpret(Expression e) {
  switch (e) {
    ...
    VariableRef: e.variable.interpret
    ...
}

def dispatch Object interpret(AbstractElement e) {
  e.expression.interpret
}
```

Using the interpreter

Xtext allows us to customize all UI aspects, as we saw in *Chapter 6, Customizing Xtext Components*. We can provide a custom implementation of **text hovering** (that is, the pop-up window that comes up when we hover for some time on a specific editor region) so that it shows the type of the expression and its evaluation. We refer to the Xtext documentation for the details of the customization of text hovering; here, we only show our implementation (note that we create a multiline string using HTML syntax):

```
import static extension org.eclipse.emf.ecore.util.EcoreUtil.*

class ExpressionsEObjectHoverProvider extends
```

```
      DefaultEObjectHoverProvider {
    @Inject extension ExpressionsTypeComputer
    @Inject extension ExpressionsInterpreter
    override getHoverInfoAsHtml(EObject o) {
      if (o instanceof Expression && o.programHasNoError) {
        val exp = o as Expression
        return '''
        <p>
        type  : <b>«exp.typeFor.toString»</b> <br>
        value : <b>«exp.interpret.toString»</b>
        </p>
        '''
      } else
        return super.getHoverInfoAsHtml(o)
    }

    def programHasNoError(EObject o) {
      Diagnostician.INSTANCE.validate(o.rootContainer).
        children.empty
    }
  }
```

Remember that our interpreter is based on the assumption that it is invoked only on an EMF model that contains no error. We invoke our validator programmatically using the EMF API that is, the `Diagnostician` class. We must validate the entire AST, thus, we retrieve the root of the EMF model using the method `EcoreUtil.getRootContainer` and check that the list of validation issues is empty. We need to write an explicit bind method for our custom implementation of text hovering in the `ExpressionsUiModule`:

```
def Class<? extends IEObjectHoverProvider>
    bindIEObjectHoverProvider() {
  return ExpressionsEObjectHoverProvider
}
```

In the following screenshot, we can see our implementation when we place the mouse over the * operator of the expression 2 * (3 + 5); the pop-up window shows the type and the evaluation of the corresponding multiplication expression:

```
example.expressions ⊠                                    ▭  ⬜
  1  var i = 0
  2
  3  var j = (i > 0 && (i < (i+1)))
  4
  5  eval j || true
  6
  7  eval (i + 10) < (2 * (3 + 5))
  8
  9  eval (i + 10) < (2  type : int     )
 10                      value : 16
                    Press 'F2' for fo
```

Finally, we can write a code generator which creates a text file (by default, it will be created in the src-gen directory):

```
import static extension
  org.eclipse.xtext.nodemodel.util.NodeModelUtils.*

class ExpressionsGenerator implements IGenerator {
  @Inject extension ExpressionsInterpreter

  override void doGenerate(Resource resource,
                        IFileSystemAccess2 fsa, IGeneratorContext
context) {
    resource.allContents.toIterable.
      filter(ExpressionsModel).forEach[
        fsa.generateFile
          ('''«resource.URI.lastSegment».evaluated''',
           interpretExpressions)
      ]
  }

  def interpretExpressions(ExpressionsModel model) {
    model.elements.map[
      '''«getNode.getTokenText» ~> «interpret»'''
    ].join("\n")
  }
}
```

Differently from the code generator we saw in *Chapter 5, Code Generation*, here we generate a single text file for each input file (an input file is represented by an EMF `Resource`); the name of the output file is the same as the input file (retrieved by taking the last part of the URI of the resource), with an additional `evaluated` file extension.

Instead of simply generating the result of the evaluation in the output file, we also generate the original expression. This can be retrieved using the Xtext class `NodeModelUtils`. The static utility methods of this class allow us to easily access the elements of the **node model** corresponding to the elements of the AST model. (Recall from *Chapter 6, Customizing Xtext Components* that the node model carries the syntactical information, for example, offsets and spaces of the textual input.) The method `NodeModelUtils.getNode(EObject)` returns the node in the node model corresponding to the passed `EObject`. From the node of the node model, we retrieve the original text in the program corresponding to the `EObject`.

An example input file and the corresponding generated text file are shown in the following screenshot:

```
example.expressions ✕
 1  var i = 0
 2
 3  var j = (i > 0 && (i < (i+1)))
 4
 5  eval j || true
 6
 7  eval 'a' + (2 * (3 + 5))
 8
 9  eval 12 / (3 * 2)
10
```

```
example.expressions.evaluated ✕
1 var i = 0 ~> 0
2 var j = (i > 0 && (i < (i+1))) ~> false
3 eval j || true ~> true
4 eval 'a' + (2 * (3 + 5)) ~> a16
5 eval 12 / (3 * 2) ~> 2
```

Optimizations and fine tuning

Now that we implemented this DSL with a test suite, we can concentrate on refactoring some parts of it in order to optimize the performance.

In the *Forward references* section, we implemented the method `variablesDefinedBefore` and we anticipated that its performance might not be optimal. Since that method is used in the validator, in the type system and in the content assist it would be good to somehow cache its results to improve the performance.

Caching usually introduces a few problems since we must avoid that its contents become stale. Xtext provides a cache that relieves us from worrying about this problem, `org.eclipse.xtext.util.IResourceScopeCache`. This cache is automatically cleared when a resource changes, thus its contents are never stale. Moreover, its default implementation is annotated as `com.google.inject.Singleton`, thus all our DSL components will share the same instance of the cache.

To use this cache we call the method:

```
<T> T get(Object key, Resource res, Provider<T> provider)
```

We must provide the key of the cache, which can be any object, the `Resource` associated with the cache, and the `Provider` whose `get()` method is called automatically if no value is associated to the specified key.

Let's use this cache in the `ExpressionsModelUtil` for the implementation of `variablesDefinedBefore`:

```
@Inject IResourceScopeCache cache
...
def variablesDefinedBefore(AbstractElement containingElement) {
  cache.get(containingElement, containingElement.eResource) [
    val allElements =
      (containingElement.eContainer as ExpressionsModel).elements

    allElements.subList(0,
      allElements.indexOf(containingElement)).typeSelect(Variable)
  ]
}
```

We specify the `AbstractElement` as the key, its resource and a lambda for the `Provider` parameter. The lambda is simply the original implementation of the method body. Remember that the lambda will be called only in case of a cache miss. This is all we have to do to use the cache.

We now run the whole test suite, including the UI tests for the content assist, to make sure that the cache does not break anything.

Another aspect that is worth caching is the type computation. In fact, the type system is used by the validator, by the interpreter and by the custom hover implementation. In particular, it is good to cache type computation for cases that are not simple, such as variable reference. For computing, the type of a variable reference we compute the type of the referred variable's initialization expressions. This is performed over and over again for all the variable references that refer to the same variable.

Remember that the cache is shared by all the components of the DSL, thus we cannot simply reuse the referred variable as the key in this case, since that would conflict with the use of cache that we do in `variablesDefinedBefore`. Thus, in the type computer, we use a "pair" for the key, where the first element is the string `"type"` and the second element is the variable. A pair can be specified in Xtend with the following syntax: `e1 -> e2`.

This is the modified part in the type computer:

```
@Inject IResourceScopeCache cache
...
def dispatch ExpressionsType typeFor(VariableRef varRef) {
    if (!varRef.isVariableDefinedBefore)
        return null
    else {
        val variable = varRef.variable
        return cache.get("type" -> variable, variable.eResource) [
            variable.expression.typeFor
        ]
    }
}
```

Again, make sure you run the whole test suite to check that nothing is broken.

You can also try and experiment with a type computer where the type computation for all kinds of expression is cached.

Another part that can be optimized is the interpretation of a variable reference in the `ExpressionsInterpreter`: instead of interpreting the same variable over and over again, we can cache the result of the interpretation of variables:

```
VariableRef: {
    // avoid interpreting the same variable over and over again
    val v = e.variable
    cache.get("interpret" -> v, e.eResource) [
        v.interpret
    ]
}
```

In the sources of this DSL, you will also find a few tests that compare the performance of the DSL with and without caching. It is important to have such tests so that you can work on fine-tuning your DSL implementation. You need to make sure that the use of cache does not introduce overhead in some contexts, or you will get the opposite effect.

Summary

In this chapter, we implemented a DSL for expressions. This allowed us to explore some techniques for dealing with recursive grammar rule definitions in Xtext grammars and some simple type checking. We also showed how to write an interpreter for an Xtext DSL.

In the next chapter, we will develop a small object-oriented DSL. We will use this DSL to show some advanced type checking techniques that deal with object-oriented features such as inheritance and subtyping (type conformance).

9
Type Checking

In this chapter we will develop a small object-oriented DSL, which can be seen as a smaller version of Java that we call **SmallJava**. We will use this DSL to show some type checking techniques that deal with object-oriented features such as inheritance and subtyping (type conformance). This will also allow you to learn other features of Xtext grammars and to see some good practices in Xtext DSL implementations.

This chapter will cover the following topics:

- A small object-oriented language implemented with Xtext
- Some additional features of Xtext grammars
- The type system for object-oriented languages
- Some best practices for Xtext DSL implementation

SmallJava

The language we develop in this chapter is a simplified version of Java, called SmallJava. This language does not aim at being useful in practice and cannot be used to write real programs such as Java. However, SmallJava contains enough language features that will allow us to explore advanced type checking techniques that can also be reused for other DSLs, which have OOP mechanisms such as inheritance and subtyping.

The implementation we see in this chapter will not be complete, since some features of this language, such as correct member access, will be implemented in the next chapter when we introduce the mechanism of local and global scoping. In a Java-like language type checking and scoping are tightly connected and complement each other; for the sake of readability, we will split typing and scoping into two separate chapters.

We will not describe how to write a code generator for SmallJava; we will focus on statically checking SmallJava programs rather than executing them. However, in the code of the SmallJava DSL, you will also find a code generator that generates the corresponding Java classes.

Let's stress that implementing the whole Java language and, in particular, its complete type system, would not be feasible in this book. If your DSL needs to access Java types and to be interoperable with Java, you may want to consider using Xbase described in *Chapter 12, Xbase*. If your DSL does not have to interact with Java, the concepts described in this chapter can be reused and adapted to fit your DSL.

Creating the project

First of all, we will use the Xtext project wizard to create the projects for our DSL (following the same procedure that we saw in the previous chapters).

Start Eclipse and perform the following steps:

1. Navigate to **File | New | Project...**; in the dialog, navigate to the **Xtext** category and click on **Xtext Project**.

2. In the next dialog, fill in the details for the following fields:

    ○   **Project name:** `org.example.smalljava`

    ○   **Name:** `org.example.smalljava.SmallJava`

    ○   **Extensions:** `smalljava`

3. Press **Finish**.

The wizard will create several projects into your workspace and it will open the `SmallJava.xtext` file that is the grammar definition.

SmallJava grammar

Before starting to develop this language, we sketch the simplifications we will adopt:

*   Classes have no explicit constructors

*   There is no cast expression

*   Arithmetic and boolean expressions are not implemented

*   Basic types (such as `int`, `boolean`, and so on) and void methods are not considered (methods must always return something)

*   There is no method overloading

- Member access must always be prefixed with the object, even if it is `this`
- Variable declarations must always be initialized
- `super` is not supported, but it will be implemented in the next chapter
- The `new` instance expression does not take arguments, since there are only implicit default constructors
- Package and imports are not supported, but they will be implemented in the next chapter

Basically, the features that we are interested in and that will allow us to have a case study for type checking and *scoping* (next chapter) are class inheritance, field and method definitions, and blocks of statements with local variable definitions.

Rules for declarations

The rules in the SmallJava grammar are prefixed with SJ to avoid confusion with the classes and terms in Java that they mimic.

The first rules are straightforward and they state that a SmallJava program is a possibly empty sequence of classes:

```
SJProgram:
  classes+=SJClass*;

SJClass: 'class' name=ID ('extends' superclass=[SJClass])? '{'
  members += SJMember*
'}' ;

SJMember:
  SJField | SJMethod ;

SJField:
  type=[SJClass] name=ID ';' ;

SJMethod:
  type=[SJClass] name=ID
  '(' (params+=SJParameter (',' params+=SJParameter)*)? ')'
  body=SJBlock ;

SJParameter:
  type=[SJClass] name=ID ;
```

Each class can have a superclass, that is, a reference to another SmallJava class and a possibly empty sequence of members. An SJMember object can be either an SJField object or an SJMethod object; note that since both fields and methods have a type and a name feature, these two features will end up in their common base class SJMember.

The body of a method is a block, that is a possibly empty sequence of SJStatement (defined later) enclosed in curly brackets:

```
SJBlock:
  '{' statements += SJStatement* '}' ;
```

If we define the rule for block as in the preceding code snippet, we get a warning:

```
The rule 'SJBlock' may be consumed without object instantiation. Add
an action to ensure object creation, for example, '{SJBlock}'.
```

In fact, the only assignment is to the feature statements, which is based on SJStatement*; if no statement is parsed, the rule will be valid, but the feature will not be assigned and no object will be instantiated (see the *Digression on Xtext grammar rules* section, *Chapter 8*, *An Expression Language* for an explanation of how object instantiation and feature assignment in a rule are connected). As suggested by the warning, we add an action to ensure object creation:

```
SJBlock:
  {SJBlock} '{' statements += SJStatement* '}' ;
```

Rules for statements and syntactic predicates

These are the rules for statements:

```
SJStatement:
  SJVariableDeclaration |
  SJReturn |
  SJExpression ';' |
  SJIfStatement
;

SJReturn:
  'return' expression=SJExpression ';'
;

SJVariableDeclaration:
  type=[SJClass] name=ID '=' expression=SJExpression ';'
;
```

```
SJIfStatement:
  'if' '(' expression=SJExpression ')' thenBlock=SJIfBlock
  (=>'else' elseBlock=SJIfBlock)?
;

SJIfBlock returns SJBlock:
  statements += SJStatement
  | SJBlock ;
```

The blocks for an `if` statement can also be specified without curly brackets; in this case, a single statement can be specified. The alternative is an `SJBlock`. In case of a single statement, we still assign it to the `statements` list feature. Since this feature is used also in `SJBlock`, we specify that the rule returns an `SJBlock` element. This way, we can treat both a method body and the blocks of an `if` statement in the same way, even in case of a single statement. This will be useful when dealing with variable declarations in nested program blocks in the next chapter.

The rule for the `if` statement shows another important feature of Xtext grammars, **syntactic predicates** represented by the symbol `=>`. These are useful to solve ambiguities in a grammar. We will use the `if` statement as an example to describe such situations. If we write the rule for the `if` statement as follows:

```
SJIfStatement:
  'if' '(' expression=SJExpression ')' thenBlock=SJIfBlock
  ('else' elseBlock=SJIfBlock)?
;
```

During the MWE2 workflow, we will get this warning in the console:

```
warning(200): Decision can match input such as "'else'" using
multiple alternatives: 1, 2

As a result, alternative(s) 2 were disabled for that input
```

This issue is also known as the **Dangling Else Problem**; if you consider this nested `if` statement:

```
if (...)
  if (...)
    statement
  else
    statement
```

The parser would not know to which `if` statement the `else` belongs to (remember that spaces and indentation are ignored by the parser); it could belong either to the outer `if` or to the inner one, and this leads to an ambiguity.

Never ignore warnings issued by the MWE2 workflow concerning the generated ANTLR parser. Each warning will surely be a source of problems if not solved, even when ambiguities are automatically resolved by the parser itself using a default strategy. Make sure each ambiguity is resolved the way you want.

Using the syntactic predicate, that is, the `=>` before the `'else'` keyword, we remove such ambiguity by directing the parser. We tell the parser that if it finds the `'else'` keyword, then it should not try to search for other ways of parsing the statement, and the `else` will belong to the inner `if`, which is the typical behavior of languages with an `if` statement.

Another way of solving ambiguities is to enable **backtracking** for the ANTLR parser generator. However, this is strongly discouraged, and it is only a source of further problems not easily detectable; thus, we will not consider this option in this book.

The rule `SJParameter` and the rule `SJVariableDeclaration` have something in common: the `type` and `name` features. Therefore, we introduce a rule for forcing the creation of a common superclass:

```
SJSymbol: SJVariableDeclaration | SJParameter ;
```

This will give us a common supertype for referring to a local variable and a parameter from within a method body, as we will see later in this chapter. Note that the rule name is grayed in the Xtext grammar editor; this highlights the fact that this rule is never called by the parser.

Finally, it is helpful to have a common type for all the elements with the feature name:

```
SJNamedElement:
    SJClass | SJMember | SJSymbol;
```

This will be useful later when checking for duplicate elements with the same name.

Rules for expressions

As we saw in the rule SJStatement, a statement can also be an expression terminated by ;. In fact, as in Java, a method invocation can be both a standalone statement and an expression, that is, the right-hand side of an assignment or the argument for another method invocation.

Also an assignment statement can itself be an expression; for instance, in Java you can write:

```
a = b = c ;
```

With the meaning that c is assigned to b and then b is assigned to a. Thus, the preceding statement should be parsed as:

```
a = (b = c) ;
```

Moreover, both the left-hand and right-hand side of an assignment can be expressions.

For all of the aforementioned reasons, and from what you learned from *Chapter 8, An Expression Language*, you should know that we will have to deal with left recursion.

The same holds when writing the rule for a member selection expression, that is, for selecting a field or a method on an object. In fact, in order to be able to write selection expressions like:

```
a.b().c.d()
```

The left-hand side of a member selection, which is usually called the **receiver** of the selection, must be an expression.

Therefore, we need to left factor the grammar using the technique introduced in *Chapter 8, An Expression Language*.

To keep the presentation simple, we will not deal with arithmetic and boolean expressions in the grammar. We will concentrate only on assignments, member selections, and some additional terminal expressions. All the other expressions can be easily added taking the Expressions DSL of *Chapter 8, An Expression Language* as inspiration.

We must write the rule for the expression with lower precedence first, that is, the rule for assignment:

```
SJExpression: SJAssignment;

SJAssignment returns SJExpression:
  SJSelectionExpression
```

```
({SJAssignment.left=current} '=' right=SJExpression)? // Right
associativity
;
```

The left factoring technique should be familiar by now. Just note that an assignment expression must be right-associative (refer to *Chapter 8, An Expression Language* for associativity). That is why we wrote the right recursive part as:

```
right=SJExpression)?        // Right associativity
```

instead of:

```
right=SJSelectionExpression)*    // Left associativity
```

Therefore, a nested assignment expression like:

```
a = b = c
```

Will be parsed as:

```
a = (b = c)
```

As required by our DSL.

The rule for member selection is as follows:

```
SJSelectionExpression returns SJExpression:
  SJTerminalExpression
  (
    {SJMemberSelection.receiver=current} '.'
    member=[SJMember]
    (methodinvocation?='('
      (args+=SJExpression (',' args+=SJExpression)*)? ')'
    )?
  )* ;
```

Remember that while the name of the rule is SJSelectionExpression, the rule will instantiate an SJMemberSelection object.

Note that this rule deals both with field selection and method invocation; for this reason, the part that deals with method invocation can have optional parentheses and arguments. We keep track of the presence of parentheses using the boolean feature methodinvocation; this will allow us to distinguish between an SJMemberSelection object that represents a field selection from one that represents a method invocation.

You might be tempted to distinguish between a field selection and a method invocation explicitly in the grammar. For instance, we could write the rule as follows:

```
// alternative DISCOURAGED implementation
SJSelectionExpression returns SJExpression:
  SJTerminalExpression
  (
    ({SJMethodInvocation.receiver=current} '.'
      method=[SJMethod]
        '(' (args+=SJExpression (',' args+=SJExpression)*)? ')')
    |
    ({SJFieldSelection.receiver=current} '.' field=[SJField])
  )* ;
```

After parsing a dot, the parser needs to scan all the way to the right parenthesis; if it finds it, then it creates an instance of SJMethodInvocation that refers directly to an SJMethod; otherwise, it parses the selection by creating an instance of SJFieldSelection, which refers directly to an SJField object. This solution has the advantage that in the AST it is straightforward to distinguish a field selection from a method invocation since they are represented by objects of different types.

However, this version of the rule will require a parser that performs additional work, and most important of all, many IDE features, such as the content assist, will not work as expected.

In general, a good practice in Xtext DSL implementations is to keep the grammar simple. It is better to have a loose grammar and a strict validation phase (*loose grammar, strict validation*, see the presentation *Zarnekow* 2012).

Therefore, we keep the selection rule in its original form, and we will deal with the cases for field selection and method invocation in the validator and in other components.

Finally, we have the rule for terminal expressions:

```
SJTerminalExpression returns SJExpression:
  {SJStringConstant} value=STRING |
  {SJIntConstant} value=INT |
  {SJBoolConstant} value = ('true' | 'false') |
  {SJThis} 'this' |
  {SJNull} 'null' |
  {SJSymbolRef} symbol=[SJSymbol] |
  {SJNew} 'new' type=[SJClass] '(' ')' |
  '(' SJExpression ')'
;
```

Note that we have a single rule for referring both to a parameter (SJParameter) and to a local variable (SJVariableDeclaration), since we have a cross-reference of type SJSymbol (see the rule we added previously to have a base class for both parameters and local variables). In our DSL, you cannot pass arguments when creating an instance (SJNew), since we simplified the language by removing explicit parameterized constructors. Finally, as in the Expressions DSL, we have a rule that allows explicit parentheses.

As we hinted in the beginning of this chapter, member access always requires a receiver expression, even if it is this. If we also wanted to handle member access with an implicit receiver expression, we could have changed the rule for SJSymbol to also include SJMember, for example:

```
SJSymbol: SJVariableDeclaration | SJParameter | SJMember;
```

The features type and name are common to SJMember as well. However, this would require some additional work when implementing other aspects of the DSL, which might distract from the real intent of the SmallJava DSL, that is, being a case study for typing and scoping.

Rule fragments

In some of the rules we have written so far, there is a recurrent fragment:

```
type=[SJClass] name=ID
```

It would be nice to avoid such duplication without adding a rule that would introduce an additional node in the AST. To this aim, we use a **parser rule fragment**. Such a rule can be called by other rules, and the result will correspond to a literal inclusion of the rule fragment content into the calling rule. For example:

```
SJField:
  SJTypedDeclaration ';' ;

SJMethod:
  SJTypedDeclaration
  '(' … as before

SJParameter:
  SJTypedDeclaration ;

SJVariableDeclaration:
  SJTypedDeclaration '=' expression=SJExpression ';' ;

fragment SJTypedDeclaration:
  type=[SJClass] name=ID ;
```

A rule fragment will correspond to a new type in the AST, and the types of the calling rules will automatically inherit from such a type. In this example, the type SJVariableDeclaration will inherit from the SJTypedDeclaration type. We do not want this to happen, since we want to manage the hierarchy of the AST types ourselves. For example, we want SJVariableDeclaration and SJParameter to have a common supertype, but we do not want SJMember to do so. To disable the creation of a type in the AST for the rule fragment and the corresponding implied inheritance relations we put an * in the rule fragment as follows:

```
fragment SJTypedDeclaration *:
  type=[SJClass] name=ID ;
```

The complete grammar

We will sum up by showing the complete grammar of the SmallJava DSL (in the next chapter, we will modify this grammar):

```
grammar org.example.smalljava.SmallJava with   org.eclipse.xtext.
common.Terminals

generate smallJava "http://www.example.org/smalljava/SmallJava"

SJProgram:
  classes+=SJClass*;

SJClass: 'class' name=ID ('extends' superclass=[SJClass])? '{'
  members += SJMember*
'}' ;

SJMember:
  SJField | SJMethod ;


SJField:
  SJTypedDeclaration ';' ;

SJMethod:
  SJTypedDeclaration
    '(' (params+=SJParameter (',' params+=SJParameter)*)? ')'
    body=SJBlock ;

SJParameter:
  SJTypedDeclaration ;
```

```
SJBlock:
  {SJBlock} '{' statements += SJStatement* '}' ;

SJStatement:
  SJVariableDeclaration |
  SJReturn |
  SJExpression ';' |
  SJIfStatement
;

SJVariableDeclaration:
    SJTypedDeclaration '=' expression=SJExpression ';'
;

SJReturn:
  'return' expression=SJExpression ';'
;

SJIfStatement:
  'if' '(' expression=SJExpression ')' thenBlock=SJIfBlock
  (=>'else' elseBlock=SJIfBlock)?
;

SJIfBlock returns SJBlock:
  statements += SJStatement
  | SJBlock ;

SJSymbol: SJVariableDeclaration | SJParameter ;

fragment SJTypedDeclaration *:
  type=[SJClass] name=ID ;


SJNamedElement:
  SJClass | SJMember | SJSymbol ;

SJExpression: SJAssignment ;

SJAssignment returns SJExpression:
  SJSelectionExpression
  ({SJAssignment.left=current} '=' right=SJExpression)? // Right
associativity
;
```

```
SJSelectionExpression returns SJExpression:
  SJTerminalExpression
  (
    {SJMemberSelection.receiver=current} '.'
    member=[SJMember]
    (methodinvocation?='('
      (args+=SJExpression (',' args+=SJExpression)*)? ')'
    )?
  )* ;


SJTerminalExpression returns SJExpression:
  {SJStringConstant} value=STRING |
  {SJIntConstant} value=INT |
  {SJBoolConstant} value = ('true' | 'false') |
  {SJThis} 'this' |
  {SJNull} 'null' |
  {SJSymbolRef} symbol=[SJSymbol] |
  {SJNew} 'new' type=[SJClass] '(' ')' |
  '(' SJExpression ')'
;
```

Utility methods

As we did for previous DSLs, we write an Xtend class, `SmallJavaModelUtil`, with utility methods for accessing the AST model of a SmallJava program:

```
class SmallJavaModelUtil {
  def fields(SJClass c) {
    c.members.filter(SJField)
  }

  def methods(SJClass c) {
    c.members.filter(SJMethod)
  }



  def returnStatement(SJMethod m) {
    m.body.returnStatement
  }

  def returnStatement(SJBlock block) {
    block.statements.filter(SJReturn).head
  }
}
```

Since the feature `members` in an `SJClass` object contains both the `SJField` and `SJMethod` instances, it is useful to have utility methods to quickly select them based on type. We will use these methods as extension methods in other Xtend classes so that we will be able to write expressions such as `c.methods` and `c.fields`. The method to quickly access the `return` statement will be useful when writing unit tests for the DSL. We will add other utility methods in the next sections.

Testing the grammar

As you should know by now, we should write unit tests for the parser as soon as we write some rules for the DSL grammar. In this chapter, we show only a few interesting cases, in particular the tests for the associativity of expressions such as assignments and member selection (see *Chapter 8, An Expression Language*, for the technique for testing associativity). We use the `SmallJavaModelUtil` utility methods to write cleaner tests:

```
import static extension org.junit.Assert.*

@RunWith(XtextRunner)
@InjectWith(SmallJavaInjectorProvider)
class SmallJavaParsingTest {
  @Inject extension ParseHelper<SJProgram>
  @Inject extension SmallJavaModelUtil


  @Test def void testMemberSelectionLeftAssociativity() {
  '''
  class A {
    A m() { return this.m().m(); }
  }
  '''.parse.classes.head.methods.head.
        body.statements.last.assertAssociativity("((this.m).m)")
  }

  @Test def void testAssignmentRightAssociativity() {
  '''
  class A {
    A m() {
      A f = null;
      A g = null;
      f = g = null;
    }
  }
  '''.parse.classes.head.methods.head.
```

```
    body.statements.last.assertAssociativity("(f = (g = null))")
}

  def private assertAssociativity(SJStatement s, CharSequence
expected) {
    expected.toString.assertEquals(s.stringRepr)
  }

  def private String stringRepr(SJStatement s) {
    switch (s) {
      SJAssignment:'''(«s.left.stringRepr» = «s.right.stringRepr»)'''
      SJMemberSelection:'''(«s.receiver.stringRepr».«s.member.
name»)'''
      SJThis: "this"
      SJNew: '''new «s.type.name»()'''
      SJNull: "null"
      SJSymbolRef: s.symbol.name
      SJReturn: s.expression.stringRepr
    }
  }
```

We also write tests for the syntactic predicate for the if statement rule:

```
@Test def void testElse() {
  '''
  class C {
    C c;
    C m() {
      if (true)
        if (false)
          this.c = null;
        else
          this.c = null;
      return this.c;
    }
  }
  '''.parse => [
    val ifS = (classes.head.methods.head.
      body.statements.head as SJIfStatement)
    ifS.elseBlock.assertNull
    // thus the else is associated to the inner if
  ]
}
```

```
@Test def void testElseWithBlock() {
  '''
  class C {
    C c;
    C m() {
      if (true) {
        if (false)
          this.c = null;
      } else
          this.c = null;
      return this.c;
    }
  }
  '''.parse => [
    val ifS = (classes.head.methods.head.
      body.statements.head as SJIfStatement)
    ifS.elseBlock.assertNotNull
    // thus the else is associated to the outer if
  ]
}
```

The additional effort in writing tests for the SmallJava DSL is that when you need to access statements and expressions, you will need to walk the AST model to access the class, then the method, and then access the desired expression or statements in the method's body statement list.

First validation rules

Before getting to the main subject of this chapter, we will first implement some constraint checks that are complementary to type checking. Correct access to fields and methods will be checked in the next chapter, where we implement a custom scoping mechanism.

Checking cycles in class hierarchies

The SmallJava parser accepts input with cyclic class hierarchies, for instance:

```
class A extends C {}

class C extends B {}

class B extends A {}
```

This cannot be checked in the parser; we must write a validator @check method to mark such situations as errors (this is similar to the validator for the Entities DSL in *Chapter 4, Validation*). As you will see later in this chapter, we will often need to traverse the inheritance hierarchy of a class to perform additional checks. Also in this case, it is our job to avoid an infinite loop in case of cycles. We write a utility method in SmallJavaModelUtil that collects all the classes in the hierarchy of a given SJClass, to avoid entering an infinite loop. Similarly to what we did for the Entities DSL, we will visit the class hierarchy inspecting the superclass feature, and we will stop the visit either when the superclass is null or when a class is already in the list of visited classes:

```
class SmallJavaModelUtil {

  def classHierarchy(SJClass c) {
    val visited = newLinkedHashSet()

    var current = c.superclass
    while (current != null && !visited.contains(current)) {
      visited.add(current)
      current = current.superclass
    }

    visited
  }...
```

When looking at the example code, you will find that testing is done in isolation in its own JUnit test class for SmallJavaModelUtil—this is not shown in this chapter.

Now it is straightforward to write the validator method for checking whether the hierarchy of a class contains a cycle; given an SJClass object, we check whether that class is contained in its own class hierarchy. Refer to the following code:

```
class SmallJavaValidator extends AbstractSmallJavaValidator {


  protected static val ISSUE_CODE_PREFIX =
    "org.example.smalljava.";
  public static val HIERARCHY_CYCLE =
    ISSUE_CODE_PREFIX + "HierarchyCycle";

  @Inject extension SmallJavaModelUtil
```

```
@Check def checkClassHierarchy(SJClass c) {
  if (c.classHierarchy.contains(c)) {
    error("cycle in hierarchy of class '" + c.name + "'",
      SmallJavaPackage.eINSTANCE.SJClass_Superclass,
      HIERARCHY_CYCLE, c.superclass.name)
  }
}...
```

Differently from what we did in *Chapter 4, Validation* for the Entities DSL, we do not build the inheritance hierarchy directly in the validator; we implemented this functionality in `SmallJavaModelUtil`, since we will use it in other parts. This validation rule can be tested as we did for the Entities DSL example in *Chapter 7, Testing*, section *Testing the validator*.

Checking member selections

As we said in the section *Rules for Expressions*, we preferred to have a simple rule for member selection. This means that we must check whether a member selection actually refers to a field and whether a method invocation actually refers to a method ("Loose grammar, Strict validation").

We therefore write a `@Check` method for checking these situations. In particular, we use the boolean feature `methodinvocation` to know what we need to check; remember that this feature is set to true if the program text contains an opening parenthesis after the member reference:

```
public static val FIELD_SELECTION_ON_METHOD =
  ISSUE_CODE_PREFIX + "FieldSelectionOnMethod"
public static val METHOD_INVOCATION_ON_FIELD =
  ISSUE_CODE_PREFIX + "MethodInvocationOnField"

@Check def void checkMemberSelection(SJMemberSelection sel) {
  val member = sel.member

  if (member instanceof SJField && sel.methodinvocation)
    error(
      '''Method invocation on a field''',
      SmallJavaPackage.eINSTANCE.
        SJMemberSelection_Methodinvocation,
      METHOD_INVOCATION_ON_FIELD)
  else if (member instanceof SJMethod && !sel.methodinvocation)
    error(
      '''Field selection on a method''',
```

```
SmallJavaPackage.eINSTANCE.
    SJMemberSelection_Member,
FIELD_SELECTION_ON_METHOD
)


}
```

Note that for an error concerning a method invocation on a field, we pass the `methodinvocation` feature when calling `error`. This way, the `error` marker will be placed on the opening parenthesis.

This validator rule is verified by the following two test methods:

```
@Test def void testInvocationOnField() {
  '''
  class A {
    A f;
    A m() {
      return this.f();
    }
  }
  ''' => [
    parse.assertError(
      SmallJavaPackage.eINSTANCE.SJMemberSelection,
      SmallJavaValidator.METHOD_INVOCATION_ON_FIELD,
      lastIndexOf("("), 1, // check error position
      "Method invocation on a field"
    )
  ]
}

@Test def void testFieldSelectionOnMethod() { // similar
}
```

Checking return statements

We must check that a `return` statement is the last statement of a block. If there were other statements after the `return` statement, they would never be executed, and thus we should issue an "Unreachable code" error, like Java does. We could have enforced this in the grammar in the rule for SJBlock , but you should know by now that this should be avoided.

In fact, such a solution would have several drawbacks. First of all, while you can easily access the return statement of a block, you cannot treat all the statements of a block uniformly, and you will need to consider the case for the return statement separately. Most important of all, in case the return statement is not the last statement of a block, the error issued by the parser does not bring much information. Indeed, several syntax errors will be generated that are hard to understand by the user. Not getting AST elements in such cases also means it is not possible (or very hard) to offer good quick fixes.

It is much better to have a loose grammar rule in combination with a strict check to provide better error messages. If we find a return statement that is not the last element of a block's statement list, then we generate an error on the statement following the return statement, specifying that it is "Unreachable code" as shown in the following code snippet:

```
public static val UNREACHABLE_CODE =   ISSUE_CODE_PREFIX +
"UnreachableCode"

@Check def void checkUnreachableCode(SJBlock block) {
  val statements = block.statements
  for (var i = 0; i < statements.length-1; i++) {
    if (statements.get(i) instanceof SJReturn) {
        // put the error on the statement after the return
        error("Unreachable code",
          statements.get(i+1),
          null, // EStructuralFeature
          UNREACHABLE_CODE)
        return // no need to report further errors
    }
  }
}
```

Note that the for loop ends at the last but one statement. Thus, we do not check the last statement, since the error is represented by the situation where we find a return that is not the last statement. We use the version of the error method that also accepts the EObject to mark with the error (if not specified, the object that is passed to the @Check method is marked). Since we pass null for the EStructuralFeature argument, the whole statement will be marked with the error.

To test that the error is actually generated on the correct statement, we rely on the type of the statement:

```
@Test def void testUnreachableCode() {
  '''
  class C {
```

```
    C m() {
      return null;
      this.m(); // the error should be placed here
    }
  }
  '''.parse.assertError(
    SmallJavaPackage.eINSTANCE.SJMemberSelection,
    SmallJavaValidator.UNREACHABLE_CODE,
    "Unreachable code"
  )
}
```

In the preceding code, we check that the error is on the statement of type
SJMemberSelection, that is, the statement after the return statement in the
test input code.

If we need a quick way of accessing the return statement of a block, we call the utility
method returnStatement in SmallJavaModelUtil.

The same utility method can be used to check that a method actually ends with a
return statement, since in SmallJava there are no void methods. The implementation
of this validator method can be found in the sources of the example. Also, in this
case, the error contains more information than what we would get if we tried to rule
out this situation in the grammar.

Checking for duplicates

In the DSL examples we have seen so far, we have always used the default validator
NamesAreUniqueValidator to check for elements of the same kind with the same
name. In this example, we will deal with such checks manually in our own validator.
To check for duplicate elements, we avoid to compare each name with other every
other name, since this would have quadratic complexity. Instead, we will populate
a multi-map, where the key is the name and the values are the elements of the same
type with that name. For the multi-map, we use com.google.common.collect.
HashMultimap; this is part of com.google.guava, on which the DSL project already
depends on. If such a map then contains a list with more than one element for a
given key, then we mark all such elements as duplicates. Using a multi-map, which
we fill upfront, will allow us to generate the exact number of errors. In contrast,
filling a plain map while inspecting the collection and generating a errors if we find
an existing element in the map with the same name, would yield too many errors.

We first implement a reusable method, which performs such check given an iterable of SJNamedElement objects and a description of the type of element to be used when reporting errors:

```
public static val DUPLICATE_ELEMENT =
  ISSUE_CODE_PREFIX + "DuplicateElement"

def private void checkNoDuplicateElements(
      Iterable<? extends SJNamedElement> elements, String desc) {
  val multiMap = HashMultimap.create()

  for (e : elements)
    multiMap.put(e.name, e)

  for (entry : multiMap.asMap.entrySet) {
    val duplicates = entry.value
    if (duplicates.size > 1) {
      for (d : duplicates)
        error(
          "Duplicate " + desc + " '" + d.name + "'",
          d,
          SmallJavaPackage.eINSTANCE.SJNamedElement_Name,
          DUPLICATE_ELEMENT)
    }
  }
}
```

Then, we will call this method with classes, fields, methods, parameters of a method, and variables of a method body. The check for duplicate variable declarations must deal with possible nested blocks, since we do not allow a local variable to shadow a previously defined variable with the same name. Instead of inspecting all possible nested blocks manually, we use the EcoreUtil2.getAllContentsOfType method, which returns the list of all elements of a given type, even the nested ones:

```
@Check def void checkNoDuplicateClasses(SJProgram p) {
  checkNoDuplicateElements(p.classes, "class")
}

@Check def void checkNoDuplicateMembers(SJClass c) {
  checkNoDuplicateElements(c.fields, "field")
  checkNoDuplicateElements(c.methods, "method")
}

@Check def void checkNoDuplicateSymbols(SJMethod m) {
```

```
    checkNoDuplicateElements(m.params, "parameter")
    checkNoDuplicateElements(
      m.body.getAllContentsOfType(SJVariableDeclaration), "variable")
}
```

Then, we write the tests for all these checks (here we only show a few of them). For members, we also write a test ensuring that a method and a field are allowed to have the same name:

```
@Test def void testDuplicateFields() {
  '''
  class C {
    C f;
    C f;
  }
  '''.toString.assertDuplicate(
      SmallJavaPackage.eINSTANCE.SJField, "field", "f")
}


@Test def void testDuplicateVariables() {
  '''
  class C {
    C m() {
      C v = null;
      if (true)
        C v = null;
      return null;
    }
  }
  '''.toString.assertDuplicate(
      SmallJavaPackage.eINSTANCE.SJVariableDeclaration, "variable",
"v")
}


@Test def void testFieldAndMethodWithTheSameNameAreOK() {
  '''
    class C {
      C f;
      C f() { return null; }
    }
  '''.parse.assertNoErrors
}


def private void assertDuplicate(String input, EClass type,
            String desc, String name) {
```

```
    input.parse => [
      // check that the error is on both duplicates
      assertError(type,
        SmallJavaValidator.DUPLICATE_ELEMENT,
        input.indexOf(name), name.length,
        "Duplicate " + desc + " '" + name + "'")
      assertError(type,
        SmallJavaValidator.DUPLICATE_ELEMENT,
        input.lastIndexOf(name), name.length,
        "Duplicate " + desc + " '" + name + "'")
    ]
  }
```

Type checking

Most of the constraint checks for an object-oriented language such as SmallJava will deal with **type checking**, that is, checking that expressions and statements are well-typed.

We have already seen how to perform a simple form of type checking in the Expressions DSL (*Chapter 8, An Expression Language*). In this chapter, we will see an advanced type checking mechanism, which includes **subtyping** or **type conformance**: an object of class C can be used in a context where an object of a superclass of C is expected.

We will follow the same strategy illustrated in *Chapter 8, An Expression Language*: we will separate the type computation from the actual type checking. We will be able to generate the error on the sub-expression or statement that is the source of the problem. As in the previous chapter, we will implement all the type system related classes in the package typing. This package must be exported in the MANIFEST.MF in order to test the classes contained in this package.

Type computer for SmallJava

The type computer for SmallJava expressions we are about to construct will compute the type of any SJExpression. The concept of type will be represented by SJClass, since SmallJava does not support primitive types, such as int, boolean, and so on.

We write a single typeFor method, which returns an SJClass object using a type switch (the default case simply returns null):

```
import static extension org.eclipse.xtext.EcoreUtil2.*

class SmallJavaTypeComputer {
  def SJClass typeFor(SJExpression e) {
```

```
switch (e) {
  SJNew: e.type
  SJSymbolRef: e.symbol.type
  SJMemberSelection: e.member.type
  SJAssignment: e.left.typeFor
  SJThis : e.getContainerOfType(SJClass)
  ...
}
}...
```

In the preceding method, the type of a new instance expression is clearly the class that we are instantiating (the feature: `type`). The type of a symbol reference is the type of the referred symbol. Similarly, the type of a member reference is the type of the referred member. The type of an assignment expression is the type of the left hand side. The type for `this` is simply the type of the containing class. Note that while at runtime the actual object replacing `this` could be an object of a subclass, statically, its type is always the class where `this` is being used. In all of the preceding cases, the type always corresponds to an existing `SJClass`.

Now we need to provide a type for the remaining terminal expressions, that is, null and the constant expressions. For these expressions, there are no existing `SJClass` instances that we can use as types; we will create static instances in `SmallJavaTypeComputer` (for convenience, we will also give them a name):

```
class SmallJavaTypeComputer {
  private static val factory = SmallJavaFactory.eINSTANCE
  public static val STRING_TYPE =
    factory.createSJClass => [name='stringType']
  public static val INT_TYPE =
    factory.createSJClass => [name = 'intType']
  public static val BOOLEAN_TYPE =
    factory.createSJClass =>[name='booleanType']

  public static val NULL_TYPE =
    factory.createSJClass => [name = 'nullType']

  def SJClass typeFor(SJExpression e) {
    switch (e) {
      ...continuation
      SJNull: NULL_TYPE
      SJStringConstant: STRING_TYPE
      SJIntConstant: INT_TYPE
      SJBoolConstant: BOOLEAN_TYPE
    }
```

```
    }

    def isPrimitive(SJClass c) {
        c.eResource == null
    }
    ...
```

Note that it is convenient to have a way of identifying the types we created for `null` and for constant expressions, which we call **primitive types**; we have a specific method for that called `isPrimitive`. An easy way to identify such types is to check that they are not part of a resource. We will need this distinction in the next chapter.

To test the type computer and keep the tests clean and compact, we implement a method that contains the skeleton of the test logic where a single passed expression is replaced. We will use the class names `R` for method return type, `P` for parameter type, and so on. This way, the actual test methods are compact and simple since they only specify the expression and the expected type name:

```
@RunWith(XtextRunner)
@InjectWith(SmallJavaInjectorProvider)
class SmallJavaTypeComputerTest {
    @Inject extension ParseHelper<SJProgram>

    @Inject extension SmallJavaModelUtil
    @Inject extension SmallJavaTypeComputer

    def private assertType(CharSequence testExp,
                            String expectedClassName) {
    '''
    class R { }
    class P { }
    class V { }
    class N { }
    class F { }

    class C {
        F f;

        R m(P p) {
            V v = null;
            «testExp»;
            return null;
        }
    }
    '''.parse => [
```

```
      expectedClassName.assertEquals(
        classes.last.methods.last.
          body.statements.get(1).statementExpressionType.name
      )
    ]
  }


  def private statementExpressionType(SJStatement s) {
    (s as SJExpression).typeFor
  }

  @Test def void thisType() {"this".assertType("C")}
  @Test def void paramRefType() {"p".assertType("P")}
  @Test def void varRefType() {"v".assertType("V")   }
  @Test def void newType() {"new N()".assertType("N")}
  @Test def void fieldSelectionType() {"this.f".assertType("F")}
...other cases...
  @Test def void intConstantType() {'10'.assertType("intType")}
  @Test def void nullType() {'null'.assertType("nullType")}
```

This technique is useful when you need a complete program to perform tests. In SmallJava you cannot type an expression without having a containing method and a containing class.

Type conformance (subtyping)

In an object-oriented language, the type system must also take **type conformance** (or **subtyping**) into account: an object of class C can be used in a context where an object of a superclass of C is expected. For instance, the following code is well-typed:

```
C c = new D();
```

Provided that D is a subclass (subtype) of C., that is, either D extends C or D extends B and, recursively, B is a subclass of C. This holds true in every context where an expression is assigned, for example, when we pass an argument in a method invocation.

We implement type conformance in a separate class, SmallJavaTypeConformance.

To check whether a class is a subclass of another class, we need to inspect the class hierarchy of the former and see whether we find the latter. We compute the class hierarchy using SmallJavaModelUtil.classHierarchy(), which computes the class hierarchy avoiding infinite loops in case of a cyclic hierarchy.

Type conformance deals with subclasses as well as other special cases. For instance, a class is not considered a subclass of itself, but it is of course conformant to itself. Another special case is the expression `null`; it can be assigned to any variable and field and passed as an argument for any parameter. The type for `null`, which is represented by the static instance NULL_TYPE in SmallJavaTypeComputer, must be conformant to any other type.

This is the initial implementation of type conformance for SmallJava:

```
import static org.example.smalljava.typing.SmallJavaTypeComputer.*

class SmallJavaTypeConformance {

  @Inject extension SmallJavaModelUtil

  def isConformant(SJClass c1, SJClass c2) {
    c1 === NULL_TYPE || // null can be assigned to everything
    c1 === c2 ||
    c1.isSubclassOf(c2)
  }

  def isSubclassOf(SJClass c1, SJClass c2) {
    c1.classHierarchy.contains(c2)
  }...
```

For the moment, we are not considering other cases (we need some additional concepts, as we will see in the next chapter).

We test this implementation as follows:

```
@RunWith(XtextRunner)
@InjectWith(SmallJavaInjectorProvider)
class SmallJavaTypeConformanceTest {
  @Inject extension ParseHelper<SJProgram>
  @Inject extension SmallJavaTypeConformance

  @Test def void testClassConformance() {
  '''
  class A {}
  class B extends A {}
  class C {}
  class D extends B {}
  '''.parse.classes => [
      // A subclass of A
      get(0).isConformant(get(0)).assertTrue
```

```
        // B subclass of A
        get(1).isConformant(get(0)).assertTrue
        // C not subclass of A
        get(2).isConformant(get(0)).assertFalse
        // D subclass of A
        get(3).isConformant(get(0)).assertTrue
        // null's type is conformant to any type
        NULL_TYPE.isConformant(get(0)).assertTrue
    ]
}...
```

Expected types

Now, we must check whether an expression has a type which conforms to the one expected by the context where it is used. The context is not necessarily an assignment or a method invocation; for instance, the expression used in an `if` statement must have the type boolean.

An obvious but not very good way of implementing this check is to write a `@Check` method in the validator for each specific context where the conformance needs to be checked. For example, the check for the assignment expression could be implemented as shown in the following code snippet:

```
@Check
def void checkAssignment(SJAssignment a) {
  val actualType = a.right.typeFor
  val expectedType = a.left.typeFor
  if (!actualType.isConformant(expectedType)) {
    error(...
  }
}
```

However, if we followed this approach, we would need to write several methods in the validator, which all have the preceding logic in common.

It is easier to compute the **expected type** and the **actual type** of an expression separately and then check for conformance rather than checking explicitly for each language construct. The expected type of an expression depends on the context where the expression is being used. We implement the method, `expectedType`, in `SmallJavaTypeComputer`.

The idea is that, given an expression, its expected type depends on its role in the container of the expression. For instance, consider this `SJVariableDeclaration`:

```
C c = new D();
```

The expected type of the expression `new D()` depends on the fact that it is contained in a variable declaration. The role, in particular, is represented by the feature of the container that contains the expression. In this example, the feature of `SJVariableDeclaration` is `expression`. We get the container using the method `eContainer` and the containing feature using the method `eContainingFeature`. Then, it is just a matter of dealing with all the cases. We will use a typed switch that allows us to specify additional conditions, using the keyword `case`. Note that the typed switch is performed on the container of the expression, and the `case` part deals with the containing feature. When an expression can only be contained in a single feature, we do not need to check the containing feature. For example, if an expression is contained in a variable declaration, then it can only be contained in the feature `expression`. Similarly, when we do not need the container, we simply check the containing feature, as in the case of the expression of an `if` statement.

To summarize, when the expression:

- Is the initialization expression of a variable declaration, the expected type is the type of the declared variable

- Is the right-hand side of an assignment, the expected type is the type of the left-hand side of the assignment

- Is the expression of a `return` statement, the expected type is the return type of the containing method

- Is the expression of an `if` statement, the expected type is boolean

- Is an argument of a method invocation, the expected type is the type of the corresponding parameter of the invoked method

The implementation is as follows:

```
static val ep = SmallJavaPackage.eINSTANCE

def expectedType(SJExpression e) {
  val c = e.eContainer
  val f = e.eContainingFeature
  switch (c) {
    SJVariableDeclaration:
      c.type
    SJAssignment case f == ep.SJAssignment_Right:
      typeFor(c.left)
    SJReturn:
      c.getContainerOfType(SJMethod).type
    case f == ep.SJIfStatement_Expression:
      BOOLEAN_TYPE
```

```
SJMemberSelection case f == ep.SJMemberSelection_Args: {
  // assume that it refers to a method and that there
  // is a parameter corresponding to the argument
  try {
    (c.member as SJMethod).params.get(c.args.indexOf(e)).type
  } catch (Throwable t) {
    null // otherwise there is no specific expected type
  }
}
}
}
```

Note that in the last case, we enclose the computation of the expected type in a try catch; in fact, there are some things that can go wrong in this case. The invoked member does not exist, it is not a method, or there is no parameter corresponding to the argument. In these cases, an exception is thrown and we simply return `null` as the expected type. If this happens, the corresponding error situation is reported by other validation checks. In general exceptions are a bad protocol; we used them here just for the sake of simplicity.

Checking type conformance

Now, we are able to write a single validator method to check type conformance for a generic expression:

```
@Inject extension SmallJavaTypeComputer
@Inject extension SmallJavaTypeConformance

public static val INCOMPATIBLE_TYPES =
  ISSUE_CODE_PREFIX + "IncompatibleTypes"

@Check def void checkConformance(SJExpression exp) {
  val actualType = exp.typeFor
  val expectedType = exp.expectedType
  if (expectedType == null || actualType == null)
    return; // nothing to check
  if (!actualType.isConformant(expectedType)) {
    error("Incompatible types. Expected '" + expectedType.name
      + "' but was '" + actualType.name + "'", null,
      INCOMPATIBLE_TYPES);
  }
}
```

To test this method in `SmallJavaValidatorTest`, we must create a test for each situation where conformance is not respected; as we did for the type computer, we write a method that contains the skeleton of the input, where the passed expression or statement is replaced (considering that B is conformant to A, but C is not conformant to A):

```
def private void assertIncompatibleTypes(CharSequence method-Body,
        EClass c, String expectedType, String actualType) {
  '''
  class A {}
  class B extends A {}
  class C {
    A f;
    A m(A p) {
      «methodBody»
    }
  }
  '''.parse.assertError(
      c, SmallJavaValidator.INCOMPATIBLE_TYPES,
      "Incompatible types. Expected '" + expectedType
        + "' but was '" + actualType + "'"
    )
}

@Test def void testVariableDeclExpIncompatibleTypes() {
  "A v = new C();".
    assertIncompatibleTypes(
      SmallJavaPackage.eINSTANCE.SJNew,"A", "C")
}

@Test def void testReturnExpIncompatibleTypes() {
  "return new C();".
    assertIncompatibleTypes(
      SmallJavaPackage.eINSTANCE.SJNew , "A", "C")
}
... test for the valid cases not shown

@Test def void testArgExpIncompatibleTypes() {
  "this.m(new C());".
    assertIncompatibleTypes(
      SmallJavaPackage.eINSTANCE.SJNew, "A", "C")
}...other cases not shown...
```

We still need to check whether the number of arguments passed to a method invocation is equal to the number of parameters of the invoked method:

```
public static val INVALID_ARGS = ISSUE_CODE_PREFIX + "InvalidArgs"

@Check def void checkMethodInvocationArguments(SJMemberSelection sel)
{
  val method = sel.member
  if (method instanceof SJMethod) {
    if (method.params.size != sel.args.size) {
      error(
        "Invalid number of arguments: expected " +
        method.params.size + " but was " + sel.args.size
        SmallJavaPackage.eINSTANCE.SJMemberSelection_Member,
        INVALID_ARGS)
    }
  }
}
```

Checking method overriding

Finally, we must check that method overrides are correct: the return type must be conformant to the type of the overridden method and the parameter types must be the same as the ones of the overridden method (of course, the parameter names can be different). In order to do that in an efficient way, we first aggregate all the methods inherited by a class into a map, where the key is the method name. Since we are not considering method overloading, using the method name as the key is sufficient. We use `SmallJavaModelUtil.classHierarchy()` to get the class hierarchy, and we get all the methods of the classes in the hierarchy. Since we want the methods in a subclass to have precedence over the homonymous methods in a superclass, we perform the following operations. We first reverse the class hierarchy so that superclasses appear first. We combine this list of lists of methods into a single `Iterable` of methods using the standard library utility method `flatten`. Then, we use the utility method `toMap` that takes a lambda for computing the key; in our case, the key is the method's name. Since adding an element to a map replaces a possible existing element with the same key, due to the way the classes in the hierarchy appear after the reversing, methods defined in subclasses will replace the homonymous methods in superclasses. We implement this method in `SmallJavaModelUtil` as follows:

```
def classHierarchyMethods(SJClass c) {
  c.classHierarchy.toList.reverseView.
    map[methods].flatten.toMap[name]
}
```

Then we can write the validator check as follows:

```
public static val WRONG_METHOD_OVERRIDE =
  ISSUE_CODE_PREFIX + "WrongMethodOverride"

@Check
def void checkMethodOverride(SJClass c) {
  val hierarchyMethods = c.classHierarchyMethods
  for (m : c.methods) {
    val overridden = hierarchyMethods.get(m.name)
    if (overridden != null &&
        (!m.type.isConformant(overridden.type) ||
         !m.params.map[type].elementsEqual(overridden.params.
map[type]))) {
      error("The method '" + m.name + "' must override a superclass
method",
        m, SmallJavaPackage.eINSTANCE.SJNamedElement_Name,
        WRONG_METHOD_OVERRIDE)
    }
  }
}
```

We search for a method in the class hierarchy with the same name as the examined method. If we find it, we check that the return type of the examined method is conformant to the one of the overridden method and that the parameter types are the same. For this latter check, we get the list of types of parameters of the two methods, and we use the standard library utility method `elementsEqual`; this checks whether the two `Iterable` instances have the same number of elements and that each element of the first `Iterable` is equal to the corresponding element of the other `Iterable`.

Improving the UI

To provide a better experience to the user of the SmallJava editor and tooling, we customize the appearance of SmallJava members (fields and methods) in several places of the UI.

First of all, we give a better string representation of members by also showing their `type` feature; thus, the string representation of a member is its name and its type's name separated by a colon :. Moreover, for methods, we also show the type of each parameter. We mimic the representation of Java members as implemented by Eclipse JDT. We then implement the methods for string representation in `SmallJavaModelUtil`:

```
def memberAsString(SJMember m) {
  m.name +
  if (m instanceof SJMethod)
```

```
      "(" + m.params.map[type.name].join(", ") + ")"
    else ""
}


def memberAsStringWithType(SJMember m) {
  m.memberAsString + " : " + m.type.name
}
```

We also borrow icons from Eclipse JDT for classes, fields, and methods. As we saw in *Chapter 6, Customizing Xtext Components*, we can specify the label representation for our DSL model elements by implementing text and image methods in SmallJavaLabelProvider. When we implement text, we can return a JFace StyledString object, which allows us to also specify the style (font, color, and so on) of the resulting label. For instance, we want to represent the part starting with : using a different style, again to mimic JDT:

```
class SmallJavaLabelProvider extends DefaultEObjectLabelProvider {
  ...

  @Inject extension SmallJavaModelUtil

  def text(SJMember m) {
    new StyledString(m.memberAsString).
      append(new StyledString(" : " + m.type.name,
        StyledString.DECORATIONS_STYLER))
  }
  ...
```

We also want a custom representation of members when they are proposed by the content assist; this will provide the user with additional information about the available members. In our SmallJavaProposalProvider class, we can simply override the getStyledDisplayString method that is automatically called by the default implementation of the proposal provider to represent the proposals. In this case, we return a custom StyledString object for representing an SJMember element, and we use a different style for representing the class containing the proposed member:

```
class SmallJavaProposalProvider extends
        AbstractSmallJavaProposalProvider {

  @Inject extension SmallJavaModelUtil

  override getStyledDisplayString(EObject element,
        String qualifiedNameAsString, String shortName) {
    if (element instanceof SJMember) {
```

```
      new StyledString(element.memberAsStringWithType).
      append(new StyledString(" - " +
        (element.eContainer as SJClass).name,
        StyledString.QUALIFIER_STYLER))
    } else
    super.getStyledDisplayString(element,
        qualifiedNameAsString, shortName)
}...
```

The result can be seen in the following screenshot (we also customized the outline view, as we did in *Chapter 6, Customizing Xtext Components*). Note all the type related information that is now available in the UI:

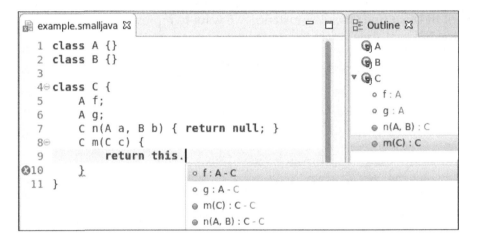

Summary

In this chapter, we presented type checking techniques that are typical for a DSL with object-oriented features. A small Java-like language was introduced to demonstrate how to parse features such as member access and inheritance and how to handle validation of type conformance. The reader might want to experiment with the caching techniques we described in the previous chapter and apply them to the implementation of the DSL.

For further reading concerning type system implementations for Xtext languages, we refer the interested reader to the articles *Bettini et al.* 2012, *Bettini* 2013, and *Bettini* 2016. In these articles, a DSL for implementing type systems for Xtext languages, **Xsemantics** is also described. Xsemantics is available as an open source project at `http://xsemantics.sourceforge.net`. There is, however, a crucial aspect that we still have to deal with—correct access to members (fields and methods). In fact, the following selection expression:

```
e.f
```

well-typed only if the field `f` is declared in the class of `e` (similarly for methods) or in any superclass of the class of `e`: If you perform some experiments, you will note that at the moment, you can access members which are not declared in the class of the receiver expression, and that you cannot access all the members of the hierarchy of the class of the receiver expression. Furthermore, local variable access does not work correctly in the current implementation; you can also refer to variables defined later and variables defined in inner blocks.

In order to correctly deal with the preceding issues, which concern cross-reference resolution, we will need to implement a custom scoping mechanism, as we will see in the next chapter. Scoping defines what is visible in a specific context so that Xtext can correctly resolve cross references.

In the next chapter, we will also add to SmallJava access level modifiers for members (that is, `private`, `protected`, and `public`). We will show you how a SmallJava program can access classes defined in other files and how to provide a library with some predefined classes (for example, `Object`, `String`, and so on).

10
Scoping

Usually, the first aspect you need to customize in your DSL implementation in Xtext is the validator. Typically, the second aspect you need to customize is **scoping**, which is the main mechanism behind visibility and cross-reference resolution. As soon as the DSL needs some constructs for structuring the code, a custom scoping implementation is required. In particular, scoping and typing are often strictly connected and interdependent especially for object-oriented languages. For this reason, in this chapter, we will continue developing the SmallJava DSL introduced in the previous chapter. We will describe both local and global scoping and explain how to customize scoping using SmallJava as a case study.

This chapter will cover the following topics:

- A detailed description of the Xtext mechanisms for local and global scoping
- How to customize the local scoping in an object-oriented language
- How to customize the global scoping with the concepts of packages and imports
- How to provide a library and a project wizard for your DSL
- How to customize the indexing of elements of your DSL

Cross-reference resolution in Xtext

Cross-reference resolution involves several mechanisms. In this section, we introduce the main concepts behind these mechanisms and describe how they interact. We will also write tests to get familiar with cross-reference resolution.

Containments and cross-references

Xtext relies on EMF for the in-memory representation of a parsed program, thus, it is necessary to understand how cross-references are represented in EMF.

In EMF, when a feature is not a **datatype** (string, integer, and so on), it is a reference, that is, an instance of `EReference`. A **containment reference** defines a stronger type of association. The association is stronger regarding the lifecycle. The referenced object is contained in the referring object, called the **container**. In particular, an object can have only one container. If you delete the container, all its contents are also automatically deleted. For non-containment references, the referenced object is stored somewhere else, for example, in another object of the same resource or even in a different resource. A **cross-reference** is implemented as a non-containment reference.

> In Ecore, the `EReference` class has a boolean property called `containment` that defines whether the reference is a containment reference or not.

Let's recall the SmallJava DSL rule for a class definition:

```
SJClass: 'class' name=ID ('extends' superclass=[SJClass])? '{'
    members += SJMember*
'}' ;
```

An `SJMember` member is contained in an `SJClass` class, that is, `members` is a multi-value containment reference. On the contrary, `superclass` is a single-value cross-reference.

Scoping deals with cross-references, that is, references with the boolean attribute `containment` set to false.

The index

The Xtext **index** stores information about all the objects in every resource. This mechanism is the base for cross-reference resolution. For technical reasons (mainly efficiency and memory overhead), the index stores the `IEObjectDescription` elements instead of the actual objects. An `IEObjectDescription` element is an abstract description of an `EObject`. This description contains the name of the object and the EMF **URI** of the object. The EMF URI is a path that includes the resource of the object and a unique identifier in the resource. The URI provides a means to locate and load the actual object when needed. The description also contains the `EClass` of the object, which is useful to filter descriptions by type.

The set of resources handled by the index depends on the context of execution. In the IDE, Xtext indexes all the resources in all the Xtext projects. The index is kept up-to-date in an incremental way using the incremental building mechanism of Eclipse, thus keeping the overhead minimal.

In a plain runtime context, where there is no workspace, the index is based on the EMF `ResourceSet`. We will see what this implies when we write JUnit tests and when we implement a standalone compiler.

In both contexts, the index is global. Visibility across resources is handled by using containers as shown later in the *The index and the containers* section.

Qualified names

The default implementation of the index uses a mechanism based on names. The computation of names is delegated to `IQualifiedNameProvider`. The default implementation of the name provider is based on the string attribute name. This is why we always defined elements that we want to refer to with a feature `name` in the grammar.

 The Xtext editor highlights the string attribute name in orange in the grammar.

Using only the simple name will soon raise problems due to duplicates, even in a simple program. Most Java-like languages use **namespaces** to allow for elements with the same name in different namespaces. Thus, for example, two different methods are allowed to have local variables with the same name, two different classes are allowed to have fields with the same name, two different packages are allowed to have classes with the same name, and so on. For this reason, the default implementation of the name provider computes a **qualified name**. It concatenates the name of an element with the qualified name of its container recursively; elements without a name are simply skipped. By default, all segments of a qualified name are separated by a dot, which is a common notation for expressing qualified names like in Java.

For example, consider the following SmallJava program (the type of declarations is not important here, thus, we use the class A that we assume as defined in the program):

```
class C {
  A f;
  A m(A p) {
    A v = null;
    return null;
  }
}
```

The containment relations are shown in the following tree figure:

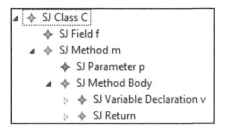

The qualified names of the elements of the preceding SmallJava class are shown in the following table:

Object	Qualified Name
SJClass C	C
SJField f	C.f
SJMethod m	C.m
SJParameter p	C.m.p
SJVariableDeclaration v	C.m.v

Note that SJMethodBody does not participate in the computation of the qualified name of the contained variable declaration, since it does not have a name feature.

 Qualified names are the mechanism also used by NamesAreUniqueValidator to decide when two elements are considered as duplicates.

Exported objects

To understand the mechanism behind scoping, it is useful to learn how to access the index. Accessing the index will also be useful for performing additional checks as shown later in this chapter. We show how to get all the object descriptions of the current resource.

The indexed object descriptions of a resource are stored in IResourceDescription, which is an abstract description of a resource. The index is implemented by IResourceDescriptions (plural form) and can be obtained through an injected ResourceDescriptionsProvider using the getResourceDescriptions(Re source) method.

Different resource descriptions are returned depending on the context they are retrieved. For example, there are resource descriptions of the files as they are on disk. However, while typing in the editor, a different resource description will be retrieved, which reflects the unsaved changes and that will shadow the resource description of the corresponding file saved on the disk. The `ResourceSet` records in which context it was created, that is why it is used as a parameter in the `ResourceDescriptionsProvider`.

Once we have the index, we get the `IResourceDescription` of a resource by specifying its URI. Once we have the `IResourceDescription`, we get the list of all the `IEObjectDescription` elements of the resource that are externally visible, that is, globally exported, using the method `getExportedObjects`. We can also filter exported elements by type:

We implement all the index-related operations in a separate class, `SmallJavaIndex`, in the package `scoping`:

```
class SmallJavaIndex {
  @Inject ResourceDescriptionsProvider rdp

  def getResourceDescription(EObject o) {
    val index = rdp.getResourceDescriptions(o.eResource)
    index.getResourceDescription(o.eResource.URI)
  }

  def getExportedEObjectDescriptions(EObject o) {
    o.getResourceDescription.getExportedObjects
  }

  def getExportedClassesEObjectDescriptions(EObject o) {
    o.getResourceDescription.
      getExportedObjectsByType(SmallJavaPackage.eINSTANCE.SJClass)
  }
}
```

We then write a learning test (see *Chapter 7, Testing*) listing the qualified names of the exported object descriptions:

```
@RunWith(XtextRunner)
@InjectWith(SmallJavaInjectorProvider)
class SmallJavaIndexTest {
  @Inject extension ParseHelper<SJProgram>
  @Inject extension SmallJavaIndex
  @Test def void testExportedEObjectDescriptions() {
    '''
```

```
class C {
  A f;
  A m(A p) {
    A v = null;
    return null;
  }
}
class A {}
'''.parse.assertExportedEObjectDescriptions
    ("C, C.f, C.m, C.m.p, C.m.v, A")
// this will have to be adapted at the end of the chapter
}
def private assertExportedEObjectDescriptions(EObject o,
                CharSequence expected) {
  expected.toString.assertEquals(
    o.getExportedEObjectDescriptions.map[qualifiedName].join(", ")
  )
}
}
```

The linker and the scope provider

The actual cross-reference resolution, that is, the linking, is performed by LinkingService. Usually, you do not need to customize the linking service, since the default implementation relies on IScopeProvider, which is the component you would customize instead. The default linking service relies on the scope obtained for a specific **context** in the model, and chooses an object whose name matches the textual representation of the reference in the program.

Thus, a **scope** provides information about:

- The objects that can be reached, that is, they are visible, in a specific part of your model, the context
- The textual representation to refer to them

You can think of a scope as a symbol table (or a map), where the keys are the names and the values are instances of IEObjectDescription. The Java interface for scopes is IScope.

The overall process of cross-reference resolution, that is, the interaction between the linker and the scope provider, can be simplified as follows:

1. The linker must resolve a cross-reference with text n in the program context c for the feature f of type t.

2. The linker queries the scope provider: "give me the scope for the elements assignable to f in the program context c".

3. The scope searches for an element whose key matches with n.

4. If it finds it, it locates and loads the EObject pointed to by the IEObjectDescription and resolves the cross-reference.

5. Otherwise, it issues an error of the shape "Couldn't resolve reference to...".

The IScopeProvider entry point is a single method:

```
IScope getScope(EObject context, EReference reference)
```

Since the program is stored in an EMF model, the context is an EObject and the reference is an EReference. Note that cross-references in an Xtext grammar specify the type of the referred elements. Thus, the scope provider must also take the types of objects for that specific reference into consideration when building the scope. The type information is retrieved from EReference that is passed to getScope.

Both scopes and the index deal with object descriptions. The crucial difference is that a scope also specifies the actual string with which you can refer to an object. The actual string does not have to be equal to the object description's qualified name in the index. Thus, the same object can be referred to with different strings in different program contexts.

To put it in another way, the index provides all the qualified names of the visible objects of a resource so that all these objects can be referred to using their qualified names. The scope provides further information, that is, in a given program context, some objects can be referred to even using simple names or using qualified names with less segments.

If in our DSL we can only use IDs to refer to objects, and objects are visible only by their fully qualified names, then we will not be able to refer to any object. Thus, being able to refer to an object by a simple name is essential.

Another important aspect of scopes is that they can be **nested**. Usually, a scope is part of a chain of scopes so that a scope can have an **outer scope**, also known as the **parent scope**. If a matching string cannot be found in a scope, it is recursively searched in the outer scope. If a matching string is found in a scope, the outer scope is not consulted. This strategy allows Xtext to implement typical situations in programming languages. For example, in a code block, you can refer to variables declared in the containing block. Similarly, declarations in a block usually shadow possible declarations with the same name in the outer context.

The default implementation of IScopeProvider reflects the nested nature of scopes using the containment relations of the EMF model. For a given program context, it builds a scope where all objects in the container of the context are visible by their simple name. The outer scope is obtained by recursively applying the same strategy on the container of the context.

Let's go back to our previous SmallJava example:

```
class C {
  A f;
  A m(A p) {
    A v = null;
    return null; // assume this is the context
  }
}
```

Let's assume that the context is the expression of the return statement; in that context, the SJMember elements will be visible by simple names and by qualified names:

```
f, m, C.f, C.m
```

In the same context, the SJSymbol elements will be visible by the following names:

```
p, v, m.p, m.v, C.m.p, C.m.v
```

This is because p and v are contained in m, which in turn is contained in C. Note that they are also visible by simpler qualified names, that is, qualified names with less segments, m.p and m.v, respectively.

In the SmallJava grammar, we can refer to members and symbols only by their simple name using an ID, not by a qualified name. Without a scope, we would not be able to refer to any of such elements, since they would be visible only by their qualified names.

A learning test that invokes the method `getScope` can help understand the default scope provider implementation (note how we specify `EReference` using `SmallJavaPackage`):

```
@RunWith(XtextRunner)
@InjectWith(SmallJavaInjectorProvider)
class SmallJavaScopeProviderTest {
  @Inject extension ParseHelper<SJProgram>
  @Inject extension SmallJavaModelUtil

  @Inject extension IScopeProvider
  @Test def void testScopeProvider() {
    '''
    class C {
      A f;
      A m(A p) {
        A v = null;
        return null; // return's expression is the context
      }
    }
    class A {}
    '''.parse.classes.head.
        methods.last.returnStatement.expression => [
          // THIS WILL FAIL when we customize scoping in the next
sections
          assertScope
          (SmallJavaPackage.eINSTANCE.SJMemberSelection_Member,
            "f, m, C.f, C.m")
          assertScope
          (SmallJavaPackage.eINSTANCE.SJSymbolRef_Symbol,
            "p, v, m.p, m.v, C.m.p, C.m.v")
        ]
  }

  def private assertScope(EObject context,
                EReference reference, CharSequence expected) {

    expected.toString.assertEquals(
      context.getScope(reference).
        allElements.map[name].join(", "))
  }
}
```

In the next diagram, we show the interaction between the linker and the scope provider for the resolution of the member in a member selection expression:

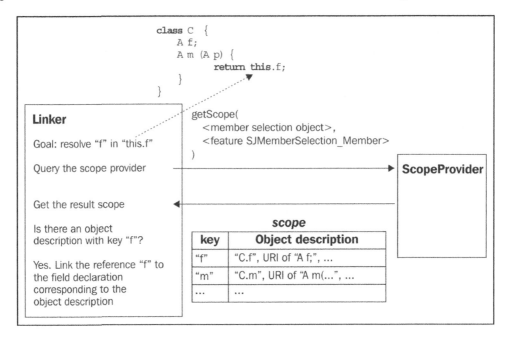

Summarizing, the default implementation of the scope provider fits most DSLs; in fact, for the Entities DSL, the cross-reference resolution worked out of the box.

 The scope provider is also used by the content assist to provide a list of all visible elements. Since the scope concerns a specific program context, the proposals provided by the content assist are actually sensible for that specific context.

Component interaction

Before getting into scope customization, we conclude this section by summarizing, in a simplified way, how all of the preceding mechanisms are executed internally by Xtext's builder:

- **Parsing**: Xtext parses the program files and builds the corresponding EMF models; during this stage, cross-references are not resolved

- **Indexing**: All the contents of the EMF models are processed; if an element can be given a qualified name, a corresponding object description is put in the index

- **Linking**: The linking service performs cross-reference resolution using the scope provider

This workflow is fixed. Consequently, we cannot rely on resolved cross-references during indexing. We need to keep that into consideration if we modify the indexing process, as we will see later in the section, *What to put in the index?*

Custom scoping

As soon as a DSL introduces more involved features, such as nested blocks or inheritance relations, the scope provider must be customized according to the semantics of the language.

The Xtext generator generates an Xtend stub class for implementing a custom scope provider. In the SmallJava DSL, it is SmallJavaScopeProvider.

In order to customize the scope provider we redefine the method getScope, and we manually check the reference and the context's class, for example:

```
override getScope(EObject context, EReference reference) {
  if (reference == SmallJavaPackage.eINSTANCE.SJSymbolRef_Symbol) {
    if (context instanceof ...)
      ...
  } else if (reference ==
        SmallJavaPackage.eINSTANCE.SJMemberSelection_Member) {
    ...
  } else {
    super.getScope(context, reference)
  }
}
```

Scope for blocks

The default scope provider can be too permissive. For example, in SmallJava, it allows an expression to refer to a variable declaration that is defined after that expression. As we have seen in *Chapter 8, An Expression Language*, forward references for variables are usually not permitted in languages. Moreover, if the language has nested code blocks, the default scope provider allows an outer block to access variable declarations of an inner block.

Let's consider an example of nested blocks in SmallJava:

```
class C {
  A m(A p) {
    A v1 = v4; // forward reference
    if (true) {
      A v2 = null;
      A v3 = v4; // forward reference
    }
    A v4 = v2; // reference to a var of an inner block
    return null;
  }
}
```

The example shows variable references that should not be valid. However, with the default scope provider, all variable declarations are visible in all contexts of the method body.

In *Chapter 8*, *An Expression Language*, we solved the problem of forward references by implementing a check in the validator, while in this chapter we show how to solve the visibility of symbols with a custom scope. The idea of the solution is basically the same; we want to build a scope consisting of the list of symbols defined before the current program context. In SmallJava, we have nested blocks, and we also need to examine containing blocks. Moreover, when examining the containing block, we still need to limit the list of visible variables to those declared before the block containing the current context. This implicitly prevents a variable definition from referring to itself in its initialization expression. Considering the previous example, when the context is the variable declaration A v3 = v4 in the if block, the scope should consist of all the variables of the container (the if block) declared before the context, that is, only v2. The outer scope should consist of all the variables of the container of the container (the method's body) declared before the container of the context, that is, only v1, and so on. The end of this recursion will be the case when the container is the method itself, in which case the scope is the list of parameters. Thus, we want to build the following nested scope for the variable declaration A v3 = v4 in the if block:

```
v2, outer: (v1, outer: (p, outer: null))
```

To actually create the scope instance, which would require us to build a list of IEObjectDescription, we can use the static utility method Scopes.scopeFor. This method takes an Iterable<EObject> and creates a scope with the corresponding IEObjectDescription elements. In particular, the object descriptions are created using the string attribute name of the passed EObject elements. This way, the descriptions will have simple names instead of qualified ones, which is what we want. You can also pass the outer scope to the method Scopes.scopeFor.

To implement the custom scoping for symbol references, we override `getScope` in `SmallJavaScopeProvider` as follows:

```
val epackage = SmallJavaPackage.eINSTANCE

override getScope(EObject context, EReference reference) {
  if (reference == epackage.SJSymbolRef_Symbol) {
    return scopeForSymbolRef(context)
  }
  return super.getScope(context, reference)
}

def protected IScope scopeForSymbolRef(EObject context) {
  val container = context.eContainer
  return switch (container) {
    SJMethod: Scopes.scopeFor(container.params)
    SJBlock:
      Scopes.scopeFor(
        container.statements.takeWhile[it != context].
          filter(SJVariableDeclaration),
        scopeForSymbolRef(container) // outer scope
      )
    default: scopeForSymbolRef(container)
  }
}
```

Since we want to customize the scope for symbol references, we check whether the passed EMF reference is `SJSymbolRef_Symbol`. In the SmallJava grammar, this is the only case where we can refer to a symbol. We delegate the computation of the scope to the recursive method `scopeForSymbolRef`. In this method, we perform a typed switch on the container of the context. The case for `SJMethod` ends the recursion by returning a scope consisting of the parameters of the method. The case for `SJBlock` builds a scope consisting of the variables in the block defined before the current context, using the Xtend library utility method `takeWhile`; the outer scope is the one returned by the recursive invocation walking the containment hierarchy. Recall that the case for `SJBlock` includes the cases for the body of an `SJMethod` and for the branches of an `SJIfStatement`. The default case simply performs another step of the recursion, without participating in the building of the scope.

The following table illustrates the recursive construction of the scope when the context is the variable declaration A v3 = v4. The table shows the container, the context, and the scope for symbols in that context:

Container	Context	Scope
If block	A v3 = v4	v2
If statement	If block	
Method body	If statement	v1
Method definition	Method body	p

Note that when the context is SJIfBlock, the container is SJIfStatement, and there is no symbol to add in the scope.

The resulting scope is as we wanted:

```
v2, outer: (v1, outer: (p, outer: null))
```

In this way, we get the correct behavior for symbol references, which can be verified in the following test (the testScopeProvider that we wrote a few sections before will now fail, since we customized the scope provider):

```
@Test def void testScopeProviderForSymbols() {
  '''
  class C {
    A m(A p) {
      A v1 = null;
      if (true) {
        A v2 = null;
        A v3 = null;
      }
      A v4 = null;
      return null;
    }
  }
  class A {}
  '''.parse.classes.head.methods.last.body.eAllContents.
  filter(SJVariableDeclaration) => [
    findFirst[name == 'v3'].expression.assertScope
      (SmallJavaPackage.eINSTANCE.SJSymbolRef_Symbol,
        "v2, v1, p")
    findFirst[name == 'v4'].expression.assertScope
      (SmallJavaPackage.eINSTANCE.SJSymbolRef_Symbol,
        "v1, p")
  ]
}
```

In this test, we verify the scope when the context is the variable declaration with name v3, and when the context is the variable declaration with name v4.

With this scope provider implementation, the variables defined in an inner block or after the program context cannot be referred; the user will get errors of the "Couldn't resolve reference to..." type.

Scope for inheritance and member visibility

The default scope provider implementation based on containments does not work for more complex relations implied by the semantics of the DSL. A typical example is the inheritance relation in object-oriented languages.

In SmallJava a subclass's method body must be able to refer to superclass's members. Note that for the moment, SmallJava does not have access level modifiers like `private` and `protected`; every member is implicitly `public`. We will add such modifiers in the next section.

For example, consider the following code snippet:

```
class C {
  A a;
  A n() { return null; }
}

class D extends C {
  A b;
  A m() {
      this.n(); // cannot access inherited method
      return this.a; // cannot access inherited field
  }
}
```

With the current scope provider, the members a and n of C will be visible only by their qualified name in the subclass D. Thus, the body of m of the subclass D is not able to refer to the members of the superclass C.

Moreover, the default scope provider implementation's strategy of considering only the containment relation cannot take into consideration the actual receiver of a member selection, which is instead needed for a valid member access.

For example, with the current scope provider implementation the following code would be considered valid:

```
class C {

}

class D {
  A b;
  A m() { return new C().b; }
}
```

While it should not be well typed in SmallJava, since the field b is not defined in the class C of the receiver new C().

We must build a custom scope for resolving an SJMember reference in an SJMemberSelection expression with the following strategy:

1. Get the type C of the receiver expression.
2. Return a nested scope consisting of:
    ◦ All the members in C
    ◦ As outer scope, all the members of the class hierarchy of C

To compute the collection of the members in the class hierarchy, we add to SmallJavaModelUtil the following method:

```
def classHierarchyMembers(SJClass c) {
  c.classHierarchy.map[members].flatten
}
```

This is similar to the method classHierarchyMethods we developed in *Chapter 9, Type Checking*, section *Checking method overriding*. The members in subclasses will appear first, which is what we need to build the scope.

We must check whether the context is of type SJMemberSelection. We modify the scope provider as follows:

```
@Inject extension SmallJavaModelUtil
@Inject extension SmallJavaTypeComputer

override getScope(EObject context, EReference reference) {
  if (reference == epackage.SJSymbolRef_Symbol) {
    return scopeForSymbolRef(context)
  } else if (context instanceof SJMemberSelection) {
    return scopeForMemberSelection(context)
```

```
  }
  return super.getScope(context, reference)
}

def protected IScope scopeForMemberSelection(SJMemberSelection sel) {
  val type = sel.receiver.typeFor
  if (type == null || type.isPrimitive)
    return IScope.NULLSCOPE

  return Scopes.scopeFor(
    type.members,
    Scopes.scopeFor(type.classHierarchyMembers)
  )
}
```

Let's examine the preceding method. If the receiver has a primitive type, we return an empty scope, since primitive types have no members. The scope will consist of all the members in the class of the receiver and the outer scope will consist of all the members in the superclasses of the receiver. If the class of the receiver has no superclass, the outer scope will be empty.

This implementation will also make field shadowing and method redefinitions work out of the box; a member in a subclass will be considered before a homonymous member in a superclass due to the way `classHierarchyMembers` is implemented.

 You should never return `null` as a scope; if you need to return an empty scope, you should return `IScope.NULLSCOPE`.

With this implementation of the scope provider, the members of a superclass will be visible in the subclass and the first example of this section is now considered valid. At the same time, only the members in the class hierarchy of the receiver will be visible in a member selection expression and the second example will be considered invalid.

The following test verifies whether references to fields are resolved correctly (a similar test can be written for methods), in particular, if fields in subclasses have the precedence over homonymous fields in superclasses:

```
@Test def void testFieldScoping() {
  '''
  class A {
    D a;
    D b;
    D c;
```

```
    }

    class B extends A {
      D b;
    }

    class C extends B {
      D a;
      D m() { return this.a; }
      D n() { return this.b; }
      D p() { return this.c; }
    }
    class D {}
  '''.parse.classes => [
      // a in this.a must refer to C.a
      get(2).fields.get(0).assertSame
        (get(2).methods.get(0).returnExpSel.member)
      // b in this.b must refer to B.b
      get(1).fields.get(0).assertSame
        (get(2).methods.get(1).returnExpSel.member)
      // c in this.c must refer to A.c
      get(0).fields.get(2).assertSame
        (get(2).methods.get(2).returnExpSel.member)
  ]
}


def private returnExpSel(SJMethod m) {
  m.returnStatement.expression as SJMemberSelection
}
```

This implementation still has a problem though, due to the fact that we allow a method and a field to have the same name, as in Java. With this implementation of scoping, methods and fields are mixed in the scope and they appear in the scope with their declaration order. Thus, when referring to a member, the first one will be linked irrespective of whether the expression is a field selection or a method invocation.

Consider the following example:

```
class C {
  A m;
  A m() {
    return this.m();
  }
}
```

The method invocation expression will wrongly refer to the field m.

Indeed, this test fails:

```
@Test def void testFieldsAndMethodsWithTheSameName() {
  '''
  class C {
    A f;
    A f() {
      return this.f(); // must refer to method f
    }
    A m() {
      return this.m; // must refer to field m
    }
    A m;
  }
  class A {}
  '''.parse.classes.head => [
    // must refer to method f()
    methods.head.assertSame(methods.head.returnExpSel.member)
    // must refer to field m
    fields.last.assertSame(methods.last.returnExpSel.member)
  ]
}
```

We must build the scope for member selection according to whether it is a method invocation or a field selection. We distinguish between a method invocation and a field selection using the feature methodinvocation. We modify the scopeForMemberSelection method as follows:

```
def protected IScope scopeForMemberSelection(SJMemberSelection sel) {
  val type = sel.receiver.typeFor
  if (type == null || type.isPrimitive)
    return IScope.NULLSCOPE

  val grouped = type.
    classHierarchyMembers.groupBy[it instanceof SJMethod]
  val inheritedMethods = grouped.get(true) ?: emptyList
  val inheritedFields = grouped.get(false) ?: emptyList

  if (sel.methodinvocation) {
    return Scopes.scopeFor(
      type.methods + type.fields,
      Scopes.scopeFor(inheritedMethods + inheritedFields)
    )
```

```
  } else {
    return Scopes.scopeFor(
      type.fields + type.methods,
      Scopes.scopeFor(inheritedFields + inheritedMethods)
    )
  }
}
```

We use the Xtend library utility method `groupBy`, using the `it instanceof` `SJMethod` lambda predicate; this way, we build a map where methods are associated to the key `true` and fields to the key `false`.

Now, the previous test succeeds.

Why do we return the other members, instead of returning only methods or fields according to the actual member selection kind? Because, without this strategy a program like the following would issue an error saying that the member `f` cannot be resolved, and this would not be informative:

```
class C {
  C f;
  C m() { return this.f(); }
}
```

Instead, with the preceding scoping implementation, `f` is resolved and our validator issues an error saying that we are trying to perform method invocation using a field (see *Chapter 9, Type Checking*); such an error is much better.

Visibility and accessibility

One important thing to understand about scoping is that it should deal with **visibility**, not necessarily with **validity**. For example, an element can be visible in a certain program context, but that context should not access it.

To illustrate this concept, we introduce in SmallJava the **access level modifiers** as in Java. To keep the example simple, we will not consider the Java package-private modifier, which is the default in Java.

Thus, we modify field and method declarations with the optional access level specification:

```
SJField:
  access=SJAccessLevel? SJTypedDeclaration ';';
SJMethod:
  access=SJAccessLevel? SJTypedDeclaration
  '(' (params+=SJParameter (',' params+=SJParameter)*)? ')'
```

```
      body=SJBlock ;
enum SJAccessLevel:
   PRIVATE='private' | PROTECTED='protected' | PUBLIC='public';
```

To express access level we use an enum rule; this will correspond to a Java enum. An **enum rule** always has an implicit default value, which corresponds to the first value. Thus, if no access level is specified in a SmallJava program, the value PRIVATE will be assumed.

> Remember that, in Java, member access is checked at class level, not at object level. Inside a class C, you can access private members on any object of class C, not only on this. We will use the same semantics in SmallJava.

To check if a member is accessible in a given program context, we need to check the subclass relation between the class containing the context and the class containing the referred member. We define a dedicated class SmallJavaAccessibility, in the package validation, as follows:

```
import static extension org.eclipse.xtext.EcoreUtil2.*

class SmallJavaAccessibility {

  @Inject extension SmallJavaTypeConformance

  def isAccessibleFrom(SJMember member, EObject context) {
    val contextClass = context.getContainerOfType(SJClass)
    val memberClass = member.getContainerOfType(SJClass)
    switch (contextClass) {
      case contextClass === memberClass : true
      case contextClass.isSubclassOf(memberClass) :
        member.access != SJAccessLevel.PRIVATE
      default:
        member.access == SJAccessLevel.PUBLIC
    }
  }
}
```

If the two classes are the same, the member can always be accessed. In a subclass, you can access only members of superclasses that are not private. In all other cases, you can only access public members.

It is straightforward to test this class, and we leave it as an exercise; as usual, the code of this example has such a test case.

Now we could modify the scope provider so that only the members that are accessible in a context are visible in that context. However, as we said at the beginning of the section, scoping should only deal with visibility, not with validity. In many ways, all members of a class are actually visible, the fact that some of them cannot be accessed is a validation issue.

Instead of restricting the scope, we write a validator rule that checks the accessibility of a referred member. With this strategy, we can provide better error information, for example, "private member is not accessible", instead of the default "couldn't resolve reference to...". In the editor, the user will still be able to navigate to the definition of a member even if the validator issues an error, since that member is still visible from the scoping point of view. This strategy is implemented by the Eclipse JDT editor as well, and it is considered a good practice (*Loose scoping, Strict validation*, see *Zarnekow* 2012).

The following is the validator rule:

```
class SmallJavaValidator extends AbstractSmallJavaValidator {
...
  @Inject extension SmallJavaAccessibility
  public static val MEMBER_NOT_ACCESSIBLE =
    ISSUE_CODE_PREFIX + "MemberNotAccessible"
...
  @Check
  def void checkAccessibility(SJMemberSelection sel) {
    val member = sel.member
    if (member.name != null && !member.isAccessibleFrom(sel))
      error(
      '''The «member.access» member «member.name» is not accessible
here''',
      SmallJavaPackage.eINSTANCE.SJMemberSelection_Member,
      MEMBER_NOT_ACCESSIBLE
      )
  }...
```

Note that before checking accessibility, we check whether the member's name is not null. If it is null, it means that the member reference cannot be resolved, and it would not make sense to generate an additional error on accessibility. An example of accessibility error is shown in the next screenshot. In the subclass D, we can access the protected field f of superclass C, but not to the private method m (remember that members are private by default in SmallJava). However, m is correctly linked to its method definition, and the reported error clearly states the problem.

```
example.smalljava ⊠

  1⊖ class C {
  2       protected C f;
  3       C m() { return this.f; }
  4  }
  5
  6⊖ class D extends C {
  7⊖     C n() {
  8           this.f = null;
  9           return this.m();
  10      }
  11 }
```

⊗ The private member m is not accessible here
Press 'F2' for focus

We adopted the same philosophy of a loose scoping and a strict validation in *Chapter 8, An Expression Language,* when checking forward references to variables. In this chapter, we rule out forward references to symbols with a restricted scope. In general, the validator approach allows you to give better feedback to the user, but it requires you to customize the content assist as shown in the following section. On the contrary, the restricted scope approach does not require customization of other aspects, but the user receives errors of the type "Couldn't resolve reference to...", which are less informative.

Now, we must update the check for correct method overriding that we implemented in *Chapter 9, Type Checking,* section *Checking method overriding*: an overriding method cannot reduce the access level of the overridden method:

```
public static val REDUCED_ACCESSIBILITY =
  ISSUE_CODE_PREFIX + "ReducedAccessibility"

@Check def void checkMethodOverride(SJClass c) {
  val hierarchyMethods = c.classHierarchyMethods
  for (m : c.methods) {
    val overridden = hierarchyMethods.get(m.name)
    if (overridden != null && … as before
    } else if (m.access < overridden.access) {
      error("Cannot reduce access from " + overridden.access +
        " to " + m.access,
        m, SmallJavaPackage.eINSTANCE.SJMember_Access,
        REDUCED_ACCESSIBILITY)
    }
  }
}
```

Due to the way the enum access levels are defined in the grammar, we have the needed ordering on access enums—`private` < `protected` < `public`.

Filtering unwanted objects from the scope

Since we are not restricting the scope of the members, the content assist will still provide all members as proposals, even the private and the protected ones, irrespective of their accessibility in that specific program context. As we saw in *Chapter 8, An Expression Language*, it is good practice to modify the proposals so that only valid ones are presented to the programmer. In that chapter, we manually built the proposals; in this chapter, since we introduced scoping, we use a different technique. The default implementation for proposals concerning a cross-reference relies on scoping; if you look at the implementation of the `AbstractSmallJavaProposalProvider.completeSJSelectionExpression_Member` method, it uses the method `lookupCrossReference`, which in turn uses the scope provider. There is an overloaded version of `lookupCrossReference` that also takes a predicate to filter proposals. In Xtend, a predicate corresponds to a lambda returning a boolean. Such a predicate receives `IEObjectDescription` as an argument, and it returns true if that description has to be included in the proposals. We override `completeSJSelectionExpression_Member` in `SmallJavaProposalProvider` and we call `lookupCrossReference` passing a lambda to filter out members that are not accessible in that context:

```
class SmallJavaProposalProvider extends
        AbstractSmallJavaProposalProvider {
  ...
  @Inject extension SmallJavaAccessibility
  override void completeSJSelectionExpression_Member
          (EObject model, Assignment a,
           ContentAssistContext context,
           ICompletionProposalAcceptor acceptor) {
    lookupCrossReference
      (a.getTerminal() as CrossReference, context, acceptor) [
        description |
        (description.getEObjectOrProxy as SJMember)
          .isAccessibleFrom(model)
      ]
  }
}
```

Note that in the lambda we retrieve the `EObject` from the description.

In the code of the SmallJava implementation, you can find some content assist tests for this customization.

You can now experiment with the content assist, which will propose only the members that are actually accessible in the current context.

Global scoping

Xtext has a default mechanism for **global scoping** that allows you to refer to elements defined in a different file, possibly in a different project of the workspace; in particular, it uses the dependencies of the Eclipse projects. For Java projects, it uses the classpath of the projects. Of course, this mechanism relies on the global index.

Global scoping is implied by the fact that the default scoping mechanism always relies on an outer scope that consists of the visible object descriptions in the index.

With the default configuration in the MWE2, this mechanism for global scoping works out of the box. You can experiment with a project with some SmallJava files. You will see that you can refer to the SmallJava classes defined in another file; content assist works accordingly.

Before proceeding to the use of global scoping, it is worthwhile to learn how to write JUnit tests that concern several input programs.

As hinted in the section *The index*, when running in a plain Java context where there is no workspace concept, the index is based on an EMF `ResourceSet`. There is an overloaded version of `ParseHelper.parse` that also takes the resource set to be used when loading the passed program string. Thus, if we want to write a test that involves several files where one of them refers to elements of the other, we need to parse all input strings using the same resource set.

This can be accomplished in two ways. You can inject a `Provider<ResourceSet>`, create a resource set through this provider, and pass it to the `parse` method as follows (we write this test in the `SmallJavaValidatorTest`):

```
@Inject Provider<ResourceSet> resourceSetProvider;
@Test def void testTwoFiles() {
  val resourceSet = resourceSetProvider.get
  val first = '''class B extends A {}'''.parse(resourceSet)
  val second = '''class A { B b; }'''.parse(resourceSet)
```

```
first.assertNoErrors
second.assertNoErrors

second.classes.head.assertSame(first.classes.head.superclass)
}
```

Note that in this test, the two input programs have mutual dependencies and the cross-reference mechanism works, since we use the same resource set.

 It is crucial to validate the models only after all the programs are loaded; remember that `ParseHelper` only parses the program, it does not try to resolve cross-references.

Alternatively, you can parse the first input and retrieve its resource set from the returned model object; then, the subsequent inputs are parsed using that resource set:

```
@Test def void testTwoFilesAlternative() {
  val first = '''class B extends A {}'''.parse
  val second = '''class A { B b; } '''.
      parse(first.eResource.resourceSet)
  ... as before
```

In the following sections, we will implement some aspects related to global scoping and the index.

Packages and imports

Since we can refer to elements of other files, it might be good to introduce the notion of **namespace** in SmallJava, which corresponds to the Java notion of a **package**.

Thus, we add an optional package declaration in the rule for `SJProgram`:

```
SJProgram:
  ('package' name=QualifiedName ';')?
  classes+=SJClass*;

QualifiedName: ID ('.' ID)* ;
```

The rule `QualifiedName` is a **data type rule**. A data type rule is similar to a terminal rule, for example, the terminal rule for `ID`, and it does not contain feature assignments. Differently from a terminal rule, a data type rule is valid only in specific contexts, that is, when it is used by another rule. A data type rule is executed by the parser, which has a much more sophisticated lookahead strategy than the lexer that executes the terminal rules. This way, it will not conflict with terminal rules; for example, the rule `QualifiedName` will not conflict with the rule `ID`.

 The Xtext editor highlights a data type rule's name in blue.

According to the default mechanism for computing a qualified name (see the section *Qualified names*), when a `SJClass` is contained in a program with a package declaration, its fully qualified name will include the package name. For example, given this program:

```
package my.pack;
class C { }
```

The class `C` will be stored in the index with the qualified name `my.pack.C`.

It now makes sense to allow the user to refer to a SmallJava class with its fully qualified name, like in Java.

When you specify a cross-reference in an Xtext grammar, you can use the complete form `[<Type>|<Syntax>]`, where `<Syntax>` specifies the syntax for referring to the element of that type. The compact form `[<Type>]` we used so far is just a shortcut for `[<Type>|ID]`. In fact, until now, we have always referred to elements by their `ID`. Now, we want to be able to refer to `SJClass` using the `QualifiedName` syntax; thus, we modify all the involved rules accordingly. We show the modified rule for `SJClass`, but also the rules for `SJTypedDeclaration` and `SJNew` must be modified accordingly:

```
SJClass:
    'class' name=ID ('extends' superclass=[SJClass|QualifiedName])?
    '{' members += SJMember* '}' ;
```

The rule for `QualifiedName` also accepts a single ID, thus, if there is no package, everything keeps on working as before. This means that all existing tests should still be successful.

We can now test class references with qualified names in separate files:

```
@Test def void testPackagesAndClassQualifiedNames() {
  val first = '''
  package my.first.pack;
  class B extends my.second.pack.A {}
  '''.parse
  val second = '''
  package my.second.pack;
  class A {
    my.first.pack.B b;
  }
  '''.parse(first.eResource.resourceSet)
  first.assertNoErrors
  second.assertNoErrors

  second.classes.head.assertSame(first.classes.head.superclass)
}
```

Now, it would be nice to have an **import** mechanism as in Java so that we can import a class by its fully qualified name once and then refer to that class simply by its simple name. Similarly, it would be helpful to have an import with wildcard * in order to import all the classes of a specific package. Xtext supports imports, even with wildcards; it only requires that a feature with name `importedNamespace` is used in a parser rule and then the framework will automatically treat that value with the semantics of an import; it also handles wildcards as expected:

```
SJProgram:
  ('package' name=QualifiedName ';')?
  imports+=SJImport*
  classes+=SJClass*;

SJImport:
    'import' importedNamespace=QualifiedNameWithWildcard ';' ;

QualifiedNameWithWildcard: QualifiedName '.*'? ;
```

The following test verifies imports:

```
@Test def void testImports() {
  val first = '''
  package my.first.pack;
  class C1 { }
  class C2 { }'''.parse

  '''
  package my.second.pack;
  class D1 { }
  class D2 { }'''.parse(first.eResource.resourceSet)

  '''
  package my.third.pack;
  import my.first.pack.C1;
  import my.second.pack.*;

  class E extends C1 { // C1 is imported
    my.first.pack.C2 c; // C2 not imported, but fully qualified
    D1 d1; // D1 imported by wildcard
    D2 d2; // D2 imported by wildcard
  }
  '''.parse(first.eResource.resourceSet).assertNoErrors
}
```

To keep the SmallJava DSL simple, we do not require the path of the `.smalljava` file to reflect the fully qualified name of the declared class as in Java. Indeed, in SmallJava, all classes are implicitly `public` and can be referred by any other SmallJava class.

The index and the containers

The index does not know anything about visibility across resources. In fact, the index is global in that respect. The Xtext index can also be seen as the counterpart of the JDT indexing mechanism for all the Java types, and the Eclipse platform indexing mechanism that keeps track of all the files in all the projects in the workspace. JDT provides the dialog "**Open Type**" that can be accessed using the menu **Navigate | Open Type** or with the shortcut *Ctrl + Shift + T*. This allows you to quickly open any Java type that is accessible from the workspace. Eclipse provides the dialog "**Open Resource**" that can be accessed using the shortcut *Ctrl + Shift + R*. This allows you to quickly open any file in the workspace. Xtext provides a similar dialog, "**Open Model Element**" that can be accessed by navigating to the **Navigate | Open Model Element** menu or with the shortcut *Ctrl + Shift + F3*. This allows you to quickly open any Xtext DSL element that is in the index, independently from the project. An example is shown in the next screenshot, where the dialog provides you quick access to all the elements of all the DSLs we implemented so far:

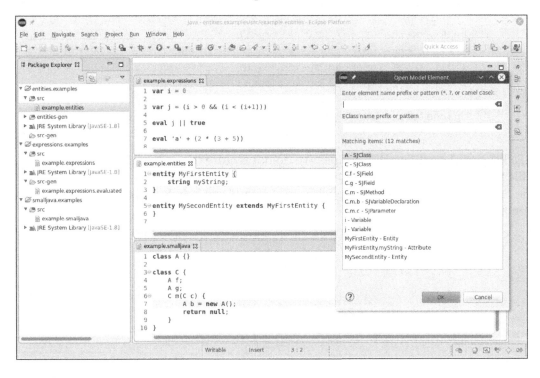

The mechanism concerning the visibility across resources is delegated to IContainer that can be seen as an abstraction of the actual container of a given resource. The inner class IContainer.Manager provides information about the containers that are visible from a given container. Using these containers, we can retrieve all the object descriptions that are visible from a given resource.

> The implementation of the containers and the managers depends on the context of execution. In particular, when running in Eclipse, containers are based on Java projects. In this context, for an element to be referable, its resource must be on the classpath of the caller's Java project and it must be exported. This allows you to reuse for your DSL all the mechanisms of Eclipse projects, and the users will be able to define dependencies in the same way as they do when developing Java projects inside Eclipse. We refer to the *About the index, containers, and their manager* section of the Xtext documentation for all the details about available container implementations.

The procedure to get all the object descriptions, which are visible from a given EObject o consists of the following steps:

1. Get the index.
2. Retrieve the resource description of the object o.
3. Use the IContainer.Manager instance to get all the containers in the index that are visible from the resource description of o.
4. Retrieve the object descriptions from the visible containers, possibly filtering them by type.

We thus add some utility methods to the class SmallJavaIndex:

```
class SmallJavaIndex {
  ...
  @Inject IContainer.Manager cm
  ...
  def getVisibleEObjectDescriptions(EObject o, EClass type) {
    o.getVisibleContainers.map[ container |
      container.getExportedObjectsByType(type)
    ].flatten
  }

  def getVisibleClassesDescriptions(EObject o) {
    o.getVisibleEObjectDescriptions
      (SmallJavaPackage.eINSTANCE.SJClass)
  }
```

```
def getVisibleContainers(EObject o) {
  val index = rdp.getResourceDescriptions(o.eResource)
  val rd = index.getResourceDescription(o.eResource.URI)
  cm.getVisibleContainers(rd, index)
}...
```

Note that the result of `map` in the preceding code is a `List<Iterable<IEO bjectDescription>>`; the `flatten` utility method from the Xtend library combines multiple iterables into a single one. Thus, the final result will be an `Iterable<IEObjectDescription>`.

In the section *Exported objects*, we created the class `SmallJavaIndex` with utility methods to retrieve all the descriptions exported by a resource. We used those methods to write learning tests to get familiar with the index. The methods we have just added to `SmallJavaIndex` will be effectively used in the rest of the chapter to perform specific tasks that require access to all the visible elements. In particular, `getVisibleClassesDescriptions` will be useful for checking duplicate classes across files, in the next section.

Checking duplicates across files

The visibility of elements is implemented in the scope provider; thus, usually the index is not used directly. One of the scenarios where you must use the index is when you want to check for duplicates across files in a given container, that is, in a project and all its dependencies. The validator for SmallJava currently only implements checks for duplicates in a single resource.

We now write a validator method to check for duplicates across files using the index. We only need to check instances of `SJClass`, since they are the only globally visible objects.

 Do not traverse the resources in the resource set (that is, visit all of them) since this is an expensive operation. Instead, use the index in these situations since this is both better and cheaper. It is OK to visit elements in the resource being processed.

The idea is to use the method `SmallJavaIndex.getVisibleClassesDescriptions` to get all the object descriptions of the type `SJClass` that are visible from the resource of a given SmallJava class and search for duplicate qualified names. These descriptions include both the elements stored in other resources and the one exported by the resource under validation. Thus, it is essential to compute the difference, so that we collect only the descriptions, corresponding to `SJClass` elements that are defined in resources different from the one under validation. To this aim, we add the following method to `SmallJavaIndex`:

```
def getVisibleExternalClassesDescriptions(EObject o) {
  val allVisibleClasses = o.getVisibleClassesDescriptions
  val allExportedClasses = o.getExportedClassesEObjectDescriptions
  val difference = allVisibleClasses.toSet
  difference.removeAll(allExportedClasses.toSet)
  return difference.toMap[qualifiedName]
}
```

To compute such difference, we first transform the descriptions to sets and use the `Set.removeAll` method. We also transform the result into a `Map`, where the key is the description's qualified name. This allows us to quickly find a description given a qualified name.

In the validator, it is just a matter of checking that for each `SJClass` c in the `SJProgram` there is no element in the preceding map with the same qualified name of c:

```
@Inject extension SmallJavaIndex
@Inject extension IQualifiedNameProvider
public static val DUPLICATE_CLASS =
  ISSUE_CODE_PREFIX + "DuplicateClass"

// perform this check only on file save
@Check(CheckType.NORMAL)
def checkDuplicateClassesInFiles(SJProgram p) {
    val externalClasses = p.getVisibleExternalClassesDescriptions
    for (c : p.classes) {
      val className = c.fullyQualifiedName
      if (externalClasses.containsKey(className)) {
        error("The type " + c.name + " is already defined",
          c,
          SmallJavaPackage.eINSTANCE.SJNamedElement_Name,
          DUPLICATE_CLASS)
      }
    }
  }
}
```

Note that we specified the `CheckType.NORMAL` in the `@Check` annotation; this instructs Xtext to call this method only on file save, not during editing as it happens normally (the default is `CheckType.FAST`). This is a good choice since this check might require some time, and if executed while editing, it might reduce the editor performance. Eclipse JDT also checks for class duplicates across files only on file save.

Providing a library

Our implementation of SmallJava does not yet allow to make references to types such as `Object`, `String`, `Integer`, and `Boolean` We could use these to declare variables initialized with constant expressions. In this section, we show how to create a library with predefined types.

One might be tempted to hardcode these classes/types directly in the grammar, but this is not the best approach. There are many reasons for not doing that; mostly, that the grammar should deal with syntax only. Moreover, if we hardcoded, for example, `Object` in the grammar, we would only be able to use it as a type, but what if we wanted `Object` to have some methods? We would not be able to express that in the grammar.

Instead, we will follow the **library approach** (see also the article *Zarnekow* 2012-b). Our language implementation will provide a library with some classes, for example, `Object`, `String`, and so on, just like Java does. Since Xtext deals with EMF models, this library could consist of any EMF model. However, we can write this library just like any other SmallJava program.

To keep things simple, we write one single file, `mainlib.smalljava`, with the following SmallJava classes:

```
package smalljava.lang;
class Object {
  public Object clone() {
    return this;
  }

  public String toString() {
    // fake implementation
    return "not implemented";
  }

  public Boolean equals(Object o) {
    // fake implementation
    return false;
  }
```

```
}

class String extends Object {}
class Integer extends Object {}
class Boolean extends Object {}
```

SmallJava does not aim at being usable and useful; thus, this is just an example implementation of the classes of SmallJava library. We also use a package name, smalljava.lang, which reminds us of the main Java library, java.lang. We create a new **Source Folder**, smalljavalib, in the main smalljava project (Right-click on the project, **New | Source Folder**). In this new source folder we create the file smalljava/lang/mainlib.smalljava. Furthermore, in the MANIFEST of the main SmallJava plug-in project, we make sure that the package smalljava.lang is exported and we add the smalljavalib folder as a source folder in the build.properties file (as usual, use the quickfix on the warning placed in the build.properties file).

Now, if we run Eclipse, create a project, and add as dependency our org.example.smalljava project, the classes of mainlib.smalljava will be automatically available. In fact, Xtext global scoping implementation takes into consideration the project's dependencies; thus, the classes of our library are indexed and available in SmallJava programs.

In the next sections, we will adapt the type system implementation in order to take into accounts the SmallJava types defined in this library.

Default imports

As we saw in the last sections, a DSL can automatically refer to elements in other files thanks to global scoping. In particular, Xtext also takes imported namespaces into consideration; if we import smalljava.lang.*, then we can refer to, for example, Object directly, without its fully qualified name. The scope provider delegates this mechanism to the class ImportedNamespaceAwareLocalScopeProvider.

At this point, in order to use library classes like Object, we have to explicitly import smalljava.lang. In Java, you do not need to import java.lang, since that is implicitly imported in all Java programs. It would be nice to implement this implicit import mechanism also in SmallJava for the package smalljava.lang. All we need to do is to provide a custom implementation of ImportedNamespaceAwareLocalScopeProvider and redefine the method getImplicitImports (the technical details should be straightforward):

```
class SmallJavaImportedNamespaceAwareLocalScopeProvider
        extends ImportedNamespaceAwareLocalScopeProvider {
  override getImplicitImports(boolean ignoreCase) {
    newArrayList(new ImportNormalizer(
```

```
        QualifiedName.create("smalljava", "lang"),
        true, // wildcard
        ignoreCase
    ))
  }
}
```

In the previous code, the important part is the creation of `ImportNormalizer`, which takes a qualified name and interprets it as an imported namespace, with a wildcard when the second argument is true. This way, it is as if all SmallJava programs contained an import of `smalljava.lang.*`.

Now, we need to bind this implementation in the runtime module `SmallJavaRuntimeModule`. This is slightly different from other customizations in the Guice module we have seen so far; in fact, we need to bind the delegate field in the scope provider:

```
override void configureIScopeProviderDelegate(Binder binder) {
    binder.bind(org.eclipse.xtext.scoping.IScopeProvider)
    .annotatedWith(
      com.google.inject.name.Names
      .named(AbstractDeclarativeScopeProvider.NAMED_DELEGATE))
      .to(SmallJavaImportedNamespaceAwareLocalScopeProvider);
}
```

With this modification, we can simply remove the import statement `import smalljava.lang.*` and still be able to refer to the classes of the SmallJava library.

Using the library outside Eclipse

Being able to load the SmallJava library outside Eclipse is important both for testing and for implementing a standalone command-line compiler for the DSL.

As we saw in the previous sections, when we write unit tests with several dependent input programs, we need to load all the resources corresponding to input programs into the same resource set. Thus, we must load our library into the resource set as well to make the library available when running outside Eclipse.

We write a reusable class `SmallJavaLib`, which deals with all the aspects concerning the SmallJava library. We start with a method that loads the library in the passed the resource set:

```
class SmallJavaLib {

  public val static MAIN_LIB = "smalljava/lang/mainlib.smalljava"
  def loadLib(ResourceSet resourceSet) {
```

```
    val url = getClass().getClassLoader().getResource(MAIN_LIB)
    val stream = url.openStream
    val resource = resourceSet.createResource(URI.createFileURI(url.
path))
    resource.load(stream, resourceSet.getLoadOptions())
  }
}
```

The important thing here is that we get the contents of `mainlib.smalljava` using the **class loader**. We use `getResource`, which returns an URL for the requested file and `URL.openStream`, which returns `InputStream` to read the contents of the requested file. The class loader will automatically search for the given file using the classpath. This will work both for JUnit tests and even when the program is bundled in a JAR as for the case of the standalone compiler. Then, we create an EMF resource and load it using the contents of the library file.

We are now able to write a test to verify that implicit imports work correctly. We use the version of the method `parse` that also takes the resource set as an argument, and we use the same resource set both for loading an input program and for loading the library using the method `SmallJavaLib.loadLib` shown previously:

```
@RunWith(XtextRunner)
@InjectWith(SmallJavaInjectorProvider)
class SmallJavaLibTest {
  @Inject extension ParseHelper<SJProgram>
  @Inject extension ValidationTestHelper
  @Inject extension SmallJavaLib
  @Inject Provider<ResourceSet> rsp
  @Test def void testImplicitImports() {
  '''
  class C extends Object {
    String s;
    Integer i;
    Object m(Object o) { return null; }
  }
  '''.loadLibAndParse.assertNoErrors
  }
  def private loadLibAndParse(CharSequence p) {
    val resourceSet = rsp.get
    loadLib(resourceSet)
    p.parse(resourceSet)
  }...
```

We also use `SmallJavaLib` to implement a standalone command-line compiler (see section *Standalone command-line compiler* of *Chapter 5, Code Generation*).

In the MWE2 workflow, we enable the following fragment:

```
generator = {
   generateXtendMain = true
}
```

 In the code of this example, you will also find a simple code generator for SmallJava, which basically generates Java classes corresponding to SmallJava classes.

We modify the generated Main Xtend class in order to load the library, load all the passed input files, and then validate all the resources in the resource set and run the generator for each resource. Remember that we must validate the resources only after all the resources have been loaded, otherwise the cross-reference resolution will fail. Here, we show the modified lines in the generated Main Xtend class:

```
class Main {
  def static main(String[] args) {
    val injector =
      new SmallJavaStandaloneSetupGenerated().
        createInjectorAndDoEMFRegistration
    val main = injector.getInstance(Main)
    main.runGenerator(args)
  }


  . . .
  @Inject SmallJavaLib smallJavaLib
  . . .

  def protected runGenerator(String[] strings) {
    val set = resourceSetProvider.get
    // Configure the generator
    fileAccess.outputPath = 'src-gen/'
    val context = new GeneratorContext => [
        cancelIndicator = CancelIndicator.NullImpl
    ]
    // load the library
    smallJavaLib.loadLib(set)
    // load the input files
    strings.forEach[s | set.getResource(URI.createFileURI(s), true)]
    // validate the resources
    var ok = true
```

```
    for (resource : set.resources) {
      println("Compiling " + resource.URI + "...")
      val issues = validator.
        validate(resource, CheckMode.ALL,
          CancelIndicator.NullImpl)
      if (!issues.isEmpty()) {
        for (issue : issues) {
          System.err.println(issue)
        }
        ok = false
      } else {
          generator.generate(resource, fileAccess, context)
      }
    }
    if (ok)
      System.out.println('Programs well-typed.')
  }
}
```

After we finished adapting the type system to using the library, we can follow the same procedure illustrated in *Chapter 5, Code Generation*, to export a runnable JAR file together with all its dependencies. The file `mainlib.smalljava` will be bundled in the JAR, and the class loader will be able to load it.

Using the library in the type system and scoping

Now that we have a library, we must update the type system and scope provider implementations in order to use the classes of the library. We declare public constants in `SmallJavaLib` for the fully qualified names of the classes declared in our library:

```
class SmallJavaLib {
  ...
  public val static LIB_PACKAGE = "smalljava.lang"
  public val static LIB_OBJECT = LIB_PACKAGE+".Object"
  public val static LIB_STRING = LIB_PACKAGE+".String"
  public val static LIB_INTEGER = LIB_PACKAGE+".Integer"
  public val static LIB_BOOLEAN = LIB_PACKAGE+".Boolean"
```

We use these constants to modify `SmallJavaTypeConformance` to define special cases as follows:

```
class SmallJavaTypeConformance {
  @Inject extension IQualifiedNameProvider
  def isConformant(SJClass c1, SJClass c2) {
    c1 === NULL_TYPE || // null can be assigned to everything
    c1 === c2 ||
    c2.fullyQualifiedName.toString == SmallJavaLib.LIB_OBJECT ||
    conformToLibraryTypes(c1, c2) ||
    c1.isSubclassOf(c2)
  }

  def conformToLibraryTypes(SJClass c1, SJClass c2) {
    (c1.conformsToString && c2.conformsToString) ||
    (c1.conformsToInt && c2.conformsToInt) ||
    (c1.conformsToBoolean && c2.conformsToBoolean)
  }

  def conformsToString(SJClass c) {
    c == STRING_TYPE ||
    c.fullyQualifiedName.toString == SmallJavaLib.LIB_STRING
  }... similar implementations for int and boolean
```

Recall that in the type computer we have constants for some types, for example, for string, integer and boolean constant expressions. We now have to match such constant types with the corresponding SmallJava classes of the library. The type of string constant expression is type conformant to the library class `String`. The cases for boolean and integer expressions are similar.

Each class is considered type conformant to the library class `Object`, as in Java, even if that class does not explicitly extend `Object`. If we introduced basic types directly in SmallJava, for example, `int` and `boolean`, we would still have to check conformance with the corresponding library classes, for example, `Integer` and `Boolean`.

The fact that every SmallJava class implicitly extends the library class `Object` must be reflected in the scope provider so that any class is able to access the methods implicitly inherited from `Object`. For example, the following SmallJava class should be well typed even if it does not explicitly extend `Object`, but the current implementation rejects it, since it cannot resolve the references to members of `Object`:

```
class C {
  Object m(Object o) {
    Object c = this.clone();
    return this.toString();
  }
}
```

To solve this problem, we first add a method in SmallJavaLib that loads the EMF model corresponding to the library Object class:

```
class SmallJavaLib {
  @Inject extension SmallJavaIndex
  . . .

  def getSmallJavaObjectClass(EObject context) {
    val desc = context.getVisibleClassesDescriptions.findFirst[
        qualifiedName.toString == LIB_OBJECT]
    if (desc == null)
      return null
    var o = desc.EObjectOrProxy
    if (o.eIsProxy)
      o = context.eResource.resourceSet.
        getEObject(desc.EObjectURI, true)
    o as SJClass
  }
```

In the preceding code, we get the object description of the library class Object using SmallJavaIndex.getVisibleClassesDescriptions. If the EObject corresponding to Object is still a proxy, we explicitly load the actual EObject from the resource set of the passed context using the URI of the object description. The preceding code assumes that the library classes are visible in the current projects. It also assumes that the EObject context is already loaded, otherwise the resolution of the proxy will fail.

Since the scope provider uses the class hierarchy computed by SmallJavaModelUtil, we just need to modify the method SmallJavaModelUtil.classHierarchy, we developed in *Chapter 9, Type Checking*, section *Checking method overriding*, so that it adds the library Object SmallJava class at the end of the hierarchy, if not already present:

```
class SmallJavaModelUtil {
  @Inject extension SmallJavaLib
  . . .
  def classHierarchy(SJClass c) {
    val visited = newLinkedHashSet()

    var current = c.superclass
    while (current != null && !visited.contains(current)) {
      visited.add(current)
      current = current.superclass
    }

    // new part
```

```
    val object = c.getSmallJavaObjectClass
    if (object != null)
      visited.add(object)

    visited

  }
}
```

Now, the scope provider will automatically retrieves also the methods defined in the library class `Object`.

Note that it is important to be able to easily modify the structure of the library classes in the future. We did hardcode as public constants the fully qualified names of library classes in `SmallJavaLib`, but not the library classes' structure, so if in the future we want to modify the implementation of the library classes, we will not have to modify the type system neither the scope provider.

The other interesting feature is that one could easily provide a different implementation of the library as long as the main library class names are kept. The current SmallJava implementation will seamlessly be able to use the new library without any change. This is another advantage of keeping the DSL and the library implementations separate.

Classes of the same package

Just like in Java, SmallJava classes should be able to refer to external classes in the same package without importing the package. However, this is not yet the case in the current implementation. For example, given the following two SmallJava files, they are not able to refer to each other without an explicit import, although they are in the same package:

```
// first file
package my.pack;

class A {
  B b;
}

// second file
package my.pack;

class B extends A {}
```

To solve this problem, we need to go back to our custom
`SmallJavaImportedNamespaceAwareLocalScopeProvider` that
we implemented in section *Default imports*. The idea is to customize
`internalGetImportedNamespaceResolvers` so that when the context is a
SmallJava program then we add an implicit import of the same package of the
current SmallJava program, if the program has a package.

To do that, we create an `ImportNormalizer`. We have already used
`ImportNormalizer` in section *Default imports*. This is the implementation of
`internalGetImportedNamespaceResolvers`:

```
class SmallJavaImportedNamespaceAwareLocalScopeProvider extends
        ImportedNamespaceAwareLocalScopeProvider {
  @Inject extension IQualifiedNameProvider

  ...

  override protected List<ImportNormalizer>
      internalGetImportedNamespaceResolvers(
          EObject context, boolean ignoreCase) {
    val resolvers = super.internalGetImportedNamespaceResolvers
            (context, ignoreCase)
    if (context instanceof SJProgram) {
      val fqn = context.fullyQualifiedName
      // fqn is the package of this program
      if (fqn != null) {
        // all the external classes with the same package of this
program
        // will be automatically visible in this program, without an
import
        resolvers += new ImportNormalizer(
          fqn,
          true, // use wildcards
          ignoreCase
        )
      }
    }
    return resolvers
  }

}
```

Now, the previous two SmallJava files compile without errors.

Dealing with super

As a final feature, we add the mechanism for invoking the implementation of a method in the superclass using the keyword super. Note that super should be used only as the receiver of a member selection expression, that is, it cannot be passed as the argument of a method. Following the practice "loose grammar, strict validation", we do not impose this at the grammar level. Thus, we add the rule for super as a terminal expression:

```
SJTerminalExpression returns SJExpression:
    ...
    {SJSuper} 'super' | ...
```

We add a validator rule that checks the correct super usage:

```
public static val WRONG_SUPER_USAGE =
    ISSUE_CODE_PREFIX + "WrongSuperUsage"

@Check def void checkSuper(SJSuper s) {
    if (s.eContainingFeature !=
            SmallJavaPackage.eINSTANCE.SJMemberSelection_Receiver)
        error("'super' can be used only as member selection receiver",
            null, WRONG_SUPER_USAGE)
}
```

Thanks to the way we implemented the scope provider, in order to make members of the superclass visible when the receiver expression is super, we only need to provide a type for super. The type for super is the superclass of the containing class:

```
class SmallJavaTypeComputer {
    def SJClass typeFor(SJExpression e) {
        switch (e) {
            ...
            SJSuper : e.getContainerOfType(SJClass).superclass
            ...as before
```

However, this way, if a class does not explicitly extend Object, it will not be able to access the methods of Object with super. To solve this, we just need to return the loaded instance of Object in case the superclass is null using SmallJavaLib.getSuperclassOrObject:

```
class SmallJavaTypeComputer {
    @Inject extension SmallJavaLib
    def SJClass typeFor(SJExpression e) {
        switch (e) {
```

```
        SJThis : e.containingClass
        SJSuper : e.getContainerOfType(SJClass).getSuperclassOrObject
        ...as before
    }

    def getSuperclassOrObject(SJClass c) {
      c.superclass ?: getSmallJavaObjectClass(c)
    }
```

What to put in the index?

As explained earlier in this chapter, everything that can be given a name will have a corresponding entry in the index; moreover, by default, each element of the index can be referred through its fully qualified name. However, only the references that use the qualified name syntax can refer to these elements using the index. In SmallJava, only classes can be referred with qualified names.

The index is also used by Xtext to keep track of dependencies among files and to determine when to rebuild other files when a file changes.

Therefore, it makes no sense to index those elements that cannot be referred from other files. In our DSL, this means that it does not make sense to index variables, since they can only be accessed from a method in the containing class. Instead, we leave the methods and their parameters in the index, because we want the other files using a method of an external class to be notified if the method changes name or parameters. Although the presence of entries in the index for local variables does not harm, still it occupies some memory space uselessly. Moreover, the indexing procedure could be optimized by removing the overhead of indexing useless elements.

To tweak the strategy for building the index we provide a custom implementation of `DefaultResourceDescriptionsStrategy` and redefine the method `createEObjectDescriptions`. This method is automatically called by Xtext when the index is built or updated when resources change. This method is expected to return `false` if the children of the passed `EObject` must not be processed. In our case, we simply return `false` when the object is an `SJBlock`:

```
@Singleton
class SmallJavaResourceDescriptionsStrategy extends
DefaultResourceDescriptionStrategy {

  override createEObjectDescriptions(EObject e,
                IAcceptor<IEObjectDescription> acceptor) {
    if (e instanceof SJBlock)
```

```
        return false
    else
        return super.createEObjectDescriptions(e, acceptor)
    }
}
```

Note that this class must be annotated with @Singleton, indicating that only one instance per injector will be used for all injections for this class.

Of course, we bind our implementation in the runtime module:

```
def Class<? extends IDefaultResourceDescriptionStrategy>
            bindIDefaultResourceDescriptionStrategy() {
    return SmallJavaResourceDescriptionsStrategy;
}...
```

This way, we improve the default indexing behavior.

 If you now run the test method testExportedEObjectDescriptions shown in the section *Exported objects*, you will see that it fails. You will need to modify it according to the descriptions found in the index after our customization.

Additional automatic features

Xtext makes use of the index to automatically provide many additional IDE features for your DSL. Some examples are shown in the next screenshot. For example, you can mark occurrences of any named element by toggling the corresponding toolbar button. In the following screenshot, it is the one right on top of the **Plug-in Development** perspective button, marked with **(1)**. The markers will be evident both in the editor and in its right-hand side ruler. This feature is based on the IResourceDescription instances stored in the index; they contain information about cross-references, possibly to other resources. Furthermore, by right-clicking on an element in the editor, you can choose the menu **References**, and in the **Search** view, you can see all the files in your project that reference the selected element. In the following screenshot, we selected the method predicate in the file example.smalljava, and the view shows all its occurrences also in the other file example2.smalljava:

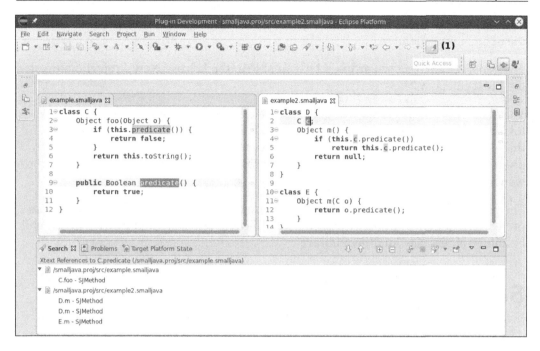

The editor for your DSL automatically supports refactoring of names: just select an element with a name, right-click on it, and choose **Rename Element**. This refactoring has the same user interface as the one of JDT; you can also access the refactoring dialog so that you can have a preview of what will be modified and possibly deselect some modifications. Refactoring works across multiple files as well. References in the same file are updated while you rename the element. External references will be updated after pressing *Enter*.

Providing a project wizard

It is nice to provide the clients of your DSL a **project wizard** that creates an Eclipse project, sets its source folders, for example, `src` and `src-gen` and adds the needed dependencies.

Xtext can generate such a project wizard for you, in the `.ui` project, if you enable this fragment in the MWE2 file in the `StandardLanguage` section:

```
newProjectWizardForEclipse = {
  generate = true
}
```

After running the MWE2 workflow, you must merge manually the `plugin.xml` and the `plugin.xml_gen`.

The generated project wizard will be available in the Eclipse **New Project** dialog, in the **Xtext** category.

The above MWE2 fragment will generate the classes for the wizard in the `src-gen` folder of the `.ui` project. Moreover, in the `src` folder, it will generate a stub class, in this example it is `SmallJavaNewProjectWizardInitialContents`, which you can use to generate some initial contents in the project created by the wizard. In our case, we will generate a simple SmallJava class.

The generated wizard will create a plug-in project, and it will add the DSL runtime project as a dependency. This way, the SmallJava projects created by the wizard will be able to access the SmallJava library.

Summary

In this chapter we described scoping, which is the main mechanism behind visibility and cross-reference resolution. In particular, scoping and typing are often strictly connected and interdependent especially for object-oriented languages. We described both local and global scoping, and we showed how to customize these mechanisms using the SmallJava DSL as a case study.

In the next chapter we will show how you can create an Eclipse update site for your DSL implementation; this way, other users can easily install it in Eclipse. Moreover, we will describe the features provided by Xtext for building and testing DSLs headlessly, for example. in a continuous integration system.

11
Continuous Integration

In this chapter, we describe how you can release your DSL implementation by creating an Eclipse update site, also known as p2 repository. In this way, others can install it in Eclipse. The Xtext project wizard can create a project for such an update site. Moreover, Xtext can create the infrastructure for building with Maven/Tycho. This will allow you to build and test your DSL implementation on a continuous integration server. We will also show how to get a web application with a web editor for your DSL; the Xtext project wizard will generate it and reuse most of the components you develop for your DSL. Finally, your DSL implementation can be easily ported to IntelliJ; to this aim, Xtext generates the infrastructure for building with Gradle, a build system alternative to Maven.

This chapter will cover the following topics:

- How to create an update site for your DSL
- Some general concepts about release engineering and continuous integration
- How to build and test your DSL with Maven/Tycho in an headless way (that is, from the command line, outside Eclipse)
- How to get a web editor for your DSL
- How to create and build with Gradle a version of your DSL to be installed in IntelliJ IDEA

Eclipse features and p2 repositories

An Eclipse **feature** groups together several related plug-ins that can be installed in an Eclipse instance. Eclipse handles installation and updates of software using the **provisioning platform** called **p2**. This provisioning technology will take care of resolving dependencies between software components; p2 will compute the complete set of required software automatically. We will go into more details about installation requirements at the end of the chapter.

Features and the plug-ins included in the features are served by a **p2 repository**. Such a repository can be put on a web server to make it available to other users. Old style Eclipse update sites have been since long deprecated and replaced by p2 repositories. Most of the sites you have been using to install new features into your Eclipse are p2 repositories; thus, you should build a p2 repository for your DSL, if you want users to easily install it in Eclipse.

> Pay attention to the fact that "p2 repositories" are almost always referred to as "update sites", since the term "**update site**" is surely more comprehensible and immediate to the user than "p2 repository". In the following, when we use "update site," we always refer to "p2 repository" and never to an old Eclipse update site.

An Eclipse feature is defined in an Eclipse **feature project**. The Xtext project wizard allows you to create a feature project and an update site project. This can be achieved in the second page of the Xtext project wizard.

By now, you should be familiar with the procedure to create an Xtext project. So, create an Xtext project and fill in the fields of the first page of the wizard as you prefer (we will not develop anything in this project). Instead of **Finish**, press **Next**. In the next page, you can specify several options for your project, and we will see some of them in this chapter. For the moment, you need to select **Create Feature** and **Create Update Site** and press **Finish**.

Besides the projects you have already seen so far, you will find two new projects, the .feature project and the .repository project for the feature of your DSL and the update site (p2 repository) of your DSL, respectively.

The .feature project contains the definition of your feature in the file feature.xml, which can be edited with the Eclipse feature editor or as an XML file. The feature. xml already includes the runtime plug-in, the .ide plug-in, and the .ui plug-in of your DSL. The .repository project contains the file category.xml, which can be edited with the Eclipse category editor or as an XML file.

An Eclipse repository can potentially contain hundreds of different features to install. **Categories** are used to structure features in a way that is meaningful to a user. The names of such categories and the features that are part of the categories are specified in the category.xml file. You have already seen categories each time you installed something in Eclipse using update sites, for example, when you installed Xtext. The category.xml already contains a category, named after your DSL name, including your DSL feature, and a category with the same name and the suffix "(Sources)" including the feature that contains the sources of your DSL. You can tweak this file as you see fit.

Note that the main.source category refers to a feature whose name is not shown, and its icon is gray. If you open category.xml with a text editor, you can see that it refers to the source feature of your DSL that does not exist. This will be created when the update site is created, as we will do in the next paragraph, so you can ignore that.

Now, you should run the MWE2 workflow and then you can generate an update site for your DSL using the Eclipse tooling:

1. Navigate to **File | Export....**
2. In the **Export** dialog, navigate to **Plug-in Development | Deployable features**.
3. In the next dialog, you need to select the feature that has been created by the Xtext project wizard. In this example, if you accepted the defaults in the Xtext project wizard dialog, it is org.xtext.example.mydsl.feature.
4. Specify a destination directory for your update site.

5. Navigate to the tab **Options**, select the options as shown in the following screenshot and select the `category.xml` of the update site project of your DSL:

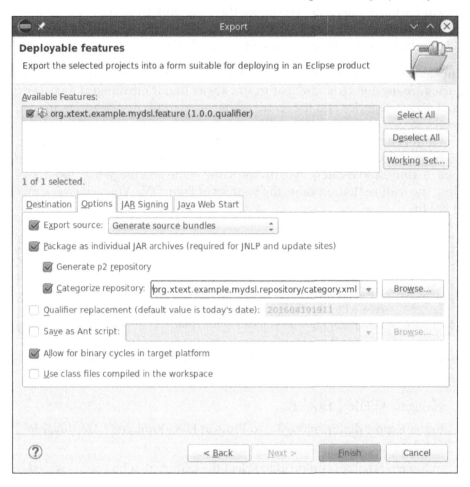

Now, press **Finish** and wait for the procedure of update site creation to terminate.

The update site is created in the output directory you specified. You can put the contents of such directory on a web server so that other users can install your DSL. You can also test this update site locally in your Eclipse: navigate to **Help | Install New Software...** and in the **Install** dialog, in the text field **Work with**, paste the full local path of your update site. Press *ENTER*, and you should see the categories **MyDsl** and **MyDsl (Sources)** categories with your DSL feature and the source feature.

If a user also installs the source feature, he/she will be able to inspect the sources of your implementation from Eclipse.

In the next sections, we will show how to make the procedure of building your DSL, testing it and creating its update site automatic so that it can be part of a continuous integration system.

Release engineering

In software engineering, **release engineering**, abbreviated as **releng**, concerns the compilation, assembly, and delivery of source code into finished products or other software components. In this section, we briefly introduce some scenarios which require release engineering mechanisms and the main concepts behind them. These will be connected to the creation of an installable version of your software, that is, an update site, and also to the capability to build and test your projects outside Eclipse, in an automatic way.

Headless builds

An important aspect when developing a DSL, and in general any project, is that you should be able to build all your projects **headlessly**, that is, from the command line outside Eclipse, in an automatic way. This will give you more confidence that your plug-ins can be installed in other Eclipse installations without problems. Installation problems easily go unnoticed, although it was possible to build the software locally. If dependencies of your components are not present in the user's environment, and you did not describe these dependencies, it will not be possible for others to install your software. While developing, these problems are easily detected. It simply will not build, but when installing, there are more considerations such as, will it install on all intended platforms, which Eclipse versions will it work with, and so on.

For all of the stated reasons, being able to build your software in isolation is a requirement in software production. This way, the headless building process will not rely on your Eclipse installation, but on a separate set of dependencies which are specified in a separate configuration.

Target platforms

A **target platform** is a set of features and plug-ins that your software depends on, for compiling, testing, and running.

Using a defined target platform, you can easily separate the tools that you need to develop your software from the actual dependencies that are required to compile and execute your software. Moreover, the tools are usually not needed during the automatic building process, thus, the target platform contains only what is actually needed to build and test your software. This way, the compilation of your plug-ins will be decoupled from the Eclipse development environment. This also holds when you test your plug-ins both with JUnit tests and when you run another Eclipse instance.

The launch configuration will run the new Eclipse instance with the plug-ins specified in the target platform, and not the ones of your Eclipse development environment.

> If no specific target platform is specified, the target platform defaults to the current Eclipse installation, that is why, even if you never explicitly define target platforms, everything works anyway.

Defining a target platform allows you to compile and test your software against dependencies without installing them in your Eclipse development environment. Defining different target platforms also allows you to test your software against different Eclipse versions.

If you develop your software in a team, all developers should use the same target platform definition. They can develop using different Eclipse installations with possibly different installed tools, but the compilation and the testing will use the same defined target platform, ensuring consistency and reproducibility.

In Eclipse, a target platform can be defined using a **target definition** file. Since such target definition files are XML files, a target definition can be easily shared in a SCM repository (such as Git) used by all the developers of the team. Later in this chapter, we will see how to use a target definition file during the development and how to customize it.

Continuous integration

If your software consists of many loosely coupled components, you probably have tests that test them in isolation; however, you should also have tests for the integration of all of them, to make sure that they are able to run altogether without problems in the final execution environment. In this book, we implemented both plain JUnit tests and JUnit Plug-in tests (see *Chapter 7, Testing*). Plain JUnit tests are expected to run really fast. On the contrary, plug-in tests require much more time since they need a running Eclipse instance and interact with the UI.

Thus, running all tests after every modification might be a burden for the programmer, decreasing the production cycle. Typically, you run tests that concern a specific task/modification/new feature that you are working on. However, single component modifications should also be tested when integrated in the whole application. With this respect, **Continuous Integration**, often abbreviated as **CI**, (see the article *Fowler*, 2006) is the practice in which isolated changes are immediately tested in the complete code base. In this way, if a bug is introduced into the application by a single component, it can be easily and quickly identified and corrected. For this reason, it is crucial to have a **build automation** mechanism, which relies on a headless building process. Usually, the actual build process is delegated to a specific software run on a dedicated server. A complete integration build can take several minutes and the developer can continue working while the server executes the build and check the result periodically.

Xtext provides a nice wizard to set up the configuration files to allow you to easily build and test your DSL headlessly and create a release of your DSL. This way, most of the setup for build automation and continuous integration is already done for you by this wizard. The resulting building infrastructure created by this wizard relies on Maven/Tycho, which we will introduce in the next section.

Introduction to Maven/Tycho

Maven is the de-facto building tool for Java projects. The configuration of a Maven build is specified in an XML file, `pom.xml`, that must be placed in the root directory of every project that must be built and tested. Maven can be extended with several plug-ins.

Tycho is a set of Maven plug-ins that allows you to build Eclipse plug-ins projects and to run tests based on Eclipse plugins. Tycho aims at bridging the Maven build system with **PDE (Plug-in Development Environment)** by taking the dependencies specified in the `MANIFEST.MF` files into consideration and by downloading dependencies from Eclipse p2 repositories. This way, it can compile Java files in Eclipse plug-in projects, create jars, create features, and update sites.

A Maven build can be run on the command line, if you install Maven on your system. You can download Maven binaries from `https://maven.apache.org/`. The Maven executable is called **mvn**. Alternatively, a Maven build can be easily run from within Eclipse if you install **M2Eclipse**, abbreviated as `m2e`, a set of Eclipse plug-ins that integrate Maven into Eclipse (`https://www.eclipse.org/m2e/`). We will use m2e in this chapter, which also has the benefit to embed the Maven binaries so that you do not need to install Maven on your computer. The feature you need to install in your Eclipse is "**m2e - Maven Integration for Eclipse**," which is available from the standard Eclipse update site.

Maven automatically downloads all the dependencies from the Internet from the **Maven Central** repository, which can be seen as the counterpart of the Eclipse update sites. Tycho instructs Maven to also download dependencies from Eclipse update sites. All these dependencies will be cached on your hard disk in the `.m2` directory in your home directory. The downloading of all the dependencies requires an Internet connection and it will take some time initially. Next builds, however, will reuse the cached downloaded dependencies, unless you change the dependencies or new versions of dependencies are found on the remote repositories.

Using the Xtext project wizard

Setting up pom files is not easy, especially if you are not familiar with Maven, Tycho, their plugins and their building lifecycle. An introduction to Maven is out of the scope of this book. On the Maven website, you find some "Getting Started" tutorials; the Tycho documentation can be found here `https://eclipse.org/tycho/documentation.php`.

Fortunately, the Xtext project wizard can create all the pom files in all the projects for you. These generated pom files are surely enough to get you started building your DSL with Maven/Tycho, and for most DSLs, they do not need to be customized at all.

In this section, we will create a new example DSL project to demonstrate the building and releasing mechanisms:

1. Navigate to **File | New | Project...**; in the dialog, navigate to the **Xtext** category and select **Xtext Project**.

2. In the next dialog, you should specify the following names:
   - **Project name:** `org.example.hellomaven`
   - **Name:** `org.example.hellomaven.HelloMaven`
   - **Extensions:** `hellomaven`

3. Press **Next**.

4. In the next page, select **Create Feature** and **Create Update Site** and choose **Maven** as the **Preferred Build System** (refer to the following screenshot).

5. Press **Finish**.

The number of projects created by the wizard and their directory layout is different from all the DSL projects we created in the previous chapters (refer to the following screenshot):

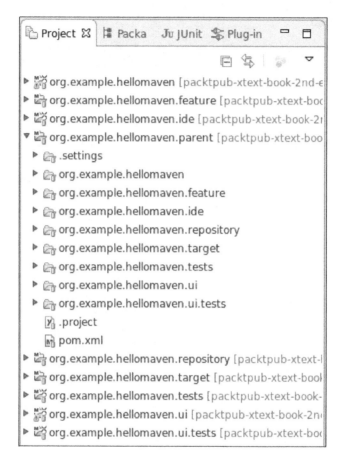

Let's now examine the new projects (we have already seen the `.feature` and `.repository` projects on the first section of this chapter):

- `org.example.hellomaven.target`: This contains the target platform definition with all the dependencies to build and test this DSL

- `org.example.hellomaven.parent`: This is the parent project for all the projects of this DSL. In fact, although Eclipse shows you all these project in a flat view, all the projects of this DSL are directories inside the `org.example.hellomaven.parent` directory.

The **parent** project is a concept that comes from the Maven world. It is used both for specifying in its pom all the common Maven configurations, which are inherited by all the contained projects, thus avoiding repetitions and enforcing consistency, and for building all the projects contained in the parent project. For this reason, the parent project is often referred to also as the **aggregator** or the **releng** project. In the parent project's pom, you can then find all the common properties, like versions of required software, common Maven and Tycho plug-ins configurations, and the list of all the projects to build. In this context, the projects are called **modules**.

We will use this example DSL only for building with Maven/Tycho, thus, we are not interested in the DSL itself; we can simply leave the default grammar as it is. However, make sure to run the MWE2 workflow at least once. We add a Plug-in JUnit test, `HelloMavenContentAssistTest`, in the `org.example.hellomaven.ui.tests` project just to have a UI test to run during the headless build. Remember that a parser test is already generated by the MWE2 workflow in the `org.example.hellomaven.tests` project.

The default for Eclipse Java projects is to generate all the `.class` files into the directory `bin`. The default for Maven is to generate the `.class` files in the directory `target/classes`. To avoid having class files into different directories, all the projects generated by the wizard are configured to generate class files into `target/classes` also when compiling from Eclipse. If you maintain your projects in a SCM repository (for example, Git, Svn, and CVS), make sure to configure the SCM repository to ignore this `target` directory.

Running the Maven build

We are now ready to run the Maven build for this project. We will do that from Eclipse. This assumes that you have already installed m2e into Eclipse, as shown at the beginning of the chapter. Right-click on the `org.example.hellomaven.parent` and select **Run As | Maven build...** and in the appearing dialog specify "clean verify" as the goals. Refer to the following screenshot:

The goal `clean` will instruct Maven to perform a clean build, thus, all the existing generated artifacts will be removed before building, for example, all Java class files will be removed before compiling. The goal `verify` will instruct Maven to compile everything, generate artifacts, for example jar files and update sites, and run all the tests.

You can now press the button **Run**, and you will see the Maven build in the **Console** view.

This requires an Internet connection, and it will take several minutes the first time, since all the requirements will be downloaded from the Internet.

Once the dependencies are resolved, each project will be compiled, one after the other. If a project contains tests, then Maven will also run the JUnit tests. When the runtime project of the DSL is built, the pom is configured to also run the MWE2 workflow during the build. Projects that contain Xtend files have a pom that instructs Maven to run the Xtend compiler during the build before running the Java compiler itself.

When the build finishes, you should see in the console the message "BUILD SUCCESSFUL". This means that during the build, there has been no compilation error and that all tests passed.

Since the pom files are configured to run the MWE2 workflow and the Xtend compiler, there is no need to store the generated sources, that is, the folders src-gen and xtend-gen, into your SCM repository.

For each plug-in project, the target folder contains one jar with the binaries and one with the sources. The same holds for feature projects. The target folder of projects with tests will contain a subdirectory, surefire-reports, with the JUnit reports, both in text format and in XML format; the latter is suitable to be imported in the JUnit view in Eclipse. Finally, the target folder of the .repository project will contain a zipped version of the update site and the subdirectory repository will contain the update site itself.

You can put the zipped repository on the web as well to offer an offline installable version of your software. The Eclipse **Install New Software...** dialog allows you to also specify a local ZIP file as the repository.

If you installed the Maven binaries in your system, you can run the same build from the command line: from the directory of the parent project just run:

```
mvn clean verify
```

Customizing the feature

The projects created by the Xtext wizard contain sensible defaults to build the update site.

The description of the feature for your DSL implementation can be found in the `feature.xml` file in the `org.example.hellomaven.feature` project. Here, you can change the name of the feature, the vendor, copyright information, and other things. Eclipse has a form-based editor for features, and we refer to the Eclipse documentation for the structure of this file.

You can create additional features for your DSL. For example, you may want to create Eclipse documentation for your DSL Eclipse editor (creation of Eclipse documentation is out of the scope of the book). If you manually create new features that you want to serve with the update site, you need to manually add such features in the `category.xml` file. You will also need to manually add pom files in the new projects. Similarly, you will have to add the references the new projects in the `modules` section in the parent pom.

Using and customizing the target platform

A defined target platform should be used during the development, in order to have a better control on the requirements of the software we are developing. As we said at the beginning of this chapter, this will also allow you to keep the plug-ins installed in your Eclipse separate from the ones of the target platform.

 For plug-ins that generate code, such as Xtext and Xtend, it is really important to install in the IDE the same version as the one in the target platform.

For all the preceding reasons, it is advisable that you use the same target definition file, which is used during the Maven/Tycho build, also in your Eclipse workbench. To activate a target platform in your Eclipse navigate to **Window | Preferences**. In the dialog, navigate to **Plug-in Development | Target Platform**. You should see that the current active target platform is the **running platform**, meaning that by default the target platform corresponds to all the installed plug-ins of your Eclipse installation. You should also see all the available target definition files contained in all the projects of the workspace (refer to the following screenshot):

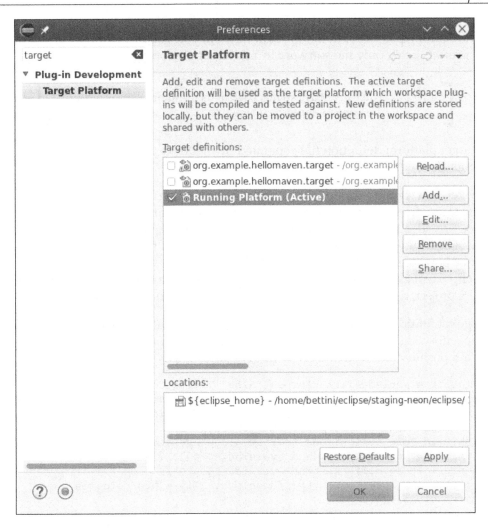

Select the checkbox of the one corresponding to the project we created and press **Apply** and **OK**.

This will start resolving and downloading all the features and plug-ins specified in the target definition file. This requires an Internet connection, and it might take several minutes depending on your network connection, since all the required features and plug-ins will be downloaded from remote p2 repositories.

 Currently, there is no way of reusing the dependencies that Maven downloads during the build also for target platform resolution in Eclipse and viceversa.

When this process finishes, your target platform will be the one that you have set, not the running platform anymore. From then on, you will be compiling and testing your projects using only the software in this target platform.

 You can always switch back to the running platform using the same preferences dialog.

The target platform definition file generated by the Xtext project wizard already contains all you need to implement a DSL in Xtext.

However, you should learn to modify the target definition file in case you need to switch to another version of Xtext or in case you need additional dependencies. Eclipse provides an editor for `.target` files, but this editor has a very bad reputation concerning its usability and its limitations. For this reason, here, we will briefly describe how to modify a target definition file, which is an XML file, manually using the Eclipse text editor. To open a `.target` file, for example the one in the `hellomaven.target` project, right-click on the file and navigate to **Open With | Text Editor**.

A target definition file is a set of `location` tags. Each location tag specifies an Eclipse p2 repository and a list of plug-ins and features identifiers to be downloaded from such a repository and installed in the target platform. For example:

```
<location includeAllPlatforms="false" includeConfigurePhase="false"
includeMode="planner" includeSource="true" type="InstallableUnit">
<unit id="org.eclipse.jdt.feature.group" version="0.0.0"/>
<unit id="org.eclipse.platform.feature.group" version="0.0.0"/>
<unit id="org.eclipse.pde.feature.group" version="0.0.0"/>
<unit id="org.eclipse.xpand" version="0.0.0"/>
<unit id="org.eclipse.xtend" version="0.0.0"/>
<repository location="http://download.eclipse.org/releases/
mars/201506241002/"/>
</location>
```

A feature can be distinguished from a plug-in from the additional `.feature.group` suffix. The version `0.0.0` means that we want the latest version available from that repository. It is also possible to specify the full version. However, if you want to be sure to always use a specific version, we suggest you use a different approach; instead of specifying the version manually, you should use an Eclipse repository, which provides only that specific version and keep the version number `0.0.0`. For example, Xtext provides an update site with all the available versions, `http://download.eclipse.org/modeling/tmf/xtext/updates/releases`, and an update site for each single version; for example, for version 2.10.0, it is `http://download.eclipse.org/modeling/tmf/xtext/updates/releases/2.10.0`. This will also make the target platform resolution faster, since the update sites to be consulted will contain fewer features.

If a new version of Xtext is released and you want to switch to that new version, you will have to install the new version in your Eclipse and modify the target platform accordingly. After a target definition file has been modified, you need to reload it with the preference dialog we described before.

If you want to install other dependencies in the target platform, you have to know the URL of their Eclipse repository and the identifiers of the features and plug-ins. This might be tricky, especially the first time. You may want to use the **Repository Explorer** view (**Show View | Oomph | Repository Explorer**), switching to **Expert Mode** (refer to the following screenshot). This way, you can easily retrieve the correct identifiers for features and plugins:

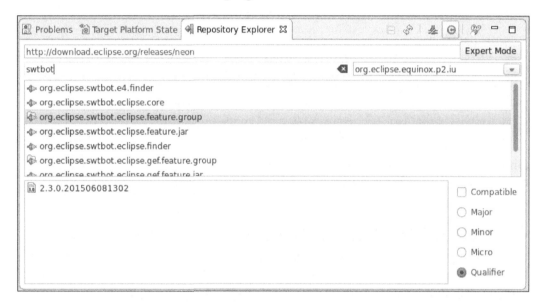

Another way to define a target platform is using the **Target Platform Definition DSL and Generator**, available from `https://github.com/mbarbero/fr.obeo.releng.targetplatform`. This provides a DSL, which is easier to use than directly editing a `.target` file. The corresponding `.target` file will then be automatically generated. Such a DSL is implemented in Xtext and it provides a rich editor with all the Eclipse tooling.

Customizing the pom files

All the pom files generated by the Xtext project wizard already contain all the configured Maven/Tycho plugins for building and testing your Xtext DSL.

You can of course modify the pom files to enable and configure other Maven/Tycho plug-ins. This is out of the scope of the book. You will have to modify at least the parent project's pom if you switch to another version of Xtext. In fact, during the Maven build, some Xtext Maven plug-ins are used to compile the Xtend files of your project. Thus, you need to make sure you specify the same version of such Xtext plug-ins as the Xtext Eclipse plugins installed in Eclipse and used in the target platform.

This is configured in the `properties` section of the parent's `pom.xml`:

```
<properties>
  <tycho-version>0.23.1</tycho-version>
  <xtextVersion>2.10.0</xtextVersion>
  <project.build.sourceEncoding>UTF-8</project.build.sourceEncoding>
  <maven.compiler.source>1.8</maven.compiler.source>
  <maven.compiler.target>1.8</maven.compiler.target>
</properties>
```

Similarly, if you want to switch to a new version of Tycho, you need to update the corresponding property accordingly.

Continuous Integration systems

Using Maven/Tycho, the building and testing of your DSL implementation can be automated, even on a continuous integration server. One of the most common open source continuous integration servers is **Jenkins** (http://jenkins-ci.org/). This subject is outside the scope of the book; we refer the interested reader to the Jenkins documentation for its installation and use. Once you get familiar with Jenkins, setting up a build job for your Xtext DSL project is really straightforward by relying on the Maven configuration files generated by the Xtext project wizard.

You can use build jobs in Jenkins for your DSL to continuously test your DSL projects when new modifications are committed to the SCM repository as we do for the examples of this book, as briefly described in the next section. You can have nightly jobs that create the p2 repository and make it available on the web; the nightly builds are common to many Eclipse projects, such as Xtext itself.

If your project is open source and hosted on **Github**, you may want to take a look at **Travis** (`http://travis-ci.org`) that allows you to build and test projects hosted on Github. This service is free for open source projects.

Some tutorials related to Maven/Tycho, the building on continuous integration servers such as Jenkins and Travis and the deployment of update sites on free cloud systems, like **Sourceforge** and **Bintray**, can be found on my blog: `http://www.lorenzobettini.it/`.

Maintaining the examples of this book

All the examples DSLs shown in this book are built using Maven/Tycho. Since I have several DSLs and I prefer to have a single headless build procedure to build and test them all, the structure and configuration of Maven projects of the examples of this book is slightly modified. In particular, there is a single shared project for the target platform, so that I do not have to duplicate it for all the DSLs. Similarly, there is a single parent project. The only exceptions are the DSLs created in this chapter, whose structure is not modified.

Furthermore, all the examples in this book are built on a personal Jenkins continuous integration server and on Travis. The examples are maintained in a Git repository on Github, and as soon as a commit is pushed to the remote Git repository, the build on Travis automatically starts. If something goes wrong during the build, Travis will send a notification email.

This allows me to continuously test all the code of the examples, especially when new versions of Xtext come out.

Your DSL editor on the Web

In this section, we briefly show the mechanisms of Xtext that allow you to port the editor for your DSL to the web. The web editor for your DSL will be implemented in **JavaScript**. This editor will then communicate to a server side component, which implements all Xtext related aspects. The server consists of a Java **servlet** and communications take place through HTTP requests. This way, the runtime implementation of your DSL will be reused by the server-side component and UI aspects will be rendered on the web accordingly. The set of UI features available on the web editor depends on the JavaScript text editor library being used. The default one is **Ace**, but **Orion** and **CodeMirror** can also be enabled. For further details and more advanced features, we refer to the *Xtext documentation*, section *Web Editor Support*.

Let's create a new Xtext project:

1. **Project name:** `org.example.hell oweb`
2. **Name:** `org.example.helloweb.HelloWeb`
3. **Extensions:** `helloweb`
4. Press **Next**.
5. In the next page, select **Web Integration** and choose **Maven** as the **Preferred Build System**.
6. Press **Finish**.

Note that when we choose the web integration, we need to also specify a build system; in this example we chose Maven.

Also in this case, the DSL itself is not important, neither is building an update site. You need to run the MWE2 workflow as usual.

This time, you will find a new project for this DSL, the `.web` project. This project is a Java project but not an Eclipse plug-in project. During the Maven build, a **WAR** file will be generated for the web project, which contains the web editor that can be deployed on an application server, for example **Tomcat**.

In the `.web` project you will also find an Xtend class `ServerLauncher`, with a main method that starts a **Jetty** server on the port 8080. This way, you can try the web editor without deploying the war file. You can run this class as a Java application and once you get the confirmation on the **Console** view that the server has started, you can open a browser and specify the URL `http://localhost:8080/`. The web editor for your DSL will appear. You can start typing and see syntax highlighting in action, use the content assist, see the error markers, and so on.

 Jetty is a web server and Java **servlet** container.

In the following screenshot, you can see the web editor of SmallJava, which you find in the source code of the examples, in action:

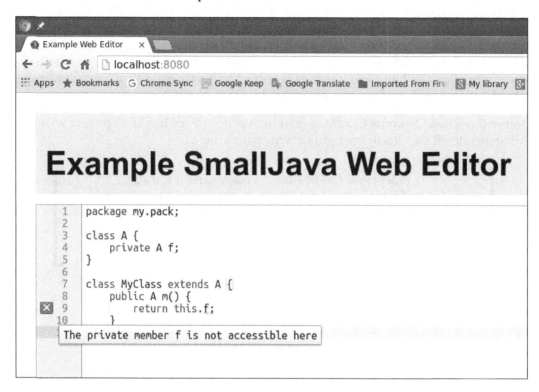

Note that the web editor generated by the Xtext wizard is just a starting point. Though all the editing and validation mechanisms work out of the box, the contents of the web editor are not saved anywhere and no generation takes place. It is up to you to implement such services in the web application.

IntelliJ and Gradle

In version 2.9, Xtext introduced the support for **IntelliJ IDEA**, another famous IDE, https://www.jetbrains.com/idea. Thus, an Xtext DSL can be developed in Eclipse but it can also target IntelliJ and an installable version of the DSL for IntelliJ can be provided to its users. In this section, we will briefly describe the procedure for achieving IntelliJ integration.

In order to compile the projects that implement IntelliJ integration of an Xtext DSL, you need to use **Gradle**, http://gradle.org. Gradle is another build system, which has been gaining lot of attention and interest lately. In particular, it is the official build system for **Android** applications. Differently from Maven, Gradle configuration files are written in **Groovy**, http://www.groovy-lang.org, not in XML, thus, they are less verbose and easier to write and read. Moreover, Gradle is much more flexible than Maven, which is known to have a rigid structure. Gradle is also able to reuse all the Java libraries available from Maven Central.

You will not need to know Gradle to read this section, since the Xtext project wizard will generate all the Gradle configuration files for you.

> In order to use Gradle from Eclipse, you need to install **Buildship**, if this is not already installed (Buildship is already installed in many Eclipse variants). Buildship is the Eclipse project that integrates Gradle into Eclipse. This can be installed from the main Eclipse update site; the feature to install is **Buildship: Eclipse Plug-ins for Gradle**.

We will now create a new Xtext project with IntelliJ integration:

1. Use the Xtext project wizard as usual with these configurations:

   ○ **Project name:** org.example.helloidea

   ○ **Name:** org.example.helloidea.HelloIdea

   ○ **Extensions:** helloidea

2. Press **Next**.

3. In the next page, select **IntelliJ IDEA Plugin** and choose **Gradle** as the **Preferred Build System**.

4. Press **Finish**.

> Currently, there is no Gradle plugin that acts as a bridge between Gradle projects and Eclipse plugin projects, such as Tycho for Maven. For this reason, building Eclipse plugins with Gradle requires much more effort and the Xtext project wizard will warn you that the Eclipse-related projects will still contain a Maven/Tycho build configuration. In case you specify no build system at all, the wizard will warn you that a Gradle build system will still be created to build the IntelliJ projects.

The first time you will have to wait for Eclipse Buildship to download a gradle distribution, if you have no gradle binaries installed on your system. Moreover, just like for the Maven projects we saw in this chapter, you will have to wait for gradle to resolve all the dependencies which will be downloaded from the gradle artifact repository. Gradle will cache all the dependencies and other artifacts in the directory `.gradle` of your home folder.

The structure and layout of the created projects are the same as the ones we saw when we created the HelloMaven DSL. However, there is an additional project, `.idea`, which contains the IntelliJ plugin for your Xtext DSL. This project will not be built with Maven, it will be built with Gradle. The `.target`, the `.ui`, and the `.ui.tests` projects will be built only with Maven. All the other projects can be built with both build tools.

To run a Gradle build from Eclipse, you need to use the **Gradle Tasks** view (navigate to **View | Gradle | Gradle Tasks**), that shows all the available build tasks in the generated Gradle configurations (refer to the following screenshot), for example, `clean`, `build`, and `test`. To run any task, just double-click on that:

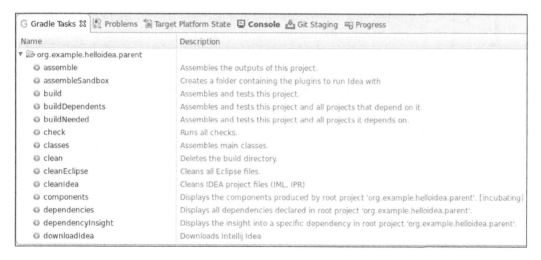

For example, let's try to run the `build` task. The status of the build will be shown in the **Gradle Executions** view, which will be opened automatically. You can also see the more verbose output in the **Console** view. During the build the MWE2 workflow will be run, Xtend files will be compiled, jar files will be created, and tests will be run (but not the UI tests which are Eclipse specific). As usual, the first time all the required dependencies will have to be downloaded from the Internet, so the first build will take a few minutes.

If you want to run the Gradle build from the command line, you can install the gradle binaries into your system. Alternatively, you can use the **Gradle Wrapper**, which is generated in the parent project. This consists of a shell script, gradlew, to be used in Linux and MacOSX, and a Windows batch file, gradlew.bat, to be used in Windows. This wrapper will automatically download a Gradle distribution and cache it in the .gradle folder. Thus, you can simply run the following:

- ./gradlew <task> (on Linux and Mac OS X)
- gradlew <task> (on Windows; this will use the batch file gradlew.bat)

In each Gradle project, the build folder contains the generated artifacts. The sub-folder libs contains the generated jar file. The sub-folder test-results of the .tests project contains the JUnit reports in XML format that can also be imported in the JUnit view in Eclipse; in the same project, the sub-folder reports/tests contains an HTML test report that can be opened in a web browser.

> If you maintain your projects in a SCM repository (for example, Git, Svn, and CVS), make sure to configure the SCM repository to ignore both the build directory and the .gradle directory that are generated in the projects.

If you run the task ideaRepository, you will find in the .idea project, folder build/ideaRepository, a repository that you can put on-line so that IntelliJ users can install your DSL plugins. This is the homologous of an Eclipse update site. Using such a repository you can try your DSL in IntelliJ.

Alternatively, there is an easier way to try your DSL in IntelliJ; you can run the task runIdea, which will download the IntelliJ SDK, install your DSL plugins and run IDEA directly from Eclipse. Once IntelliJ IDEA has started you can configure it, create a project and try your DSL.

It is out of the scope of this book to describe IntelliJ IDEA, so if you want to try your DSL inside IntelliJ you need to have a look at IntelliJ IDEA documentation, concerning creating a new project.

Pitfalls with Maven/Tycho

There are few things that you need to be aware of when using Maven/Tycho for building and testing your DSL. As we said in this chapter, Tycho is a valuable plug-in that reuses most information specified in the Eclipse plugin projects so that they can be built with Maven. However, a few pieces of information must be duplicated in the pom files. Moreover, tests run from Eclipse do not always behave exactly the same way when run from the Maven build.

Versioning

Eclipse plug-ins and features have version numbers of the shape `major.minor.micro.qualifier`. By default, your DSL projects will then have version `1.0.0.qualifier` (in the `MANIFEST.MF` for plug-in projects and in the `feature.xml` for feature projects). The qualifier segment of the version will be automatically replaced, in the produced jar files, with a timestamp when the update site is generated. For example, in the update site, you will find jars of the `org.example.hellomaven.feature_1.0.0.201605021231.jar org.example.hellomaven_1.0.0.201605021231.jar` shape depending on the date and time the jars are produced. Maven projects' versions have a similar shape, but the qualifier is specified with the suffix `-SNAPSHOT`, for example `1.0.0-SNAPSHOT`. The versions in the pom files and the versions in the Eclipse projects must be kept consistent; otherwise, the Maven build will fail. Keeping the versions in sync might be tricky if you have many projects and you want to change the versions.

Tycho provides a specific plug-in to set a new version in all the Eclipse projects and in all the pom files in a consistent way. This can be executed on the command line. For example, if you want to change all the versions of the `hellomaven` example projects to 1.1.0 you need to run this command from the directory of the parent project (this assumes that you installed Maven binaries on your system):

```
mvn org.eclipse.tycho:tycho-versions-plugin:set-version
-DnewVersion=1.1.0-SNAPSHOT -Dtycho.mode=maven
```

This will make sure that all the pom files will be modified with the new version `1.1.0-SNAPSHOT` and, consistently, all the `MANIFEST.MF` and `feature.xml` files will be modified with the new version `1.1.0.qualifier`.

PDE test problems

If you have plug-in JUnit tests that rely on the PDE (Plug-in Development Environment), then some test cases that succeed when run from Eclipse might fail during the Maven/Tycho build.

For example, in *Chapter 10*, *Scoping*, we enriched the SmallJava DSL implementation with a project wizard. The project wizard will create a plugin project, and it will add the DSL runtime project as a dependency. This way, the SmallJava projects created by the wizard will be able to access the SmallJava library. In order to test that the wizard generates the project correctly we write a Plug-in JUnit test that creates a project with the wizard and checks that the project compiles without errors. This checks that the added dependency to the DSL runtime project can be found by PDE, that is, that the SmallJava library can be loaded correctly. This is implemented in the project `org.example.smalljava.ui.tests` in the test `SmallJavaNewProjectWizardTest.xtend`. Without any additional configuration, this test succeeds when run from Eclipse but fails when run by the Maven/Tycho build. Indeed, during the Maven/Tycho build, PDE is not able to find the dependency on the SmallJava runtime project. The details are quite technical and can be found on these two bugs: `https://bugs.eclipse.org/bugs/show_bug.cgi?id=343152` and `https://bugs.eclipse.org/bugs/show_bug.cgi?id=343156`. The workaround is to programmatically set the target platform for the plugin JUnit test when it is run during the build. The implementation of the workaround can be found in the sources of the examples of the book.

Concluding remarks

We conclude this chapter by describing a few additional concepts.

Installation requirements

After you provide an update site for your DSL, other users will be able to install your DSL Eclipse plugins into their Eclipse installation. When Eclipse installs plug-ins it also makes sure that all the required software of the plug-ins being installed is also installed, using the p2 provisioning mechanisms. If the required software is not already installed, all the required features and plugins will be searched for in the update sites that are already configured in Eclipse. For this reason, the checkbox "**Contact all update sites during install to find required software**" in the "**Install New Software**" dialog should always be selected when you install new plug-ins into your Eclipse. Your DSL users should do the same.

For example, if your users have not already installed Xtext plugins in their Eclipse, when they install your Xtext DSL from your update site, all the required Xtext plug-ins will be automatically installed as well from the other update sites. However, this assumes that the update sites configured in your users' Eclipse contain the version of Xtext required by your DSL.

If that is not the case, you should document the installation procedure so that the main Xtext update site is added to the Eclipse installation before installing your DSL.

Alternatively, you can instruct Tycho to create a **self-contained p2 repository**, which will include, besides your own software, also all the requirements. This way, users can install your DSL from such an update site without having to contact other Eclipse repositories. To achieve that, you need to add this plugin configuration in the pom of the .repository project:

```
<build>
  <plugins>
    <plugin>
      <groupId>org.eclipse.tycho</groupId>
      <artifactId>tycho-p2-repository-plugin</artifactId>
      <version>${tycho-version}</version>
      <configuration>
        <includeAllDependencies>true</includeAllDependencies>
      </configuration>
    </plugin>
  </plugins>
</build>
```

Keep in mind that this way the generated update site, and its zipped version, will consist of a few hundreds of Mb.

Make contributions easy

If you want to make contributions to your DSL easy, you should provide an automatic setup procedure for the development environment. This holds both if your DSL is an open-source project and if you work in a team. Using a target definition file is a first step toward development environment reproducibility. However, the contributors are still left with the burden of downloading and installing a specific Eclipse version and install the required plug-ins, using the right version, for example, the right version of Xtext. Then, the sources of your DSL have to be taken from a SCM repository, for example Git, and the projects have to be imported in the development workspace. The right target platform has to be set in the workspace. It is best practice not to put generated sources in the SCM repository; this implies that once the projects are imported in the workspace, some additional commands have to be performed manually be the developer, for example, running the MWE2 workflow. All these manual tasks require lot of time.

The Eclipse project **Oomph**, `https://projects.eclipse.org/projects/tools.oomph`, aims at making all the preceding tasks completely automatic. You have to create a setup file, where you specify all the preceding tasks (how to create such a setup file is documented here: `https://wiki.eclipse.org/Eclipse_Oomph_Authoring`). The contributors will only need to download the Oomph **Eclipse Installer**, choose a starting Eclipse distribution, a setup file from the Oomph catalog, a few local paths for the Eclipse installation, the projects and the workspace to be created and then Oomph will do all the rest. It will download the Eclipse distribution, install all the plugins, download the sources from the SCM repository, install the target platform, import all the projects into the workspace, and run all the additional tasks for generating additional sources. This procedure will still take time, especially for downloading all the software from the Internet and for running the MWE2 workflow. However, it will be completely automatic. At the end of the procedure, the developer is ready to contribute to the project.

The examples of this book consist of many DSLs. The instructions to use Oomph and the corresponding setup file for the examples can be found on the Git repository of the examples of the book. Then, you can use the Oomph installer to have an Eclipse installed on your machine, with all the required plugins and all the imported projects.

Summary

In this chapter we only skimmed the surface of release engineering and continuous integration in the context of Xtext DSL implementations. Xtext helps the programmer also in the context of release engineering and continuous integration. Using the Xtext project wizard, it is easy to build a p2 repository for releasing your DSL implementation. It is also easy to set up a headless build process based on Maven/Tycho or Gradle that can be executed in a continuous integration server.

The configuration files for building with Maven/Tycho and Gradle generated by the Xtext project wizard provide a nice starting point for build automation of your Xtext DSL.

In the next chapter, we will briefly present Xbase, a reusable expression language completely interoperable with the Java type system. When you use Xbase in your DSL, you will not only inherit the grammar of its expressions, but also its Java type system, its code generator, and all its IDE aspects.

12
Xbase

In this chapter we briefly present Xbase, a reusable expression language completely interoperable with the Java type system. Using Xbase in your DSL, you will inherit the mechanisms for performing type checking according to the Java type system and the automatic Java code generation. Xbase also comes with many default implementations of UI aspects. The Xbase expression language is rich and has all the features of a Java-like language, such as object instantiation, method invocation, exceptions, and so on, and more advanced features such as lambda expressions and type inference. The Xtend programming language itself is built on Xbase.

This chapter will cover the following topics:

- An introduction to the main concepts and features of Xbase
- Two DSLs implemented with Xbase
- Some additional features of Xbase applied to an example DSL

Introduction to Xbase

As we have seen throughout the examples of this book, it is straightforward to implement a DSL with Xtext. This is particularly true when you only need to care about structural aspects; in the Entities DSL of *Chapter 2, Creating Your First Xtext Language*, we only defined the structure of entities. Things become more complicated when it comes to implementing expressions in a DSL; as we have seen in *Chapter 8, An Expression Language*, we need to define many rules in the grammar using left factoring to avoid left recursion, even when we only deal with a limited number of expressions. Besides the grammar, the validation part also becomes more complex due to type checking. When we mix structures and expressions, such as in the SmallJava DSL, the complexity increases again; in addition to advanced type checking (*Chapter 9, Type Checking*), we also need to take care of scoping (*Chapter 10, Scoping*), that is implied by relations such as inheritance. An inheritance relation also requires type conformance (subtyping) in the type system, and this introduces additional complexity.

To simplify many of these tasks, when the DSL needs to implement behavioral aspects like expressions and functions or methods, Xtext provides Xbase, an expression language that can be reused in a DSL (see the article *Efftinge et al.* 2012). Xbase expressions have a rich Java-like syntax, which includes standard expressions (arithmetic and boolean), control structures (for example, `if` statements and loops), exceptions and object-oriented expressions (for example, method invocation and field selection). Moreover, it provides advanced features such as lambda expressions. Indeed, Xtend method bodies are based on Xbase, thus, if you use Xbase in your DSL, you will have the expressive power of Xtend expressions. However, Xtend-specific extensions such as templates, anonymous classes, extension variables, and extension parameters are not available in Xbase.

A DSL based on Xbase will inherit the syntax of such Java-like expressions and all its language infrastructure components, such as its type system, scoping, validation, and the compiler that generates Java code. The Xbase type system is completely interoperable with the Java type system: a DSL that uses Xbase will be able to seamlessly access all Java types and use any Java library, just like in Xtend.

Note that Xbase only deals with expressions; your DSL will have to deal with structural features such as functions and class hierarchies.

In this chapter, we only give a brief introduction to Xbase. It also provides an interpreter for Xbase expressions, but we will not describe it in this book. We refer to the Xtext official documentation, section *Integration with Java* and to the seven languages examples, `https://github.com/xtext/seven-languages-xtext`. Furthermore, by navigating to **File** | **New** | **Example...** | **Xtext Examples** | **Xtext Domain-Model Example**, you can import the **Domain-Model Example** that ships with Xtext into your workspace; this is another example of how Xbase can be used in a DSL. In *Chapter 13, Advanced Topics*, we will show a more advanced example using Xbase.

Keep in mind that when using Xbase, your DSL will be tightly coupled with Java, which might not always be what you need. We will get back to this in the final section, *Summary*.

The common Java type model

Before getting into the details on how to embed Xbase in a DSL, we will first describe the main concept behind Xbase. It provides interoperability with the Java type system using a **Common Java Type model**, abbreviated from now as **Java model**. This model represents Java concepts like types (that is, classes, interfaces, enumerations, and annotations), fields, constructors, and methods. Xbase automatically creates such a model from the Java source files and the Java classes available in a Java project.

The basic idea underlying a DSL that uses Xbase is to map the DSL concepts into this common Java model of Xbase. Then, Xbase will be able to automatically resolve references to Java types and Java members using the common Java model, also respecting Java visibility and accessibility constraints.

This means that once the DSL concepts are mapped into the common Java model, Xbase will take care of performing cross-reference resolution. That includes scoping, type checking, and validation, without any further intervention from the language implementor. Moreover, Xbase is also able to generate Java code directly from the mapped model.

Summarizing, the main task that the language implementor has to perform is the mapping of the DSL concepts to the Xbase Java model.

This mapping is performed by implementing an `IJvmModelInferrer` interface, that we will describe in more detail in the forthcoming sections. The Xbase expressions used in your DSL will then have to be associated to a Java model method, which becomes the expression's logical container. Such mapping and association will let Xbase automatically implement a proper scope for the expressions so that scoping and type checking will work out of the box.

The interactions among the Xbase components and the tasks implemented by the DSL implementor are shown in the following diagram:

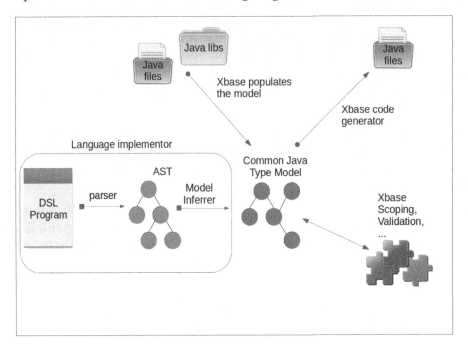

The Expressions DSL with Xbase

For the first example of the use of Xbase, we implement a DSL similar to the Expressions DSL that we presented in *Chapter 8, An Expression Language*, which we call as Xbase Expressions DSL; this DSL is inspired by the **Scripting Language** DSL of the seven languages examples.

Creating the project

Let's create a new project with the following settings:

- **Project name:** `org.example.xbase.expressions`
- **Name:** `org.example.xbase.expressions.Expressions`
- **Extensions:** `xexpressions`

Before running the MWE2 generator for the first time, you should modify the grammar so that it uses the Xbase grammar, not the Terminals grammar:

```
grammar org.example.xbase.expressions.Expressions with
    org.eclipse.xtext.xbase.Xbase
```

Since our grammar now inherits from the Xbase grammar, all the Xbase grammar rules are in effect in our DSL.

> When using Xbase, some files in the projects will contain lots of warnings of the shape:
>
> ```
> Discouraged access: The method ... from the type
> ... is not accessible due to restriction on
> required library org.eclipse.xtext.xbase_....jar
> ```
>
> This is due to the fact that a part of the Xbase API is still provisional, and it could be subject to changes in the future possibly breaking backward compatibility. When a new version of Xbase is released, you might have to run the MWE2 workflow again, and possibly modify your code to be compatible with the new version. In any case, a test suite helps to make sure that your code is still working with a new version of Xbase. To ignore the warnings, refer to *Chapter 6, Customizing Xtext Components*, section *Custom formatting*.

We want to recreate a DSL similar to the Expressions DSL we introduced in *Chapter 8, An Expression Language*. A program in this DSL is like a big code block. Xbase has a specific rule for dealing with code blocks: XBlockExpression.

> The most generic form of Xbase expression, which also corresponds to the base class of all Xbase expressions, is XExpression.

Since Xbase has its own validator that implements lots of useful constraint checks, and since, like all the validators we implemented in this book, it is based on the types of the elements being validated, we should make the main rule for our DSL return an XBlockExpression object. This way, our DSL root element will be conforming to XBlockExpression and it will be automatically validated accordingly by Xbase. In the Expressions DSL of *Chapter 8, An Expression Language*, we also made sure that variable references are validated so that a variable can only refer to variables already defined; this check is not necessary anymore when we use Xbase since it is automatically implemented for the XBlockExpression elements.

We start writing the grammar as follows:

```
grammar org.example.xbase.expressions.Expressions with   org.eclipse.
xtext.xbase.Xbase

generate expressions "http://www.example.org/xbase/expressions/
Expressions"

import "http://www.eclipse.org/xtext/xbase/Xbase"

ExpressionsModel returns XBlockExpression:...
```

Remember that when we use `returns` in a rule, we specify a type, not a rule name. Since this type, `XBlockExpression`, is defined in Xbase EMF metamodel, we need to import this metamodel. We do this by specifying the EMF namespace corresponding to Xbase (recall that each Xtext grammar defines an EMF namespace; it is the one defined after the `generate` section).

Now, we want our `ExpressionsModel` to consist of variable declarations and single expressions. Xbase has a specific rule for that: `XExpressionOrVarDeclaration`; thus, we can simply reuse that rule:

```
ExpressionsModel returns XBlockExpression:
  {ExpressionsModel}
  (expressions+=XExpressionOrVarDeclaration ';'?)*;
```

The feature `expressions` is part of `XblockExpression`. With this simple grammar, we have a working parser that allows to write programs consisting of variable declarations and single expressions. These have the same syntax as Xtend expressions. If you want to experiment with this DSL, you can start Eclipse, create a plug-in project in the workspace, and, in the src folder, create a new .xexpressions file (remember to accept the conversion to an Xtext project). You should also add the bundle `org.eclipse.xtext.xbase.lib` as a dependency in the *Dependencies* section of the `MANIFEST.MF` editor.

> The `org.eclipse.xtext.xbase.lib` bundle contains the Xbase runtime library classes that are used by Xbase during type checking, validation, and code generation. Moreover, it contains several static methods that are automatically available as extension methods.

The IJvmModelInferrer interface

Besides the grammar rules which can be reused in a DSL, the interesting feature of Xbase is the integration with Java. The same integration you have already experienced in Xtend can be reused in any DSL based on Xbase. This means that the entire type system of Xbase, which corresponds to the type system of Java, together with the additional type inference mechanisms that you enjoyed in Xtend, will be a part of your DSL as well.

In order to reuse the Xbase type system in your DSL, it is not enough to use Xbase grammar rules; you also need to give your model elements a *context* so that Xbase can check your model elements according to that context. You basically need to tell Xbase how your model elements are mapped to the Java model elements. The Xbase expressions which are contained in your model elements will then be typed and checked by Xbase as parts of the mapped Java model elements.

You basically have to map your model elements to Java types (classes and interfaces), fields, and methods. This mapping is a model to model mapping, since you map your DSL model elements to the Java model elements. When you map a model element to a Java model method, you can specify that its body is represented by an Xbase expression. Given that, Xbase will be able to type and check that Xbase expression, since it will consider it in the context of a Java method, which in turn is part of a Java class, which can extend another Java class, and so on. If that Xbase expression uses `this`, Xbase will know what it refers to. It is similar for `super`, method parameters, and so on. Unless you extend the Xbase expression language itself, just specifying this mapping to Java elements will be enough; you will not need to provide a custom scoping, since Xbase will be able to compute the scope using the mapped Java elements.

This mapping is specified by implementing an `IJvmModelInferrer` interface, since we use Xbase in our grammar, the MWE2 workflow generates an Xtend stub class, `ExpressionsJvmModelInferrer` in the `jvmmodel` subpackage. The stub class has an empty `dispatch` method named `infer`, which is the method where you specify the mapping to Java elements:

```
def dispatch void infer(ExpressionsModel element,
    IJvmDeclaredTypeAcceptor acceptor,
    boolean isPreIndexingPhase)
```

In this method, you will create Java model elements, associate them to your DSL elements, and pass them to the acceptor; this implements the mapping. The Java elements themselves are created using the injected extension `JvmTypesBuilder`, already part of the stub class. This provides a useful API to create Java model elements, for instance, `toClass`, `toMethod`, `toField`, and so on. All these methods take the source element as the first parameter. Besides creating a Java model element, these methods also record the association with the original source element. Xtext uses this association to provide a default implementation of many UI concepts.

> Note that with `JvmTypesBuilder`, you will not create effective
> Java elements (for example, `java.lang.Class`, `java.
> lang.reflect.Method`, `java.lang.reflect.Field`,
> and so on), but their representation in the Xbase EMF model
> for Java model elements (for example, `JvmGenericType`,
> `JvmOperation`, `JvmField`, and so on).

For our DSL, given an `ExpressionsModel` object, we map it to a Java class with a single main method. Since `ExpressionsModel` is itself an `XBlockExpression` object, we can directly associate the `ExpressionsModel` object itself with the body of the main method. The implementation of our `inferrer` is as follows:

```
class ExpressionsJvmModelInferrer extends AbstractModelInferrer {
    @Inject extension JvmTypesBuilder

    def dispatch void infer(ExpressionsModel element,
            IJvmDeclaredTypeAcceptor acceptor,
            boolean isPreIndexingPhase) {
        val className = element.eResource.URI.trimFileExtension.
lastSegment
        acceptor.accept(element.toClass(className)) [
            members += element.toMethod('main', typeRef(Void.TYPE)) [
                // add a parameter String[] args
                parameters +=
                    element.toParameter("args", typeRef(String).
addArrayTypeDimension)
                // make the method static
                static = true
                // Associate the model with the body of the main method
                body = element
            ]
        ]
    }
}
```

Let's comment on this code. First of all, we name the Java class after the input file, without the file extension. Note that the class, an instance of `JvmGenericType`, is created using the `JvmTypesBuilder` method `toClass`. However, further initialization operations concerning this class are deferred to the lambda passed as the last argument. In fact, the inferrer is used by Xtext first on the indexing phase (see *Chapter 10, Scoping*) and again after the indexing phase has finished. The lambda is evaluated in the second step. In the first step, the index has not been completely built, thus you cannot rely on cross-references having been resolved. In the indexing phase, you just create Java classes or interfaces for your model elements; after the indexing has finished, you can add elements to the created Java types. This mechanism allows for circular references between classes.

In the previous code, we add a method to the Java model class, an instance of `JvmOperation`, using `JvmTypesBuilder.toMethod`, passing the name of the method and its return type. When we specify types for Java model elements, we must always use instances of class `JvmTypeReference`. To create a type reference to an existing Java type, we use the method `typeRef` that takes a Java `Class` object. For the `main` method, the return type must be `void`, thus we use the static instance `java.lang.Void.TYPE`.

Once we created a Java method, we can further initialize it with a lambda that gets the created Java model `JvmOperation` as parameter. In this example, we add a parameter named `args` of type `String[]` to the created Java method using the `JvmTypesBuilder` API; we also specify that the method is static.

Finally, we associate the whole Xbase expression of the program with the body of the method (recall that `ExpressionsModel` is an `XBlockExpression`). As said before, this will allow Xbase to build a proper scope for the expressions and to perform type checking and validation of expressions.

You can now restart Eclipse and try the editor for this DSL again (we assume you have already created the project as detailed before). The result is shown in the following screenshot. Here, you can see that in the `xexpressions` file we can declare variables with the Xbase syntax, which corresponds to the same syntax for variable declaration in Xtend:

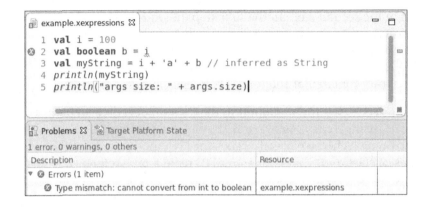

Note that all the type checking is automatically performed by Xbase. In the preceding screenshot, you can see an error due to wrong types in the expressions. Note also that the conversion to string type, when using the operator +, is performed automatically. Indeed, besides the `IJvmModelInferrer` interface, we did not have to specify anything else, neither a custom scoping nor a custom validator.

Moreover, although the `args` variable is not defined anywhere in our program, we can still refer to it since the whole expression block has been associated with the body of a method with the `args` parameter. The association we specified in the inferrer corresponds to the fact that the parameter `args` is available in the program with the specified type. Since in the `inferrer`, we specified that `args` is an array of String, we can call the method `size` on `args` in our program as follows:

```
println("args size: " + args.size)
```

Code generation

When using Xbase, we get code generation for free. This can be observed by saving an error-free .xexpressions file in the IDE. When you do so, a src-gen source folder is automatically created in your project. We have already seen this behavior in *Chapter 5, Code Generation*, when we wrote a code generator for the Entities DSL. However, this time, we did not write any code generator.

This automatic Xbase code generator mechanism is based on the `IJvmModelInferrer` interface that we implemented. The Xbase code generator uses the mapped Java model to generate Java code. See the following screenshot:

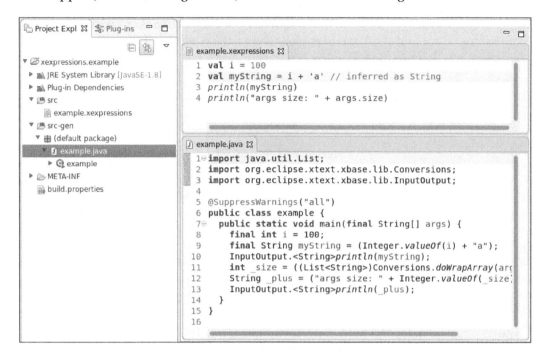

This is an extremely useful feature, since when using Xbase we only need to write the `IJvmModelInferrer` interface correctly. Xbase will take care of all the rest, including type checking and code generation.

> The automatic code generation mechanism is performed by `JvmModelGenerator`, which is automatically bound in the Guice module generated during the MWE2 workflow. Of course, you could still write your own code generator and override the Guice binding; it is recommended to rely on the automatic Xbase code generator though, since writing a code generator manually for a DSL that uses Xbase would require some effort.

Debugging

With Xbase, you can debug your DSL sources instead of the generated Java code—just like when working with Xtend. This is another valuable feature you get for free.

You can try and set a breakpoint in the `.xexpressions` program, and then right-click on the generated Java file and navigate to **Debug As | Java Application** (this menu is available since the generated Java file contains a `main` method). Now, when the execution reaches the line corresponding to the set breakpoint in the `.xexpressions` file, you will see that the debugger perspective is opened with the Expressions editor and the **Variables** view shows the contents of the variables of your program. Refer to the following screenshot:

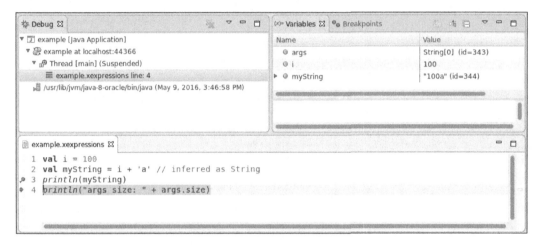

Just like when debugging Xtend code, if you need to debug the generated Java code, you can do so by right-clicking on the **Debug** view and by navigating to **Show Source | Java**.

The Entities DSL with Xbase

We will now implement a modified version of the Entities DSL that we implemented in *Chapter 2, Creating Your First Xtext Language*. This will allow us to implement a more complex DSL where, inside entities, we can also write operations apart from attributes. This is inspired by the Xtext Domain-Model example.

Creating the project

We create a new Xtext project with the following settings:

- **Project name:** `org.example.xbase.entities`
- **Name:** `org.example.xbase.entities.Entities`
- **Extensions:** `xentities`

Defining attributes

We define the rules for attributes using some rules inherited from the Xbase grammar:

```
grammar org.example.xbase.entities.Entities
  with org.eclipse.xtext.xbase.Xbase

generate entities "http://www.example.org/xbase/entities/Entities"

Model:
  entities+=Entity*;

Entity:
'entity' name=ID ('extends' superType=JvmParameterizedTypeReference)?
'{'
  attributes += Attribute*
'}';

Attribute:
  'attr' (type=JvmTypeReference)? name=ID
  ('=' initexpression=XExpression)? ';';
```

The rule for Entity is similar to the corresponding rule of the Entities DSL of *Chapter 2, Creating Your First Xtext Language*. However, instead of referring to another Entity in the feature superType, we refer directly to a Java type; since Xbase implements the Java type system, an entity can extend any other Java type. Moreover, since an Entity will correspond to a Java class (we will implement this mapping in the inferrer), it will still be able to have an entity as a super type, though it will specify it through the corresponding inferred Java class.

We refer to a Java type using the Xbase rule JvmParameterizedTypeReference. As the name of the rule suggests, we can also specify type parameters, for instance, we can write:

```
entity MyList extends java.util.LinkedList<Iterable<String>> {}
```

Similarly, for attributes, we use Java types for specifying the type of attribute. In this case, we use the Xbase rule JvmTypeReference; differently from JvmParameterizedTypeReference, this rule also allows to specify types for lambdas. Thus, for instance, we can define an attribute as follows:

```
attr (String,int)=>Boolean c;
```

We also allow an attribute to specify an initialization expression using a generic Xbase expression, XExpression. Note that both the type and the initialization expression are optional; this design choice will be clear after looking at the model inferrer:

```
class EntitiesJvmModelInferrer extends AbstractModelInferrer {
  @Inject extension JvmTypesBuilder

  def dispatch void infer(Entity entity,
              IJvmDeclaredTypeAcceptor acceptor, boolean
  isPreIndexingPhase) {
     acceptor.accept(entity.toClass("entities." + entity.name)) [
        documentation = entity.documentation
        if (entity.superType != null)
          superTypes += entity.superType.cloneWithProxies
        for (a : entity.attributes) {
          val type = a.type ?: a.initexpression?.inferredType
          members += a.toField(a.name, type) [
            documentation = a.documentation
            if (a.initexpression != null)
              initializer = a.initexpression
          ]
          members += a.toGetter(a.name, type)
          members += a.toSetter(a.name, type)
        }
     ]
  }
}
```

Note that, in this example, we provide an infer method for Entity, not for the root Model. In fact, the default implementation of the superclass AbstractModelInferrer can be summarized as follows:

```
public void infer(EObject e, ...) {
  for (EObject child : e.eContents()) {
    infer(child, acceptor, preIndexingPhase);
  }
}
```

It simply calls the infer method on each element contained in the root of the model. Thus, we only need to provide a dispatch method infer for each type of our model that we want to map to a Java model element. In the previous example, we needed to map the whole program, that is, the root model element, while in this example we map every entity of a program.

As we did in the previous section, we use an injected `JvmTypesBuilder` extension to create the Java model elements and associate them with the elements of our DSL program AST.

First of all, we specify that the superclass of the mapped class will be the entity's `superType` if one is given.

> Note that we clone the type reference of `superType`. This is required since `superType` is an EMF containment reference. The referred element can be contained only in one container; thus, without the clone, the feature `superType` would be set to `null` after the assignment.
>
> The clone is performed using `cloneWithProxies`, which clones an EMF object without resolving cross references.

For each attribute, we create a Java field using `toField`, which returns a `JvmField` instance, and a getter and setter method using `toGetter` and `toSetter`, respectively (these are part of `JvmTypesBuilder`). If an initialization expression is specified for the attribute, the corresponding Java field will be initialized with the Java code corresponding to the `XExpression`.

The interesting thing in the mapping for attributes is that we use Xbase type inference mechanisms; if no type is specified for the attribute, the type of the Java field will be automatically inferred by Xbase using the type of the initialization expression. If neither the type nor the initialization expression is specified, Xbase will automatically infer the type `Object`. If we specify both the type of the attribute and its initialization expression, Xbase will automatically check that the type of the initialization expression is conformant to the declared type. The following screenshot shows a validation error issued by Xbase:

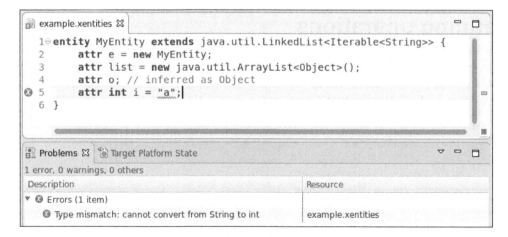

Both for the mapped Java model class and Java model field we set the documentation feature using the documentation attached to the program element. This way, if in the program we write a comment with /* */ before an entity or an attribute, in the generated Java code this will correspond to a JavaDoc comment, as illustrated in the following screenshot:

```
example.xentities ⊠
1  /* my entity */
2⊖ entity MyEntity {
3      /* my attribute */
4      attr String s;
5  }
```

```
MyEntity.java ⊠
1  package entities;
2
3⊖ /**
4   * my entity
5   */
6  @SuppressWarnings("all")
7  public class MyEntity {
8⊖   /**
9     * my attribute
10    */
11   private String s;
12
13⊖  public String getS() {
14     return this.s;
15   }
16
17⊖  public void setS(final String s) {
18     this.s = s;
19   }
20 }
```

Defining operations

Now we add operations to our entities, which will correspond to Java methods. Thus, we add the rule for Operation. To keep the example simple and to concentrate on Xbase, we did not introduce an abstract element for both attributes and operations, and we require that operations are specified after the attributes:

```
Entity:
'entity' name=ID ('extends' superType=JvmParameterizedTypeReference)?
'{'
    attributes += Attribute*
    operations += Operation*
'}';
```

```
Operation:
  'op' (type=JvmTypeReference)? name=ID
  '(' (params+=FullJvmFormalParameter (','
       params+=FullJvmFormalParameter)*)? ')'
  body=XBlockExpression;
```

Here, we use the Xbase rule `FullJvmFormalParameter` to specify parameters; parameters will have the syntactic shape of Java parameters, that is, a `JvmTypeReference` stored in the feature `parameterType` and a name. However, the keyword `final` is not considered by the `FullJvmFormalParameter` rule, in fact, just like in Xtend, Xbase parameters are implicitly `final`. The body of an `operation` is specified using the Xbase rule `XBlockExpression`, which includes the curly brackets.

In our inferrer, we add the mapping to a Java model method with the following code:

```
for (op : entity.operations) {
  members += op.toMethod(op.name, op.type ?: inferredType) [
    documentation = op.documentation
    for (p : op.params) {
      parameters += p.toParameter(p.name, p.parameterType)
    }
    body = op.body
  ]
}
```

This is similar to what we did in the first example of this chapter. We still use `toMethod`; however, this time, we have a corresponding element in our DSL, `Operation`. Thus, we create a Java model parameter for each parameter defined in the program, and we use the `Operation` instance's body as the body of the mapped Java model method. Also, for the operation, the return type can be omitted; in that case, the corresponding Java model method will have the return type that Xbase infers from the operation's `XBlockExpression`.

The association of the method's body with the operation's body implicitly defines the scope of the `XBlockExpression` object. Since an operation is mapped to a non-static Java method, in the operation's expressions you can automatically refer to the attributes and operations of the containing entity and of the entity's `superType`, since they are mapped to Java fields and methods, respectively.

This can be seen in the following screenshot, where the operation accesses the entity's fields and the inherited method `add`; Xbase automatically adds other tooling features, such as information hovering and the ability to jump to the corresponding Java method:

```
example.xentities ☒
1⊖ entity MyList extends java.util.LinkedList<String> {
2      attr String s;
3⊖     op insert(Object o) {
4          add(s)
5          add(o.toString)
6      }   ⊚ ⌂ boolean LinkedList.add(String e)
7 }
            Appends the specified element to the end of this list.

            This method is equivalent to addLast.

            Specified by: add(...) in List, add(...) in Deque. Overrides: add(...) in AbstractList
            Parameters:
                  e element to be appended to this list
            Returns:
                  true (as specified by Collection.add)
                                                              Press 'F2' for focus
```

In fact, the scope for `this` is implied by the association between the operation and the Java model method. The same holds for `super`, as shown in the following example, where the operation `m` overrides the one in the `supertype` and can access the original version with `super`:

```
entity Base {
  op m() { "Base" }
}

entity Extended extends Base {
  op m() { super.m() + "Extended" }
}
```

Indeed, associating an Xbase expression with the body of a Java model method corresponds to making the expression **logically contained** in the Java method. This logical containment defines the scope of the Xbase expression.

 An Xbase expression can have only one logical container.

In the examples we have shown so far, we have always associated an `XExpression` with the body of a Java method or with the initializer of a field. There might be cases where you want to add a method to the Java model that does not necessarily correspond to an element of the DSL.

In these cases, you can specify an Xtend template string as the body of the created method. For instance, we can add to the mapped Java class a `toString` method as follows:

```
members += entity.toMethod("toString", typeRef(String)) [
  body = '''
    return
      "entity «entity.name» {\n" +
        «FOR a : entity.attributes»
          "\t«a.name» = " + «a.name».toString() + "\n" +
        «ENDFOR»
      "}";
  '''
]
```

For instance, given this entity definition:

```
entity C {
  attr List l;
  attr s = "test";
}
```

The generated Java method will be:

```
public String toString() {
    return
      "entity C {\n" +
      "\tl = " + l.toString() + "\n" +
      "\ts = " + s.toString() + "\n" +
      "}";
}
```

As usual, remember to write JUnit tests for your DSL (see *Chapter 7, Testing*); for instance, this test checks the execution of the generated `toString` Java method:

```
@RunWith(XtextRunner)
@InjectWith(EntitiesInjectorProvider)
class EntitiesCompilerTest {
  @Inject extension CompilationTestHelper
  @Inject extension ReflectExtensions

  @Test def void testGeneratedToStringExecution() {
    '''
    entity C {
      attr l = newArrayList(1, 2, 3);
      attr s = "test";
```

```
      }'''.compile[
        val obj = it.compiledClass.newInstance
        '''
        entity C {
          l = [1, 2, 3]
          s = test
        }'''.toString.assertEquals(obj.invoke("toString"))
      ]
    }
  }
```

Imports

We saw in *Chapter 10, Scoping,* that Xtext provides support for namespace-based imports for qualified names. Xbase provides an automatic mechanism for imports of Java types and many additional UI features for the Eclipse editor. To include such feature in a DSL that uses Xbase it is enough to use the rule XImportSection; for instance, in our Xbase Entities DSL we modify the root rule as follows:

```
Model:
    importSection=XImportSection?
    entities+=Entity*;
```

The addition of this rule automatically adds to the DSL the same import mechanisms that you saw in Xtend; in addition to the standard Java imports, including static imports, you can now write import static extension statements for static methods and those static methods will be available as extension methods in the program.

Besides this enhanced import statements, Xbase adds nice UI features in the editor of the DSL that reflect the ones of JDT and Xtend:

- Warnings for unused imported types

- An **Organize Imports** menu, available also with the keyboard shortcut *Ctrl + Shift + O* (*CMD + Shift + O* on Mac)

- Automatic insertion of import statements: When you use the autocompletion for specifying a Java type reference in the program, the corresponding import statement is automatically added

 Remember to merge the files plugin.xml and plugin.xml_gen in the UI project after running the MWE2 workflow; this is required to add the **Organize Imports** menu items in the editor.

Validation

Xbase automatically performs type checking and other validation checks on the Xbase expressions used in your DSL. Other validation checks, concerning the structural parts of the DSL, are left to the language implementor. For example, we still need to implement checks on possible cycles in the inheritance hierarchy. In *Chapter 4*, *Validation*, we implemented a similar validation check. In this example, though, we cannot walk the hierarchy of entities, since an entity, in this DSL, does not extend another entity, it extends any Java type (superType is a JvmParameterizedTypeReference).

Thus, the search for possible cycles must be performed on the inferred Java model, in particular on JvmGenericType objects, which are the ones created in the inferrer with the method toClass. This is performed by the following recursive method:

```
def private boolean hasCycleInHierarchy(JvmGenericType t,
        Set<JvmGenericType> processed) {
    if (processed.contains(t))
        return true
    processed.add(t)
    return t.superTypes.map[type].filter(JvmGenericType).
        exists[hasCycleInHierarchy(processed)]
}
```

We use this method in this validator check method:

```
protected static val ISSUE_CODE_PREFIX =
    "org.example.xbase.entities.";
public static val HIERARCHY_CYCLE =
    ISSUE_CODE_PREFIX + "HierarchyCycle";

@Inject extension IJvmModelAssociations

@Check def checkNoCycleInEntityHierarchy(Entity entity) {
    val inferredJavaType = entity.jvmElements.filter(JvmGenericType).
head
    if (inferredJavaType.hasCycleInHierarchy(newHashSet())) {
        error("cycle in hierarchy of entity '" + entity.name + "'",
            EntitiesPackage.eINSTANCE.entity_SuperType,
            HIERARCHY_CYCLE)
    }
}
```

We call the recursive method passing the inferred `JvmGenericType` for the given entity. The mapping between DSL elements and Java model elements is handled by Xbase. You can access such mapping by injecting an `IJvmModelAssociations`. Note that, in general, you can infer several Java model elements from a single DSL element, that is why the method `IJvmModelAssociations.getJvmElements` returns a set of associated inferred elements.

Additional Xbase features

In this section, we will show a few additional Xbase features, and we will apply them to the Xbase Entities DSL we implemented so far.

Annotations

Xbase provides support for Java-like annotations. This support is not enabled in the standard Xbase grammar. If you want to use Xbase annotations in your DSL, then you must use `org.eclipse.xtext.xbase.annotations.XbaseWithAnnotations` as the super grammar:

```
grammar org.example.xbase.entities.Entities
    with org.eclipse.xtext.xbase.annotations.XbaseWithAnnotations
```

Now, you can use the Xbase grammar rules for annotations. In this example, we will add annotations to entities and attributes:

```
Entity:
annotations+=XAnnotation*
'entity' name=ID ('extends' superType=JvmParameterizedTypeReference)?
'{'
    attributes += Attribute*
    operations += Operation*
'}';


Attribute:
  annotations+=XAnnotation*
  'attr' (type=JvmTypeReference)? name=ID
  ('=' initexpression=XExpression)? ';';
```

We run the MWE2 generator in order to update our DSL infrastructure to deal with annotations. Now, we need to translate the Xbase annotations of our DSL elements into the corresponding annotations in the Java model. We do that in the inferrer, implementing a reusable method for this purpose:

```
def dispatch void infer(Entity entity,
               IJvmDeclaredTypeAcceptor acceptor, boolean
   isPreIndexingPhase) {
     acceptor.accept(entity.toClass("entities." + entity.name)) [
       documentation = entity.documentation
       if (entity.superType != null)
         superTypes += entity.superType.cloneWithProxies
       translateAnnotations(entity.annotations)
       for (a : entity.attributes) {
         val type = a.type ?: a.initexpression?.inferredType
         members += a.toField(a.name, type) [
           translateAnnotations(a.annotations)
           documentation = a.documentation
   . . .


   def private void translateAnnotations(JvmAnnotationTarget target,
                      Iterable<XAnnotation> annotations) {
     target.addAnnotations
       (annotations.filterNull.filter[annotationType != null])
   }
```

The JvmAnnotationTarget is a common superclass for all Java model elements that can have annotations, for example, JvmGenericType (representing any Java type), JvmField (representing a Java field), and JvmOperation (representing a Java method). Now, the Entities DSL supports annotations for entities and attributes, and the Xbase infrastructure will take care of handling them both during the type checking and in the code generator.

Reusing Java error markers

As we saw in section *Validation*, validation checks, concerning the structural parts of the DSL, are left to the language implementor. Since we added annotations to the Entities DSL, we should check whether an annotation is valid on a specific DSL element.

For example, let's consider the `com.google.inject.Inject` annotation, which is defined as follows:

```
@Target({ METHOD, CONSTRUCTOR, FIELD })
@Retention(RUNTIME)
public @interface Inject {
```

This means that using `@Inject` on a Java type is disallowed by Java. In the Entities DSL, you can annotate an entity with `@Inject`, and you will get no validation error, but the generated Java code will contain an error.

Checking the validity of annotations should be performed in the `EntitiesValidator`, but it would not be straightforward. You may want to check how Xtend performs this check, and other checks on annotations, by looking at the Xtend implementation, in particular, the `XtendValidator`.

While it is not nice to generate invalid Java code, it is even worse not to mark the corresponding DSL element that led to specific Java errors. Xbase has a mechanism for reusing error markers in the generated Java code so that they are reported also on the original DSL program. This can be enabled by customizing `XbaseConfigurableIssueCodes` as follows:

```
import org.eclipse.xtext.preferences.PreferenceKey
import org.eclipse.xtext.util.IAcceptor
import org.eclipse.xtext.validation.SeverityConverter
import org.eclipse.xtext.xbase.validation.IssueCodes
import org.eclipse.xtext.xbase.validation.XbaseConfigurableIssueCodes

class EntitiesConfigurableIssueCodes extends
XbaseConfigurableIssueCodes {
  override protected initialize(IAcceptor<PreferenceKey> iAcceptor) {
    super.initialize(iAcceptor)
    iAcceptor.accept(create(IssueCodes.COPY_JAVA_PROBLEMS,
        SeverityConverter.SEVERITY_ERROR))
  }
}
```

Then, we bind this implementation in the `EntitiesRuntimeModule`:

```
override bindConfigurableIssueCodesProvider() {
  EntitiesConfigurableIssueCodes
}
```

With this modification, if the Java code generated by the Entities DSL contains errors, like the one concerning the wrong use of annotations, the error marker will be reported also on the original DSL source file, with the prefix `"Java problem:"`. An example is shown in the following screenshot. We created a Plug-in project, with dependencies `org.eclipse.xtext.xbase.lib` and `com.google.inject`. We then created an `.xentities` file, we wrote the `@Inject` annotation on an entity and we saved the file. The generated Java code contains a compilation error, which is also reported on the `.xentities` source file.

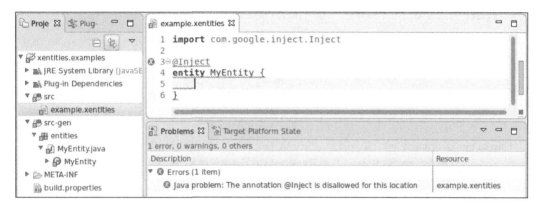

Using 'extension'

Using `XImportSection`, as we did in section *Imports*, your DSL source files can use `'extension'` in static imports so that all the imported `static` methods can be used as extension methods inside Xbase expressions. We can add a keyword `extension` also to entities' attributes in order to have the same semantics of extension fields in Xtend classes:

```
Attribute:
    annotations+=XAnnotation*
    'attr' (extension?='extension')? (type=JvmTypeReference)? name=ID
    ('=' initexpression=XExpression)? ';';
```

We could do the same for parameters and variable declarations, but this would require to redefine the corresponding Xbase rules, which we will not do in this chapter.

Xbase will be able to handle our entities' attributes as **extension methods providers** if we simply add a Java annotation to the Java model element inferred from our attributes. The Java annotation to add is `org.eclipse.xtext.xbase.lib. Extension`:

```
members += a.toField(a.name, type) [
    if (a.extension) {
```

```
        annotations += annotationRef(Extension)
    }
    ...
```

The `annotationRef` method is similar to `typeRef` that we have already used, but it is specific for Java annotations.

Now, we can write in our Entities DSL programs like the following one, which make use of attributes as extension methods providers:

```
import java.util.List

entity ListExtension {
        op void printList(List<String> l) {
                // implementation
        }
}

entity MyEntity {
        attr extension ListExtension listExtension = new
ListExtension();
        op void m(List<String> list) {
                // equivalent to listExtension.printList(list)
                list.printList
        }
}
```

Using type parameters

In this section, we introduce in the Entities DSL the possibility of declaring entities with type parameters. Xbase provides a specific grammar rule for type parameters `JvmTypeParameter`, which also deals with type parameters bounds and wildcards, with the same syntax as Java type parameters. We modify the rule for entities as follows:

```
Entity:
annotations+=XAnnotation*
'entity' name=ID
('<' typeParameters+=JvmTypeParameter (','
        typeParameters+=JvmTypeParameter)* '>')?
('extends' superType=JvmParameterizedTypeReference)? '{'
    attributes += Attribute*
    operations += Operation*
'}';
```

In a similar way, we could add type parameters to operations, thus mimicking Java generic methods (this is left as an exercise).

Then, we need to map the type parameters of our entities into type parameters of the corresponding Java model elements. We create the following method for this purpose:

```
def private void copyTypeParameters(JvmTypeParameterDeclarator target,
            List<JvmTypeParameter> typeParameters) {
    for (typeParameter : typeParameters) {
        target.typeParameters += typeParameter.cloneWithProxies
    }
}
```

The `JvmTypeParameterDeclarator` is a common superclass for all Java model elements that can have type parameters, for example, `JvmGenericType` (representing any Java type), `JvmConstructor` (representing a Java constructor), and `JvmOperation` (representing a Java method). If you add generic types to entity operations, you can reuse this method in the inferrer.

We call this method to set the type parameters of the `JvmGenericType` inferred for an entity:

```
acceptor.accept(entity.toClass("entities." + entity.name)) [
  copyTypeParameters(entity.typeParameters)
```

Now, we can write programs like the following one, which make use type parameters for entity definitions (note that you can declare bounds for type parameters just like in Java):

```
import java.util.List

entity ListExtension<T extends Comparable<T>> {
    op void printList(List<T> l) {
            // implementation
    }
}

entity MyEntity {
    attr ListExtension<String> stringListExtension;
    attr ListExtension<Integer> intListExtension;
    op void m(List<String> stringList, List<Integer> intList) {
        stringListExtension.printList(stringList)
        intListExtension.printList(intList)
    }
}
```

Formatter

Xbase has a default formatter for all the Xbase expressions and type references. If you enable the formatter in the MWE2 as we saw in *Chapter 6, Customizing Xtext Components*, section *Custom formatting*, the generated Xtend stub class `EntitiesFormatter` will extend the Xbase formatter.

We implement the `EntitiesFormatter` for this DSL similarly to the one for the Entities DSL in *Chapter 6, Customizing Xtext Components*, section *Custom formatting*. For elements that are related to Xbase, we simply delegate to the Xbase formatter base class, which will take care of formatting them. Thus, the formatting for import statements, Java type references and all Xbase expressions will be inherited from Xbase.

Here are some examples:

```
def dispatch void format(Model model,
                    extension IFormattableDocument document) {
    model.getImportSection.format
    val lastEntity = model.entities.last
    for (entity : model.entities) {
        ... similar to the EntitiesFormatter of Chapter 6
    }
}


def dispatch void format(Entity entity,
                extension IFormattableDocument document) {
    for (annotation : entity.getAnnotations()) {
        annotation.format
        annotation.append[newLine]
    }
    for (typeParameter : entity.getTypeParameters()) {
        typeParameter.format
    }
    entity.regionFor.keyword("<").append[noSpace]
    entity.regionFor.keyword(">").prepend[noSpace]

    entity.getSuperType.format
    ...
```

Further Customizations

Depending on the complexity of your DSL, you might want to customize the default implementation of several components of Xbase, such as scoping. This can be achieved by subclassing the corresponding Xbase classes and by specifying the bindings in the Guice module.

It is also possible to override some rules of the Xbase grammar in order to change the syntactic shape of some expressions. Moreover, you can change an Xbase expression rule in order to add syntax for new expressions, which are specific to your DSL. In this case, you also need to provide custom implementations for some classes of Xbase, such as the type computer and the compiler. In particular, you need to specify how to type your expressions and how they compile to Java. We will show an example in the next chapter.

Summary

Xbase can add a powerful Java-like expression language to your DSL, and by implementing the model inferrer, you will automatically reuse the Xbase Java type system implementation and the generation of Java code. This does not imply that all the concepts described in all the previous chapters (validation, code generation, scoping, and so on) are useless. In fact, knowing the main concepts underlying Xtext is required to effectively implement a DSL even when using Xbase. Moreover, in case you need to modify or add expressions to a DSL that uses Xbase, you may have to provide a custom scoping and validation as well.

When using Xbase, your DSL will be tightly coupled with Java, which might not always be what you need. Your DSL could be used only for writing specifications or simpler structures, and in that case, you will not need Xbase expressions; these would only add unwanted complexity. Alternatively, your DSL might not be bound to Java and might require code generation into another target language; also in this case, you cannot use Xbase.

13
Advanced Topics

In this chapter, we will describe a few advanced topics concerning an Xtext DSL implementation, and some advanced techniques. In the first part of the chapter, we will show how to manually maintain the Ecore model for the AST of an Xtext DSL. This way, you will have full control on the shape of the AST, instead of delegating that to the automatic Xtext Ecore inference mechanisms. Of course, the Xtext grammar and the Ecore model will still have to be consistent, but you will be able tweak the AST structure. You will also be able to add to the AST some **derived state**, which is computed from the DSL program, but which is not directly present in the program itself. In the first section, we will show how to create an Xtext DSL starting from an existing Ecore model, while in the second section, we will show how to switch to a manually maintained Ecore model, starting from the one generated by Xtext. In the third section, we will use Xcore to maintain the Ecore model for the AST. These first three sections of the chapter assume that you are already familiar with EMF and the Ecore model. In the last section, we will show how to extend an Xbase DSL with new expressions. This will require to customize the Xbase type system and the Xbase compiler in order to handle the new Xbase expressions.

This chapter will cover the following topics:

- How to create an Xtext project from an existing Ecore model
- How to switch to an imported Ecore model
- How to add to the AST some derived state
- How to use Xcore with Xtext
- How to extend Xbase and customize its compiler and type system

Creating an Xtext project from an Ecore model

In this section, we will implement an Xtext DSL starting from an existing Ecore model, which will represent the structure of AST.

Defining the Ecore model

We assume that we already have an EMF Ecore model for representing schools with students and teachers.

This Ecore model has the following structure:

- `SchoolModel`: This is the root element. The feature `schools` is a multi-value containment reference of `School` objects.

- `School`: The feature `persons` is a multi-value containment reference of `Person` objects.

- `Person`: This is an abstract class.

- `Student` is a `Person`: The `registrationNum` attribute is an integer, `teachers` is a multi-value non-containment reference of `Teacher` objects, that is, a student can refer to several teachers.

- `Teacher` is a `Person`.

- `Named` is an abstract class, which is the base class for `School` and `Person`. It contains the string attribute `name`.

During this section, we will modify this Ecore model. If you want to implement the example DSL in this section yourself, while reading, you can download the initial version of the project containing the Ecore model from here: `https://github.com/LorenzoBettini/emf-school-model`. On the other hand, the sources of the examples of the book contain the Ecore model already modified according to the contents of this chapter.

The class diagram of this model is shown in the next screenshot:

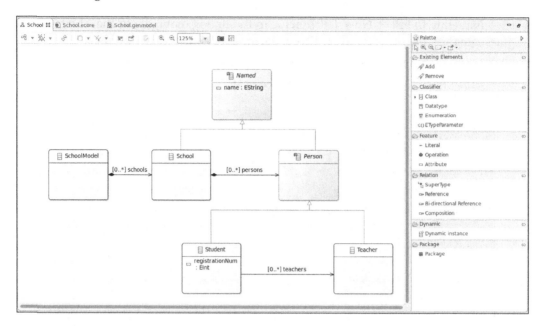

 We implemented this Ecore model using the **Ecore diagram editor**, which is shown in the preceding screenshot. If you want to try that, you can install the feature "**Ecore Diagram Editor (SDK)**", if that is not already installed in your Eclipse. Alternatively, you can edit the Ecore model using the standard EMF Ecore tree editor.

Creating the Xtext project

We will now create a new Xtext project starting from an existing Ecore model.

 Xtext grammar can refer to an existing Ecore model as long as the project containing the Ecore model is an Xtext project. If this is not the case, the Xtext grammar will show lots of errors when referring to the model classes. If the project is not already an Xtext project, you can convert it to an Xtext project by right-clicking on the project and navigating to **Configure | Convert to Xtext Project**.

In order to create the Xtext project, perform the following steps:

1. Navigate to **File | New | Project...**; in the dialog, navigate to the **Xtext** category and click on **Xtext Project From Existing Ecore Models**.

2. In the next dialog, press the **Add...** button to select a GenModel.

3. Select the `School.genmodel` and press **OK**, refer to the following screenshot:

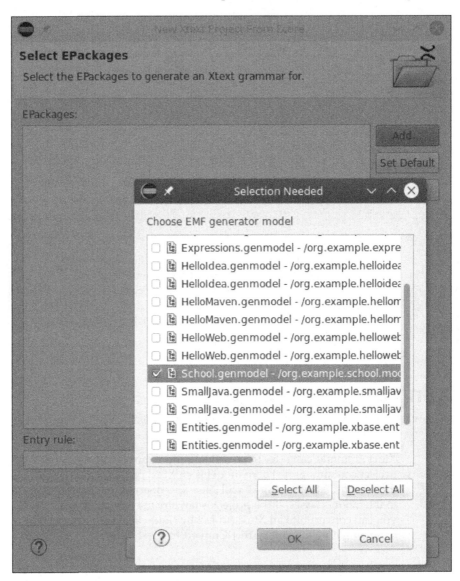

4. Specify `SchoolModel` for the **Entry rule**, refer to the following screenshot:

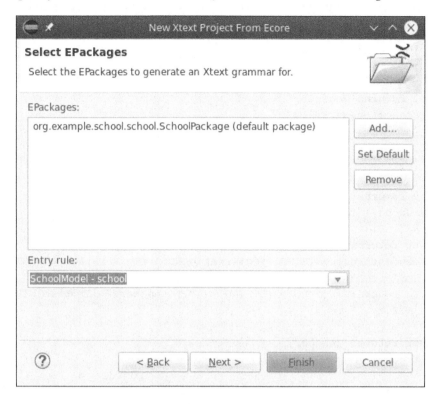

5. After you press **Next**, the dialogs are the same as the ones you have already seen in previous examples. Fill in the details for the following fields and press **Finish**:

 ° **Project name:** `org.example.school`

 ° **Name:** `org.example.school.School`

 ° **Extensions:** `school`

The first part of the grammar is slightly different from the grammars we have seen so far, since, instead of the `generate` line there is an `import` line. In fact, this time Xtext will not generate the Ecore model:

```
grammar org.example.school.School
        with org.eclipse.xtext.common.Terminals

import "http://www.example.org/school"
```

The `School.xtext` contains an initial grammar deduced by the Xtext project wizard from the Ecore model. The generated grammar rules are meant only as an initial content. We replace the rules completely with these grammar rules:

```
SchoolModel returns SchoolModel:
    schools+=School*;

School returns School:
    'school' name=STRING
    '{'
        persons+=Person*
    '}';

Person returns Person:
    Student | Teacher;

Student returns Student:
    'student' name=STRING 'registrationNum' registrationNum=INT
    ('{'
        teachers+=[Teacher|STRING] ( "," teachers+=[Teacher|STRING])*
    '}')?;

Teacher returns Teacher:
    'teacher' name=STRING;
```

The programs of this DSL will have the following shape:

```
school "A school" {
  student "A student" registrationNum 100 {
    "A teacher"
  }
  teacher "A teacher"
}
school "Another school" {
  teacher "Another teacher"
}
```

Note that in this DSL the names are specified as strings, not as IDs; cross references are declared accordingly, using the `[<Type>|<Syntax>]` form, that is `[Teacher|STRING]`.

You can now run the MWE2 workflow. Of course, you will get no `model/generated` folder in the project and no automatically inferred Ecore model.

Fixing the StandaloneSetup

If we now start writing JUnit tests, for example by modifying the generated stub `SchoolParsingTest`, and we try to run such tests, we get an exception during the execution of the shape:

```
java.lang.IllegalStateException: Unresolved proxy http://www.example.
org/school#//School. Make sure the EPackage has been registered.
```

In fact, the generated `StandaloneSetup` class for DSLs based on an imported Ecore model does not perform any registration of the EMF package. We need to do that ourselves explicitly. In this example, we must modify the `SchoolStandaloneSetup` as follows:

```
class SchoolStandaloneSetup extends SchoolStandaloneSetupGenerated {
...
  override register(Injector injector) {
    if (!EPackage.Registry.INSTANCE.containsKey(SchoolPackage.eNS_
URI)) {
      EPackage.Registry.INSTANCE.put(SchoolPackage.eNS_URI,
          SchoolPackage.eINSTANCE);
    }
    super.register(injector)
  }
}
```

If you take a look at the `StandaloneSetup` generated classes of the other DSLs we implemented so far, you can see that similar instructions are performed.

All the other aspects of an Xtext DSL implementation based on an imported Ecore model work exactly the same as all the other DSLs we implemented so far. For example, we can implement validator checks about possible duplicate elements of the same kind. We can follow the same approach shown in *Chapter 9*, *Type Checking*, section *Checking for duplicates*, based on the fact that the Ecore model has a base class for all elements with a name, `Named`:

```
class SchoolValixtends extends AbstractSchoolValidator {

  protected static val ISSUE_CODE_PREFIX = "org.example.school."
  public static val DUPLICATE_ELEMENT = ISSUE_CODE_PREFIX +
    "DuplicateElement"

  @Check def void checkNoDuplicateSchools(SchoolModel e) {
    checkNoDuplicateElements(e.schools, "school")
  }

  @Check def void checkNoDuplicatePersons(School e) {
```

```
        checkNoDuplicateElements(e.persons.filter(Teacher), "teacher")
        checkNoDuplicateElements(e.persons.filter(Student), "student")
}

def private void checkNoDuplicateElements(
            Iterable<? extends Named> elements, String desc) {
    val multiMap = HashMultimap.create()

    for (e : elements)
      multiMap.put(e.name, e)

    for (entry : multiMap.asMap.entrySet) {
      val duplicates = entry.value
      if (duplicates.size > 1) {
        for (d : duplicates)
          error("Duplicate " + desc + " '" + d.name + "'",
            d, SchoolPackage.eINSTANCE.named_Name,
            DUPLICATE_ELEMENT)
      }
    }
  }
}
```

Tweaking the Ecore model

As we did for other DSLs, in the School DSL, we do not impose any order in the definition of students and teachers within a school, and they can even be interleaved. All students and teachers are saved into the feature persons in the School class. In fact, in the preceding validator, we filtered the list of persons based on their type, either Student or Teacher, because we allow a teacher and a student to have the same name. We might need to perform such filtering in other parts of the DSL implementation, for example, in the generator. In other DSLs, we implemented utility methods in a model utility class that we used as extension methods. Since now we have complete control on the Ecore model, we can add such utility mechanisms directly in the Ecore model itself.

We first add a new EMF EDataType in the Ecore model, Iterable, whose **Instance Type Name** is java.lang.Iterable, and we add an **ETypeParameter**, say T, to the data type.

Then we add two EMF operations to the School class, getStudents() and getTeachers(), that return an Iterable with a **EGeneric Type Argument** argument Student and Teacher, respectively.

The relevant parts in the Ecore XMI file are as follows:

```
<eClassifiers xsi:type="ecore:EClass" name="School"
                          eSuperTypes="#//Named">
  <eOperations name="getStudents">
    <eGenericType eClassifier="#//Iterable">
      <eTypeArguments eClassifier="#//Student"/>
    </eGenericType>
  </eOperations>
  <eOperations name="getTeachers">
    <eGenericType eClassifier="#//Iterable">
      <eTypeArguments eClassifier="#//Teacher"/>
    </eGenericType>
  </eOperations>
...
</eClassifiers>
...
<eClassifiers xsi:type="ecore:EDataType" name="Iterable"
                          instanceClassName="java.lang.Iterable">
  <eTypeParameters name="T"/>
</eClassifiers>
```

The resulting Ecore model in the Ecore tree editor will be as in the following screenshot:

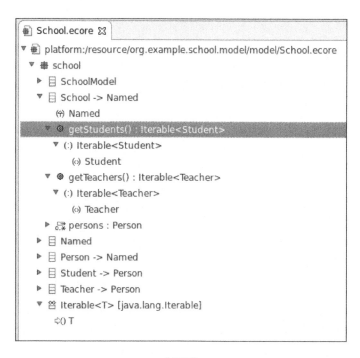

If we now regenerate the Java model code from the modified Ecore model, the `SchoolImpl` Java class will contain two unimplemented methods for the added operations, of the shape:

```
/**
 * @generated
 */
public Iterable<Student> getStudents() {
    // TODO: implement this method
    // Ensure that you remove @generated or mark it @generated NOT
    throw new UnsupportedOperationException();
}

/**
 * @generated
 */
public Iterable<Teacher> getTeachers() {
    // TODO: implement this method
    // Ensure that you remove @generated or mark it @generated NOT
    throw new UnsupportedOperationException();
}
```

We implement these methods using the static utility method `com.google.common.collect.Iterables.filter` (this is the same method we used in Xtend, since it is available as an extension method), which is part of `com.google.guava`, so we first need to add this as a dependency in the `school.model` project:

```
/**
 * @generated NOT
 */
public Iterable<Student> getStudents() {
    return Iterables.filter(getPersons(), Student.class);
}

/**
 * @generated NOT
 */
public Iterable<Teacher> getTeachers() {
    return Iterables.filter(getPersons(), Teacher.class);
}
```

Note that we marked these methods as `@generated NOT` so that a further EMF generation will not overwrite them.

In the validator, we can use these additional methods and avoid the manual filtering:

```
@Check def void checkNoDuplicatePersons(School e) {
    checkNoDuplicateElements(e.teachers, "teacher")
```

```
    checkNoDuplicateElements(e.students, "student")
}
```

> Mixing generated and manually written code is bad since it makes it much harder to maintain such code. In the following sections, we will show some alternatives that allow you to customize the model code without mixing generated and manually written code.

Derived State

In this section, we describe another mechanism, provided by Xtext, which allows you to add some additional state to the AST model.

For example, let's add another `EClass` to the `School` Ecore model, `SchoolStatistics`, with the integer fields `studentsNumber` and `teachersNumber` and the `Iterable<Student>` field `studentsWithNoTeacher`, with the obvious semantics. We then add a field in the `School` class called `statistics`, which is a containment reference of type `SchoolStatistics`. This is a **transient** feature, so that it will not be saved when the model is serialized. Refer to the following screenshot:

We would like `statistics` to be computed once and for all, each time the AST is modified.

Xtext allows you to do that by implementing an `org.eclipse.xtext.resource.IDerivedStateComputer`. This interface has two methods that you need to implement `installDerivedState` and `discardDerivedState`. These are called by Xtext after the AST has been created and when the program is going to be reparsed, respectively. In this example, we will implement the `installDerivedState` so that for each `School` object we create and fill a `SchoolStatistics` instance and set it in the `School` object. The `discardDerivedState` method will simply unset the `statistics` field of each `School` object:

```
class SchoolDerivedStateComputer implements IDerivedStateComputer {
  override discardDerivedState(DerivedStateAwareResource resource) {
    resource.allContents.filter(School).forEach [
      statistics = null
    ]
  }

  override installDerivedState(DerivedStateAwareResource resource,
            boolean preLinkingPhase) {
    if (!preLinkingPhase)
      resource.allContents.filter(School).forEach [ school |
        school.statistics = SchoolFactory.eINSTANCE.
createSchoolStatistics => [
          studentsNumber = school.students.size
          teachersNumber = school.teachers.size
          studentsWithNoTeacher = school.students.filter[teachers.
empty]
        ]
      ]
  }
}
```

The `preLinkingPhase` parameter tells you whether this method is called before the indexing phase (see *Chapter 10, Scoping*) or after the indexing phase; it has the same semantics as in the `JvmModelInferrer` (*Chapter 12, Xbase*). Since we do not need to index the statistics, we create and set the statistics when the method is called after the indexing phase.

We then need to specify a few custom Guice bindings in `SchoolRuntimeModule`:

```
import org.eclipse.xtext.resource.DerivedStateAwareResource
import
  org.eclipse.xtext.resource.
DerivedStateAwareResourceDescriptionManager
import org.eclipse.xtext.resource.IDerivedStateComputer
```

```
import org.eclipse.xtext.resource.IResourceDescription
import org.example.school.resource.SchoolDerivedStateComputer

class SchoolRuntimeModule extends AbstractSchoolRuntimeModule {
  override bindXtextResource() {
    DerivedStateAwareResource
  }

  def Class<? extends IDerivedStateComputer>
bindIDerivedStateComputer() {
    SchoolDerivedStateComputer
  }

  def Class<? extends IResourceDescription.Manager>
      bindIResourceDescriptionManager() {
    DerivedStateAwareResourceDescriptionManager
  }
}
```

Note that, besides our custom derived state computer, we need to tell Xtext to use a special XtextRe source and a special IResourceDescriptionManager that are aware of derived state.

> When using Xbase, you must not specify the additional bindings for Xtext resource and resource description manager, since Xbase already has its own implementations for these classes and should not be overwritten. Similarly, Xbase has its own default implementation of IDerivedStateComputer. This is the one responsible of calling your JvmModelInferrer implementation: all the mapped Java model elements will be part of the derived state of the resource. If you need to install additional derived state in an Xbase DSL, you can do that directly in the model inferrer.

We can now use this additional statistics field to issue warnings in the validator, in case a school has teachers and a student does not have any teacher:

```
public static val STUDENT_WITH_NO_TEACHER =
  ISSUE_CODE_PREFIX + "StudentWithNoTeacher"

@Check def void checkStudentsWithNoTeachers(School e) {
  val statistics = e.statistics
  if (statistics.teachersNumber > 0) {
    for (s : statistics.studentsWithNoTeacher) {
      warning(
        "Student " + s.name + " has no teacher",
```

```
      s,
      SchoolPackage.eINSTANCE.named_Name,
      STUDENT_WITH_NO_TEACHER)
    }
  }
}
```

Similarly, we can write a code generator using both the custom operations and the derived statistics. In this example, the generator simply generates a text file with the information about the schools and its contents:

```
class SchoolGenerator extends AbstractGenerator {
  override void doGenerate(Resource resource, IFileSystemAccess2 fsa,
                  IGeneratorContext context) {
    resource.allContents.toIterable.filter(SchoolModel).forEach [
      fsa.generateFile
        ('''«resource.URI.lastSegment».txt''', generateSchools)
    ]
  }

  def generateSchools(SchoolModel schoolModel) {
    schoolModel.schools.map [
      '''
      school «name»
        students number «statistics.studentsNumber»
        students with no teacher «statistics.studentsWithNoTeacher.
size»
        teachers number «statistics.teachersNumber»
        teachers
          «generateTeachers(teachers)»
        students
          «FOR it : students»
            «name» registration number «registrationNum»
              student's teachers
                «generateTeachers(teachers)»
          «ENDFOR»
      '''
    ].join("\n")
  }

  def generateTeachers(Iterable<Teacher> teachers) '''
    «FOR it : teachers»
    «name»
    «ENDFOR»
  '''
}
```

Finally, we customize the label provider so that statistics information will appear in the **Outline** view:

```
class SchoolLabelProvider extends DefaultEObjectLabelProvider {
  def text(Named e) {
    e.eClass.name + " " + e.name
  }

  def String text(SchoolStatistics s) {
    '''teachers «s.teachersNumber», students «s.studentsNumber»›››
  }
}
```

In the following screenshot, we show the new node with the statistics of a `school`:

```
My.school ☒                                    Outline ☒
1⊖ school "a school" {                         ▼ My
2⊖     student "a student" registrationNum 10    ▼ School a school
3      {                                            teachers 1, students 1
4          "a Teacher"                              Student a student
5      }                                            Teacher a Teacher
6      teacher "a Teacher"|
7  }
```

If we modify the the input file, the statistics will be updated consistently, as shown in the following screenshot (note the number of teachers is updated):

```
*My.school ☒                                   Outline ☒
1⊖ school "a school" {                         ▼ My
2⊖     student "a student" registrationNum 10    ▼ School a school
3      {                                            teachers 2, students 1
4          "a Teacher"                              Student a student
5      }                                            Teacher a Teacher
6      teacher "a Teacher"                          Teacher null
7      teacher|
8  }
```

In fact, the nice thing of the derived state computer mechanism is that we do not need to worry about when to update the derived state; Xtext will automatically call our derived state computer at the right moments.

Adding new rules to the language

Since now the Ecore model is not automatically inferred and generated by Xtext, you cannot simply add a new rule to the DSL, since the classes for the new rules and the features inside the new rules must already be present in the Ecore model. Thus, when your DSL is based on an imported Ecore model, you first need to add the classes and their features in the Ecore model and then you can add the corresponding rules in the DSL.

Thus, the advantage of manually maintaining the Ecore model is that you have full control on that, and it is easier to have in the AST derived features. The drawback is that you need to keep the Ecore model consistent with your DSL grammar.

Switching to an imported Ecore model

During the development of a more complex Xtext DSL, at some point, you might find the automatic Xtext Ecore inference mechanism too restrictive and you might want to have full control on the Ecore model of the AST. The Ecore model is also a very important API to all kinds of Xtext services, which you may want to to control more directly. In such cases, you can decide to switch to an imported and manually maintained Ecore model, starting from the one Xtext inferred for you from the grammar. In this section, we will detail the manual procedure to perform such a switching. we will detail the manual procedure to perform such a switching.

First of all, we create a new DSL that we will use as an example, using the following settings:

- **Project name:** `org.example.customgreetings`.
- **Name:** `org.example.customgreetings.Greetings`.
- **Extensions:** `greetings`.

Press **Next**.

In the next page, choose **Maven** as the **Preferred Build System**.

The DSL itself is not important, so we simply use the default grammar for greetings. Now, we run the MWE2 for the first time.

Let's assume we want to switch to a manually maintained Ecore model. Of course, we start from the one that Xtext generated for us, which can be found in the `model/generated` directory of the runtime project. This directory contains both the `Greetings.ecore` file, which contains the Ecore model, and `Greetings.genmodel`, which is used by the EMF generator. We rename the folder into `model/custom`.

You should perform this renaming from Eclipse, using the context menu **Refactor | Rename...**; this way, Eclipse will take care of renaming references to the directory in the plugin.xml file and in build.properties.

The .genmodel is configured to generate the EMF model Java classes into the src-gen folder, which is perfectly fine when the Ecore is handled by Xtext. Since we want to handle the Ecore model and the EMF generation ourselves, we cannot rely on the src-gen folder, since that will be completely removed when running the MWE2 workflow. For this reason, we modify the .genmodel file as follows: we open the Greetings.genmodel file with its default GenModel tree editor, we select the root element, and in the **Properties** view (which can be opened by double-clicking on the tree), we navigate to the **Model** section and we modify the **Model Directory** property from src-gen to emf-gen. Refer to the following screenshot:

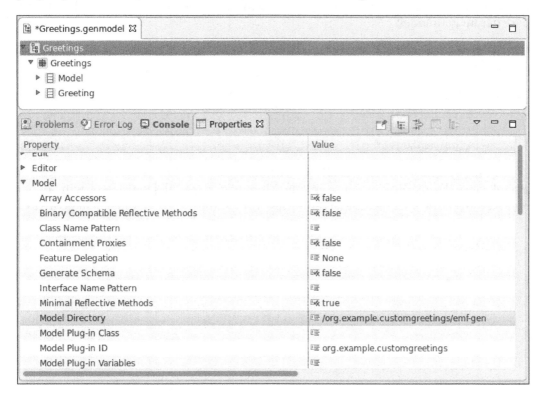

We save the file and we run the EMF generator manually, by right-clicking on the root element and select **Generate Model Code**. A new emf-gen folder will be created in the runtime project. We must set this folder as a source folder (right-click on and navigate to **Build Path | Use as Source Folder**). As usual, when adding a new source folder to a project, remember to update the build.properties accordingly. The new source folder will contain compilation errors due to duplicate Java classes: in fact the EMF Java model classes are present both in this new source folder emf-gen and in the src-gen folder. We can ignore these errors for the moment.

In the grammar, we must turn off the generation of the Ecore model, and replace that line with the import of the Ecore model, using its **namespace URI**:

```
//generate greetings "http://www.example.org/customgreetings/
Greetings"
import "http://www.example.org/customgreetings/Greetings"
```

In the MWE2, in the StandardLanguage section, we must add a resource reference to our custom genmodel:

```
language = StandardLanguage {
  name = "org.example.customgreetings.Greetings"
  fileExtensions = "greetings"
  // lines to refer to our custom genmodel
  referencedResource =
"platform:/resource/org.example.customgreetings/model/custom/
Greetings.genmodel"
```

We can now run the MWE2 workflow. This time, Xtext will not generate an Ecore model, since it will reuse our custom one. Moreover, the EMF Java classes will be removed from the src-gen folder, and the errors in the emf-gen folder will go away.

The layout of the directories in the project will be as in the following screenshot:

```
▼ 🗂 org.example.customgreetings [packtpub-xtext-book-2nd-examples r
  ▶ 📁 src
  ▼ 📁 src-gen
    ▶ ⊞ org.example.customgreetings
    ▶ ⊞ org.example.customgreetings.parser.antlr
    ▶ ⊞ org.example.customgreetings.parser.antlr.internal
    ▶ ⊞ org.example.customgreetings.scoping
    ▶ ⊞ org.example.customgreetings.serializer
    ▶ ⊞ org.example.customgreetings.services
    ▶ ⊞ org.example.customgreetings.validation
  ▶ 📁 xtend-gen
  ▼ 📁 emf-gen
    ▼ ⊞ org.example.customgreetings.greetings
      ▶ 📄 Greeting.java
      ▶ 📄 GreetingsFactory.java
      ▶ 📄 GreetingsPackage.java
      ▶ 📄 Model.java
    ▶ ⊞ org.example.customgreetings.greetings.impl
    ▶ ⊞ org.example.customgreetings.greetings.util
  ▶ 📚 JRE System Library [JavaSE-1.8]
  ▶ 📚 Plug-in Dependencies
  ▶ 📁 META-INF
  ▼ 📁 model
    ▼ 📁 custom
        Greetings.ecore
        Greetings.genmodel
```

Thus, the EMF Java classes are not generated anymore by Xtext in the `src-gen` folder, and they will be generated in the `emf-gen` folder by manually running the EMF generator.

From now on, it is our responsibility to modify the Ecore model and possibly add new classes or change the structure of existing classes if we want to modify the DSL grammar, as we said in the previous section *Adding new rules to the language*. Each time we modify the Ecore model, we also must rerun the EMF generator.

As we saw in the *Fixing the StandaloneSetup* section, to make JUnit tests work, we need to modify GreetingsStandaloneSetup as follows:

```
class GreetingsStandaloneSetup extends
GreetingsStandaloneSetupGenerated {
...
   override register(Injector injector) {
     if (!EPackage.Registry.INSTANCE.containsKey(GreetingsPackage.eNS_
URI)) {
        EPackage.Registry.INSTANCE.put(GreetingsPackage.eNS_URI,
          GreetingsPackage.eINSTANCE);
     }
   }
}
```

Generating EMF classes during the build

If we want to follow the good practice of not putting generated sources in the SCM repository, we must tweak the Maven build for this DSL so that the EMF Java classes are generated during the Maven build itself.

To do that, we create a new MWE2 file, say GenerateGreetingsModel.mwe2, and we use a component which is shipped with MWE2: org.eclipse.emf.mwe2.ecore. EcoreGenerator. This is configured with the path of the .genmodel file, the property genModel, and it will run the EMF generator for generating the EMF Java classes. We also enable the component org.eclipse.emf.mwe.utils.DirectoryCleaner, to clean up the emf-gen folder so that we are sure that each generation will remove possibly stale classes. The MWE2 file is as follows:

```
module org.example.customgreetings.GenerateGreetingsModel

import org.eclipse.xtext.xtext.generator.*
import org.eclipse.xtext.xtext.generator.model.project.*

var rootPath = ".."
var project = "org.example.customgreetings"

Workflow {
  bean = org.eclipse.emf.mwe.utils.StandaloneSetup {
    scanClassPath = true
  }
  component = org.eclipse.emf.mwe.utils.DirectoryCleaner {
    directory = "${rootPath}/${project}/emf-gen"
  }
```

```
    component = org.eclipse.emf.mwe2.ecore.EcoreGenerator {
      genModel =
        "platform:/resource/${project}/model/custom/Greetings.genmodel"
      srcPath = "platform:/resource/${project}/src"
    }
}
```

The additional `StandaloneSetup` bean is required to make the workflow find the `genmodel`. The additional `srcPath` property is required by the `EcoreGenerator` component and will be useful when we customize the EMF Java classes as shown later.

You can try and run the MWE2 workflow to make sure it works correctly.

During the Maven build, the MWE2 workflow will be run using the `exec-maven-plugin` and the Maven artifacts will be used during the execution, not the Eclipse bundles. The `genmodel` that Xtext originally generated is configured to use EMF 2.12, but there is no such a version of EMF available as Maven artifact. When running the MWE2 during the Maven build you will get a failure of the shape `The value '2.12' is not a valid enumerator of 'GenRuntimeVersion'`. To fix the problem, you need to downgrade the targeted EMF runtime version to 2.11; in the genmodel editor, using the **Properties** view, navigate to the **All** section and set the **Runtime Version** property to 2.11.

The `pom` file generated by the Xtext project wizard in the runtime project already contains the `exec-maven-plugin` configuration to run the MWE2 workflow `GenerateGreetings.mwe2` that generates the Xtext artifacts. We just need to add another execution of that plug-in to run also our new `GenerateGreetingsModel.mwe2` workflow. The final configuration of the Maven plug-in is as follows:

```
<plugin>
  <groupId>org.codehaus.mojo</groupId>
  <artifactId>exec-maven-plugin</artifactId>
  <version>1.4.0</version>
  <executions>
    <execution>
      <!-- new execution for generating EMF classes -->
      <id>mwe2GenerateEMFClasses</id>
      <phase>generate-sources</phase>
      <goals><goal>java</goal></goals>
      <configuration>
        <mainClass>
```

```
                org.eclipse.emf.mwe2.launch.runtime.Mwe2Launcher
              </mainClass>
              <arguments>
                <argument>
                /${project.basedir}/src/org/example/customgreetings/
  GenerateGreetingsModel.mwe2
                </argument>
                <argument>-p</argument>
                <argument>rootPath=/${project.basedir}/..</argument>
              </arguments>
              <classpathScope>compile</classpathScope>
              <includePluginDependencies>true</includePluginDependencies>
              <cleanupDaemonThreads>false</cleanupDaemonThreads>
            </configuration>
          </execution>
          <execution>
            <!-- execution already present -->
            <id>mwe2Launcher</id>
            <phase>generate-sources</phase>
            <goals><goal>java</goal></goals>
            <configuration>
            <mainClass>
            org.eclipse.emf.mwe2.launch.runtime.Mwe2Launcher
            </mainClass>
            <arguments>
              <argument>
              /${project.basedir}/src/org/example/customgreetings/
  GenerateGreetings.mwe2
              </argument>
```

Now, the EMF Java classes will be generated during the Maven build.

Customizing the EMF Java classes

EMF generated code contains Javadoc comments with the annotation @generated. If you want to customize a generated Java method, you need to remove that annotation or specify @generated NOT. This way, the next time you run the EMF generator, the custom methods will not be overwritten. We cannot use this technique if we generate the EMF Java classes using the MWE2 workflow approach we described in the previous section.

However, the org.eclipse.emf.mwe2.ecore.EcoreGenerator component still allows you to manually customize the EMF Java classes using the **generation gap** pattern.

For example, let's say we want to customize the `toString()` method of the `GreetingImpl` Java class. What we need to do is create in the `src` folder a class in the same package of `GreetingImpl`, `org.example.customgreetings.greetings.impl`, named `GreetingImplCustom` that extends `GreetingImpl` and redefine the `toString()` method:

```
package org.example.customgreetings.greetings.impl;

public class GreetingImplCustom extends GreetingImpl {
  @Override
  public String toString() {
    return "Hello " + getName();
  }
}
```

If we run the `GenerateGreetingsModel.mwe2` workflow, the generated EMF `GreetingsFactoryImpl` will create `Greeting` objects by instantiating our custom `GreetingImplCustom` classes:

```
/**
 * @generated
 */
public Greeting createGreeting()
{
  GreetingImplCustom greeting = new GreetingImplCustom();
  return greeting;
}
```

This can also be verified with a JUnit test:

```
@RunWith(XtextRunner)
@InjectWith(GreetingsInjectorProvider)
class GreetingsParsingTest{
  @Inject ParseHelper<Model> parseHelper

  @Test def void testCustomGreetingToString() {
    val result = parseHelper.parse('''
      Hello Xtext!
    ''')
    Assert.assertEquals("Hello Xtext", result.greetings.head.toString)
  }
}
```

The advantage of this approach, based on the generation gap pattern, is that it is easy to keep the custom code separated from the generated code. The drawback is that you cannot use the EMF generator manually to generate the EMF Java model classes; you need to run the MWE2 workflow.

Xcore

If you often find yourself customizing the Ecore model with operations or redefining existing methods, you might want to try **Xcore** for maintaining your Ecore model. Xcore is a DSL for Ecore. It is implemented in Xtext and Xbase, allowing you to specify the Ecore model with a Java-like syntax. Besides the structure of the model, you can also use Xcore to specify the behavior of operations, derived features, and provide custom implementation of methods. Moreover, the mapping of data types to Java types is more straightforward in Xcore. Being a DSL based on Xtext/Xbase, with Xcore you do not need a `.genmodel` file to generate the Java code for your model; you just edit your file, and the Java code will be automatically generated on save.

In order to use Xcore, you need to install the feature "**EMF - Eclipse Modeling Framework Xcore SDK**" into your Eclipse, unless it is already installed.

In this section, we will implement a new Xtext DSL, for specifying libraries, books, and authors. The Ecore model will be specified with Xcore.

Creating the Xcore project

Let's create an Xcore project for defining the Ecore model for the DSL that we are going to implement in this section. Steps are as follows:

1. Navigate to **File** | **New** | **Project...**; in the dialog, navigate to the **Xcore** category and click on **Xcore Project**.
2. Specify `org.example.library.model` as the project name and press **Finish**.

In the model directory of the project, create an `.xcore` file, for example, `Library. xcore`. Here we define the Ecore model, using a Java-like syntax:

```
package org.example.library

class LibraryModel {
    contains Library[] libraries
}

abstract class Named {
    String name
}

class Library extends Named {
    contains Writer[] writers
    contains Book[] books
```

```
}

class Writer extends Named {
}

class Book {
    String title
    refers Writer[] authors
}
```

As soon as you save the file, the Java code for the Ecore model will be automatically generated in the `src-gen` folder. Containment references are specified with the keyword `contains`, while cross-references with the keyword `refers`. The fact that a reference is a multi-value reference is specified with the `[]`. Of course, you can use the content assist while editing an Xcore file. The documentation of Xcore is `https://wiki.eclipse.org/Xcore`.

Creating the Xtext project from an existing Xcore model

We will now create a new Xtext project starting from the Ecore model implemented in Xcore.

 An Xcore project is an Xtext project, so you can directly use its Ecore model in your Xtext DSL.

In order to create the Xtext project, perform the following steps:

1. Navigate to **File | New | Project...**; in the dialog, navigate to the **Xtext** category and click on **Xtext Project From Existing Ecore Models**.
2. In the next dialog, press the **Add...** button to select a GenModel.
3. Select the `Library.xcore` and press **OK**.
4. Specify `LibraryModel` for the **Entry rule**.
5. After you press **Next**, fill in the details for the following fields and press **Finish**:

    ○ **Project name:** `org.example.library`
    ○ **Name:** `org.example.library.Library`
    ○ **Extensions:** `library`

As in the School DSL, the first part of the grammar uses an `import` line to refer to the existing Ecore model:

```
grammar org.example.library.Library
     with org.eclipse.xtext.common.Terminals

import "org.example.library"
```

We replace the rules of the `Library.xtext` grammar completely with these grammar rules:

```
LibraryModel returns LibraryModel:
  libraries+=Library*;

Library returns Library:
  'library' name=STRING
  '{'
    ('writers' '{' writers+=Writer ( "," writers+=Writer)* '}' )?
    ('books' '{' books+=Book ( "," books+=Book)* '}' )?
  '
Writer returns Writer:
  name=STRING;

Book returns Book:
  'title' title=STRING
  ('authors' authors+=[Writer|STRING] ( "," authors+=[Writer|STRING])*
)?
;
```

Valid programs for this DSL have the following shape:

```
library "A library" {
    writers {
        "A writer", "Another writer", "Third writer"
    }
    books {
        title "A book",
        title "Another book"
            authors "Third writer", "A writer"
    }
}

library "An empty library" {

}
```

Remember to fix the `LibraryStandaloneSetup` before running any JUnit tests:

```
override register(Injector injector) {
  if (!EPackage.Registry.INSTANCE.containsKey(LibraryPackage.eNS_URI))
{
   Epackage.Registry.INSTANCE.put(LibraryPackage.eNS_URI,
      LibraryPackage.eINSTANCE);
  }
  super.register(injector)
}
```

Modifying the Xcore model

As in the previous DSLs, let's assume that we want to modify the Ecore model. Since we use Xcore, everything will be much easier since we can write a model operation directly in the Xcore file, keeping in mind that the body of an operation in Xcore uses the Xbase syntax. For example, we add a datatype `Books` that corresponds to the Java type `Iterable<Book>`, and we implement in the `Writer` class the `getBooks` operation:

```
type Books wraps Iterable<Book>

class Writer extendsextends Named {
    op Books getBooks() {
        (eContainer as Library).books.
            filter[authors.contains(this)]
    }
}
```

That's all we need to do. On saving the file, Xcore will automatically regenerate the Java code. We do not need to modify the generate code and specify the Javadoc @ `generated NOT`, neither we need to create a separate Java file with `ImplCustom`.

The same holds if we want to give a custom implementation of methods such as `toString`. Differently from what we had to do in the previous example DSL, with Xcore it's just a matter of writing:

```
class Book {
...
  op String toString() {
    'title: "' + title + '"' +
      if (!authors.empty)
        ", by " + authors.map[name].join(", ")
  }
}
```

We can use the added operation in the validator, in the code generator, and in other parts of the DSL. This is left as an exercise.

Building an Xtext DSL that is based on Xcore with Maven/Tycho requires some ad-justments to the pom files. You can also generate the Java code from the Xcore model during the Maven build, using the **xtext-maven-plugin**. In the source code of the examples of the book, you will find all the pom files for this example DSL configured to use Xcore. Further and advanced details about using Xcore with Xtext can be found in the presentation Schill 2015.

Extending Xbase

In this section, we will extend the Xbase Expressions DSL presented in the previous chapter with a new Xbase expression. We will add the new XExpression **eval** to the DSL, which takes as an argument any Xbase expression.

In order to present the aspects of Xbase that need to be customized when adding new expressions, we want our new EvalExpression to have the following semantics:

- It can be used both as a statement and as an expression inside any other expression
- It has a String type and the argument expression must not have type void
- When it is used as a statement, it will be compiled into a Java System.out. println statement with the evaluation of the argument expression
- When it is used inside another expression, it will be compiled into a Java String expression corresponding to the string representation of the evaluated argument expression.

 This semantics does not necessarily make sense, but it allows us to explore many aspects of the customization of Xbase.

Overriding a rule in an Xtext grammar

Since we want to add another expression to the Xbase primary expression list, we need to override the corresponding Xbase grammar rule. By looking at the Xbase grammar (you can navigate to the grammar by pressing *F3* on the Xbase grammar reference after the with keyword), we find that the rule we need to override is XPrimaryExpression. Before Xtext 2.9, you were forced to copy the whole rule and paste it into your grammar to add a new rule element. Xtext 2.9 introduced the possibility to refer from within an overridden rule to the original rule in the super grammar, similar to the Java super mechanism in an overridden method. Thus, it is enough to write:super mechanism in an overridden method. Thus, it is enough to write:

```
grammar org.example.xbase.expressions.Expressions with
    org.eclipse.xtext.xbase.Xbase
```

```
generate expressions "http://www.example.org/xbase/expressions/
Expressions"

import "http://www.eclipse.org/xtext/xbase/Xbase"

ExpressionsModel returns XBlockExpression:
  {ExpressionsModel}
  (expressions+=XExpressionOrVarDeclaration ';'?)*;

XPrimaryExpression returns XExpression:
  {EvalExpression} 'eval' expression=XExpression |
  super;
```

This way, we extend the Xbase grammar rule XPrimaryExpression with our new expression while keeping also all the original expressions.

Some parsing tests make sure that our new eval expressions are parsed as expected:

```
@Test def void testEvalExpressionAsReceiver() {
  '''
  val i = 0
  (eval i).toString
  '''.parse.expressions.last => [
      assertTrue(
        (it as XMemberFeatureCall).
          actualReceiver instanceof EvalExpression)
  ]
}

@Test def void testEvalExpressionAssociativity() {
  '''
  val i = 0
  eval i.toString
  '''.parse.expressions.last => [
      assertTrue((it as EvalExpression).
        expression instanceof XMemberFeatureCall)
  ]
}
```

Note that if we want to use an eval expression inside another expression, we need to put it inside parenthesis.

Customizing the type system

The two preceding JUnit tests succeed, but the console shows some exceptions thrown by Xbase of the shape `java.lang.UnsupportedOperationException`: `Missing type computation for expression type: EvalExpression`. In fact, Xbase does not know how to type our new expression.

In order to customize the Xbase type system, we must implement our custom `XbaseTypeComputer` derived class, `ExpressionsTypeComputer` and bind it in the Guice module:

```
class ExpressionsRunule extends AbstractExpressionsRuntimeModule {
  def Class<? extends ITypeComputer> bindITypeComputer() {
    ExpressionsTypeComputer
  }
}
```

In the previous chapters, when we implemented a type system, we simply returned the computed type of our DSL expressions; the types were computed on demand. The Xbase type system works in a **batch mode**; all types are computed in a single batch operation for all the expressions of a program. The Xbase internal framework calls the type computer passing both the expression and the type computation state `ITypeComputationState`. Instead of returning the computed type, we must add information about the computed types in the passed state, and Xbase will then take care of using such type state information to perform type inference and type checking. Moreover, we must explicitly compute the types of the subexpressions. When computing the types of subexpressions, we can also impose some type expectations. If such expectations are not satisfied, the Xbase type system will automatically generate the appropriate **type mismatch errors** so that we will not have to implement any validator rules for that.

This is the implementation of our custom type computer:

```
class ExpressionsTypeComputer extends XbaseTypeComputer {
  def dispatch void computeTypes(EvalExpression eval,
          ITypeComputationState state) {
    state.withNonVoidExpectation.computeTypes(eval.expression)
    state.acceptActualType(getRawTypeForName(String, state));
  }
}
```

Given a type computation state, we can create new states with additional expectations. We want the argument expression to have a type different from void, and we declare that using withNonVoidExpectation. We then declare that an EvalExpression has type String by calling the method acceptActualType. This is enough for the Xbase type system to do all the rest.

 In an Xbase DSL, both in the grammar and in the JvmModelInferrer, we refer to Java types using JvmTypeReference objects. In the Xbase type computer, instead, we must always use LightweightTypeReference objects. Conversions between the two references are possible.

Testing the type computer

As said in the previous section, we cannot call the Xbase type computer directly. If we want to test our custom type computer, we need to inject an IBatchTypeResolver, trigger type resolution by calling resolveTypes, which returns an IResolvedTypes object, and get the actual type of an expression by calling getActualType on the IResolvedTypes object:

```
import org.eclipse.xtext.xbase.typesystem.IBatchTypeResolver
...
import static extension org.junit.Assert.*

@RunWith(XtextRunner)
@InjectWith(ExpressionsInjectorProvider)
class ExpressionsTypeComputerTest {
  @Inject extension ParseHelper<ExpressionsModel>
  @Inject IBatchTypeResolver typeResolver;

  @Test
  def void testEvalExpressionActualType() {
    '''
    val i = 0
    eval i
    '''.parse.expressions.last => [
      "java.lang.String".assertEquals(
          typeResolver.resolveTypes(it).getActualType(it).identifier
      )
    ]
  }
}
```

This is the standard mechanism to use the types computed by the Xbase type system. We will use this technique later for using the types in the compiler.

For further details about the Xbase type system, we refer to the presentation (*Zarnekow* 2015).

Customizing the validator

In our custom type computer, we specified expectations on the `eval` expression argument. Xbase will automatically generate mismatch errors accordingly. We can verify this behavior with the following tests. Since `println()`, without arguments, is a `void` method, we expect Xbase to generate an error when we use it as the argument of an `eval`; any other expression with a type different from `void` should instead be a valid argument:

```
import org.eclipse.xtext.xbase.validation.IssueCodes

@RunWith(XtextRunner)
@InjectWith(ExpressionsInjectorProvider)
class ExpressionsValidatorTest {
  @Inject extension ParseHelper<ExpressionsModel>
  @Inject extension ValidationTestHelper

  @Test def void testEvalExpressionWithVoidArgument() {
    '''
    eval println()
    '''.parse.assertError(
        XbasePackage.eINSTANCE.XfeatureCall, // error on println()
        IssueCodes.INCOMPATIBLE_TYPES,
        "Type mismatch: type void is not applicable at this location"
    )
  }

  @Test def void testValidEvalExpression() {
    '''
    val i = 0;
    eval i;
    '''.parse.assertNoErrors
  }
}
```

The first test succeeds as expected, but the second one fails with the "(`org.eclipse.` `xtext.xbase.validation.IssueCodes.invalid_inner_expression`) `'This` `expression is not allowed in this context, since it doesn't cause` `any side effects.'`" error. The Xbase validator checks that all expressions are valid in the context they are used. In particular, an expression like the variable reference i does not cause any side effect unless it is used in a context where a value is expected, for example, as the last expression of a method body or as the argument of a method call. Xbase does not know anything about our new `EvalExpression`, so it cannot detect that the variable reference is actually used in a context where a value is expected, and marks it as invalid. For this reason, we need to override the Xbase validator method `isValueExpectedRecursive` so that it returns `true` if the container of an expression is an `EvalExpression`:

```
class ExpressionsValidator extends AbstractExpressionsValidator {
  override protected isValueExpectedRecursive(XExpression expr) {
    return expr.eContainer instanceof EvalExpression ||
      super.isValueExpectedRecursive(expr)
  }
}
```

Now, the preceding `testValidEvalExpression` succeeds as expected. Of course, we also must make sure that validation errors are still raised by Xbase on expressions, that are invalid:

```
@Test def void testInvalidExpressionWithNoSideEffect() {
  '''
  val i = 0;
  i;
  '''.parse.assertError(
    XbasePackage.eINSTANCE.XFeatureCall,
    IssueCodes.INVALID_INNER_EXPRESSION,
    "This expression is not allowed in this context, since it doesn't
cause any side effects."
  )
}
```

In fact, in the preceding input program, the variable reference is invalid.

We also check that Xbase does not generate any error when an `EvalExpression` is used as a `String` object:

```
@Test def void testValidEvalExpressionAsStringReceiver() {
  '''
  val i = 0;
  val s = (eval i).trim; // trim is a method of String
  '''.parse.assertNoErrors
}
```

Customizing the compiler

Now that the Xbase type system knows how to type our `EvalExpression`, we must tell Xbase how to generate Java code for that. We must implement an `ExpressionsCompiler` that extends `XbaseCompiler` and bind it in the runtime module:

```
class ExpressionsRuntimeModule extends
AbstractExpressionsRuntimeModule {
...
  def Class<? extends XbaseCompiler> bindXbaseCompiler() {
    ExpressionsCompiler
  }
}
```

We want to compile our `EvalExpression` differently depending on whether it is used a statement or inside another expression.

Let's deal with the statement case first. Remember that in this case, we want to generate a Java `System.out.println` statement with the value of the eval expression argument. We must override the `doInternalToJavaStatement` method, which is passed the expression to compile, an `ITreeAppendable` instance that we use to generate the Java code and a boolean parameter that tells you whether the result of the compilation of that expression is going to be used in other compiled expressions:

```
import org.eclipse.xtext.xbase.compiler.XbaseCompiler
import org.eclipse.xtext.xbase.XExpression
import org.eclipse.xtext.xbase.compiler.output.ITreeAppendable
import orle.xbase.expressions.expressions.EvalExpression

class ExpressionsCompiler extends XbaseCompiler {
  override protected doInternalToJavaStatement(XExpression obj,
             ITreeAppendable a, boolean isReferenced) {
    if (obj instanceof EvalExpression) {
      obj.expression.internalToJavaStatement(a, true)
      a.newLine
      a.append('''System.out.println(''')
      obj.expression.internalToJavaExpression(a)
      a.append(");")
    } else
      super.doInternalToJavaStatement(obj, a, isReferenced)
  }
}
```

Let's comment on this implementation. First we compile the eval argument expression, using `internalToJavaStatement`. In case the eval argument expression requires intermediate compilation of subexpressions, the compilation of the subexpressions will be generated accordingly in the same appendable instance. Since we specify `true` as the second argument, we require the Xbase compiler to generate in the Java code an additional variable with the result of the evaluation of subexpressions. When later we call `internalToJavaExpression` Xbase will generate a reference to such a variable. If the eval argument expression does not contain any subexpression or it can be compiled directly as a Java expression, for example, a constant expression, then `internalToJavaStatement` will not generate any additional code and `internalToJavaExpression` will directly generate the Java code corresponding to the eval argument expression.

For example, given this input file, where the eval argument expression is a simple constant expression:

```
eval 0
```

The compiler will generate this Java code:

```
System.out.println(0);
```

While given this input file, where the eval's argument expression requires compilation of subexpressions:

```
eval if (args.length > 0) args.get(0) else ""
```

The compiler will generate the following Java code:

```
String _xifexpression = null;
int _length = args.length;
boolean _greaterThan = (_length > 0);
if (_greaterThan) {
  _xifexpression = args[0];
} else {
  _xifexpression = "";
}
System.out.println(_xifexpression);
```

Now, let's deal with the case when the eval is used inside another expression. Remember that in this case we want it to be compiled into a Java `String` expression corresponding to the string representation of the evaluation of the eval argument expression.

For this case, we need to take into consideration how the Xbase compiler workflow takes place. We saw that in some cases the subexpressions of a given expression e must be first recursively compiled, the intermediate result must be stored in a variable and then that variable must be used as the result of the compilation of e. The additional **synthetic variables** created during the compilation of subexpressions are automatically handled by Xbase and stored in the appendable object. Each new created synthetic variable is associated to the original expression. The appendable will also make sure that no two synthetic variables have the same name, by appending incremental suffixes.

When subexpressions require recursive compilation, the Xbase compiler will first compile the subexpressions as Java statements, using the method doInternalToJavaStatement, passing true as the last argument. Then, it calls the internalToConvertedExpression method.

Thus, we must implement doInternalToJavaStatement, taking into consideration the isReferenced parameter; if isReferenced is true, it means that our eval expression is used inside another expression. So, we create a synthetic variable with a proposed name and generate Java code that assigns to that variable the result of the compilation of the eval argument expression. Xbase will automatically append an incremental suffix to the proposed name in case a variable with the same name has already been used:

```
class ExpressionsCompiler extends XbaseCompiler {
  override protected doInternalToJavaStatement(XExpression obj,
            ITreeAppendable a, boolean isReferenced) {
    if (obj instanceof EvalExpression) {
      obj.expression.internalToJavaStatement(a, true)
      a.newLine
      if (isReferenced) {
        val name = a.declareSyntheticVariable(obj, "_eval")
        a.append('''String «name» = "" + ''')
        obj.expression.internalToJavaExpression(a)
        a.append(";")
      } else {
        a.append('''System.out.println('''')
        obj.expression.internalToJavaExpression(a)
        a.append(");")
      }
    } else
      super.doInternalToJavaStatement(obj, a, isReferenced)
  }
```

Note that since we generate in the Java code an assignment to a String variable, which is consistent with the fact that our eval expressions are given type String in the type system, we must make sure that the assigned Java expression has always type String; we do that by generating an explicit string concatenation with an empty string.

Then, we implement internalToConvertedExpression by simply generating in the Java code a reference to the synthetic variable associated to the original eval expression:

```
override protected internalToxpression(XExpression obj,
                ITreeAppendable a) {
    if (obj instanceof EvalExpression)
        a.append(getVarName(obj, a))
    else
        super.internalToConvertedExpression(obj, a)
    }
}
```

The implementations of these two methods must be consistent: if you implement internalToConvertedExpression assuming that a synthetic variable has been generated for an expression, you also must make sure that in the doInternalToJavaStatement implementation you always generate such a synthetic variable when the isReferenced parameter is true. Otherwise, you might end up generating Java code, which is invalid.

Given this input file, where eval is used inside another expression:

```
val i = eval 0
val j = eval true
```

The generated Java code will be:

```
String _eval = "" + 0;
final String i = _eval;
String _eval_1 = "" + true;
final String j = _eval_1;
```

Note that each synthetic variable has a unique name.

As said earlier, the Xbase compiler performs the compilation of statements and expressions and their subexpressions also taking into consideration whether a given Xbase expression can be directly compiled into a Java expression without additional Java statements. Xbase knows this information for all its expressions, but when we add new Xbase expressions we must explicitly provide such information.

Thus, we must override the `internalCanCompileToJavaExpression` method, specifying that an `EvalExpression` cannot be compiled directly into a Java expression:

```
override protected internalCanCompileToJavaExpression(XExpression e,
            ITreeAppendable a) {
  if (e instanceofinstanceof EvalExpression)
    return false
  else
    super.internalCanCompileToJavaExpression(e, a)
}
```

This allows our eval expression to be compiled correctly even in contexts where the Xbase compiler needs to generate Java code with additional compilation of subexpressions. For example, given this input.

```
var i = 0
while (!(eval args.get(i)).empty) {
  println(args.get(i++))
}
```

The generated Java code will be:

```
int i = 0;
String _get = args[i];
String _eval = "" + _get;
boolean _isEmpty = _eval.isEmpty();
boolean _not = (!_isEmpty);
boolean _while = _not;
while (_while) {
  int _plusPlus = i++;
  String _get_1 = args[_plusPlus];
  InputOutput.<String>println(_get_1);
  String _get_2 = args[i];
  String _eval_1 = "" + _get_2;
  boolean _isEmpty_1 = _eval_1.isEmpty();
  boolean _not_1 = (!_isEmpty_1);
  _while = _not_1;
}
```

Later in this section, we will modify our custom compiler in order to reduce the size of the generated Java code.

Using the type system in the compiler

The Xbase type system can be used also in the compiler to generate Java code according to the types of the expression being compiled. For example, in this DSL, we could avoid to generate the explicit string concatenation with an empty string when the eval argument expression is a String expression.

As we saw in the *Testing the type computer* section, we need to inject an IBatchTypeResolver, trigger type resolution by calling resolveTypes, and get the actual type by calling getActualType. We generate the explicit string concatenation with an empty string only when the actual type of the eval argument expression is not String:

```
@Inject IBatchTypeResolver batchTypeResolver

override protected doInternalToJavaStatement(XExpression obj,
            ITreeAppendable a, boolean isReferenced) {
...
    if (isReferenced) {
      val e = obj.expression
      val name = a.declareSyntheticVariable(obj, "_eval")
      a.append('''String «name» = ''')
      e.generateStringConversion(a)
      e.internalToJavaExpression(a)
      a.append(";")
    } else {
...
}

def private generateStringConversion(XExpression e, ITreeAppendable a)
{
  val actualType = batchTypeResolver.resolveTypes(e).getActualType(e)
  if (!actualType.isType(String)) {
    a.append('''"" + ''')
  }
}
```

In *Chapter 8, An Expression Language*, section *Optimizations and fine tuning*, we used the Xtext caching mechanism, IResourceScopeCache, to cache the results of type computations, in order to avoid to compute the type for the same expressions over and over again. We do not need this technique when using Xbase, since the default implementation of IBatchTypeResolver, that is CachingBatchTypeResolver, already implements caching.

Testing the compiled code

In *Chapter 7, Testing,* section *Testing code generation,* we showed how to test the compiled code, including checking that the generated Java code is valid Java code, and checking the runtime behavior of the generated Java code. In that section, we instantiated the compiled generated Java class and called methods on the instance. In this DSL, we generate a Java class with a `main` method so, while we can still call such a method, we cannot use the returned value to perform checks, since the generated Java `main` method only prints something on the standard output.

In such a scenario, in order to test that the generated code prints what we expect on the standard output, we can temporarily replace the `System.out` with a new output stream, run the main method on the created instance, and check that the output stream contains what we expect. A way to do that is illustrated in the following test of the `ExpressionsCompilerTest`:

```
@Test def void testEvalExpressionInWhileExecution() {
  '''
  var i = 0
  while (!(eval args.get(i)).empty) {
    println(args.get(i++))
  }
  '''.assertExecuteMain('''
  1
  2
  ''', #["1", "2", "", "3"])
}

def private assertExecuteMain(CharSequence file,
              CharSequence expectedOutput, String[] args) {
  val classes = newArrayList()
  file.compile [
    classes += compiledClass
  ]
  val clazz = classes.head
  val out = new ByteArrayOutputStream()
  val backup = System.out
  System.setOut(new PrintStream(out))
  try {
    val instance = clazz.newInstance
    clazz.declaredMethods.findFirst[name == 'main'] => [
      accessible = true
      invoke(instance, #[args])
    ]
  } finally {
```

```
    System.setOut(backup)
  }
  assertEquals(expectedOutput.toString, out.toString)
}
```

Improving code generation

Once we have fully tested our Xbase custom compiler, we can take some time
to improve the generated Java code. The way we previously implemented
`internalCanCompileToJavaExpression` does not take into consideration the
eval argument expression. If the eval argument expression can be directly compiled
into a Java expression, we can also compile the entire eval expression as a single
Java expression.

Going back to the previous example:

```
var i = 0
while (!(eval args.get(i)).empty) {
  println(args.get(i++))
}
```

The Xbase compiler is able to compile the eval argument expression, `args.get(i)`,
directly into a Java expression, without all the additional intermediate Java
compilations. So, instead of generating:

```
int i = 0;
String _get = args[i];
String _eval = "" + _get;
boolean _isEmpty = _eval.isEmpty();
boolean _not = (!_isEmpty);
boolean _while = _not;
while (_while) {
  int _plusPlus = i++;
  String _get_1 = args[_plusPlus];
  InputOutput.<String>println(_get_1);
  String _get_2 = args[i];
  String _eval_1 = "" + _get_2;
  boolean _isEmpty_1 = _eval_1.isEmpty();
  boolean _not_1 = (!_isEmpty_1);
  _while = _not_1;
}
```

We should be able to generate smaller Java code, which has the same semantics:

```
int i = 0;
while ((!(args[i]).isEmpty())) {
  int _plusPlus = i++;
  String _get = args[_plusPlus];
  InputOutput.<String>println(_get);
}
```

That is, we should be able to compile `eval args.get(i)` simply as `args.get[i]`.

To do that, we implement the `internalCanCompileToJavaExpression` method, in terms of the `EvalExpression` argument expression:

```
override protected internalCanCompileToJavaExpression(XExpression e,
            ITreeAppendable a) {
  if (e instanceof EvalExpression)
    return e.expression.internalCanCompileToJavaExpression(a)
  else
    super.internalCanCompileToJavaExpression(e, a)
}
```

Then, we need to update our implementation of `internalToConvertedExpression` accordingly. We cannot assume that a synthetic variable for an eval expression has always been generated. If a synthetic variable for an eval expression has not been generated in the appendable, then we can assume that our eval expression can be compiled directly into a Java expression:

```
override protected internalToConvertedExpression(XExpression obj,
                ITreeAppendable a) {
                ITreeAppendable a) {
  if (obj instanceof EvalExpression) {
    if (a.hasName(obj)) {
      a.append(getVarName(obj, a))
    } else {
      // compile the eval directly as a Java expression
      val e = obj.expression
      a.append("(")
      e.generateStringConversion(a)
      e.internalToJavaExpression(a)
      a.append(")")
    }
  } else
    super.internalToConvertedExpression(obj, a)
}
```

Note that we the generated Java expression for an eval expression is enclosed in parenthesis in order to ensure the right associativity in the generated Java code.

Smoke tests

A **smoke test** verifies that the basic features of your software are not completely broken, meaning that the software can deal with critical and corner cases. The Xbase testing framework provides a utility class, org.eclipse.xtext.xbase. junit.typesystem.TypeSystemSmokeTester, that checks that your custom implementation of the Xbase type system can deal also with incomplete programs by gracefully failing, without throwing exceptions. It also checks that the expected invariants of the Xbase type system hold, for example, that all the expressions of the program are visited by the type computation and are given a type. Broken invariants would essentially break almost all the downstream components that want to use the results of the type system.

You use the TypeSystemSmokeTester in conjunction with the XtextSmokeTestRunner to run your existing JUnit tests as a test suite, for example:

```
@RunWith(XtextSmokeTestRunner)
@ProcessedBy(
    value=TypeSystemSmokeTester,
    processInParallel=false
)
@SuiteClasses(
    ExpressionsParsingTest,ExpressionsCompilerTest,
    ExpressionsTypeComputerTest, ExpressionsValidatorTest
)
class ExpressionsSmokeTest {

}
```

The TypeSystemSmokeTester will intercept all the input programs used in your tests that are being parsed and performs some permutations on them, for example, it simulates typing from the first to the last character. It then verifies that the type system can still handle such invalid inputs. Note that when running your tests as a test suite with the TypeSystemSmokeTester the assertions in your tests will not be executed. Thus, the preceding test suite does not replace your JUnit tests that check the validity of your DSL implementation.

Since the TypeSystemSmokeTester performs many permutations for each test case, the preceding test suite takes much longer to execute.

Summary

In this chapter, we showed many advanced topics and techniques related to an Xtext DSL implementation. When your DSL grows in features, you may want to take some of the techniques described in this chapter into consideration. These could be useful to make the implementation cleaner and more maintainable, to make a few aspects easier to implement and to improve the overall performance.

Finally, we showed how Xbase can be extended with new expressions, by customizing the type system, the validator, and the compiler accordingly.

14
Conclusions

By the end of this book, you should have a good knowledge of Xtext and Xtend and their mechanisms. You should be able to implement even a complex DSL and all its aspects, both concerning the runtime and the UI. If your DSL needs to inter-operate with Java and its type system, you should really consider adopting Xbase in your DSL, since this will save you from implementing most aspects, including the type system and the code generator.

However, this book could not cover all the details of Xtext, so while developing your DSL you might have to face problems that this book did not even mention.

For this reason, you should always keep the official Xtext documentation at hand. As we said in the book, you find the documentation online at: `https://www.eclipse.org/Xtext/documentation/`. Remember that the Xtext documentation is also available in your Eclipse, navigating to **Help | Help Contents | Xtext Documentation**. The same holds for the Xtend programming language, whose documentation can be found online at `https://eclipse.org/xtend/documentation/` or in Eclipse navigating to **Help | Help Contents | Xtend User Guide**.

The **Xtext forum** is also a good source for finding help about Xtext problems and for discovering new features. The forum is accessible on the web, `https://www.eclipse.org/forums/index.php/f/27/`, and as a **newsgroup**, `eclipse.modeling.tmf`, using the news server `news.eclipse.org`. In both cases, you need to register in order to be able to post messages. You can also use **StackOverflow** to find help for Xtext, `http://stackoverflow.com/questions/tagged/xtext`.

Finally, you may want to have a look at some blogs on the web about Xtext. Many users and Xtext committers, including myself, constantly write some blog posts about tips and tricks on Xtext and tutorials.

My blog is `http://www.lorenzobettini.it/`. And these are some blogs and website I always keep an eye on for new Xtext articles:

- `http://blogs.itemis.com/topic/xtext.`
- `http://typefox.io/blog`
- `http://christiandietrich.wordpress.com`
- `http://blog.efftinge.de`
- `http://koehnlein.blogspot.com`
- `http://kthoms.wordpress.com`
- `http://blog.moritz.eysholdt.de`
- `http://xtextcasts.org`

You may also want to follow the official Xtext Twitter account `@xtext`.

Finally, I hope that you enjoyed this book as much as I enjoyed writing it! If you had never used Xtext before, I hope that this book gave you enough knowledge to get started and get productive in developing DSLs with Xtext and Xtend. If you were already familiar with Xtext, I hope that this book increased your knowledge about this framework and that the methodologies and best practices illustrated throughout the chapters will make you more productive.

Keep your code clean and well tested!

Bibliography

Aho, A.V., Lam, M.S., Sethi, R., Ullman, J.D. (2007). *Compilers: principles, techniques,* and tools. 2nd edition. *Addison Wesley.*

Beck, K., (2002). *Test Driven Development: By Example. Addison-Wesley.*

Bettini, L., Stoll, D., Völter, M., Colameo, S., (2012). *Approaches and Tools for Implementing Type Systems in Xtext. Software Language Engineering.* 392-412. *Volume 7745 of LNCS. Springer.*

Bettini, L., (2013). *Implementing Java-like languages in Xtext with Xsemantics. Proceedings of the* 28th *Annual ACM Symposium on Applied Computing.* 1559-1564. *ACM.*

Bettini, L., (2016). *Implementing type systems for the IDE with Xsemantics. Journal of Logical and Algebraic Methods in Programming. 85(5):655--680. Elsevier.*

Brown, D., Levine, J., Mason, T. (1995) *lex & yacc. O'Reilly.*

Cardelli, L. (1996). *Type Systems. ACM Computing Surveys,* 28(1):263–264.

Efftinge, S., Eysholdt, M., Köhnlein. J., Zarnekow, S., Hasselbring, W., von Massow, R., Hanus, M. (2012). *Xbase: Implementing Domain-Specific Languages for Java. Proceedings of the* 11th *International Conference on Generative Programming and Component Engineering,* 112-121, ACM.

Efftinge, S. (2016). *Parsing Expressions With Xtext,* `http://typefox.io/parsing-expressions-with-xtext`.

Fowler, M. (2004). *Inversion of Control Containers and the Dependency Injection pattern.* `http://www.martinfowler.com/articles/injection.html`.

Fowler, M. (2006). *Continuous Integration.* `http://martinfowler.com/articles/continuousIntegration.html`.

Fowler, M. (2010). *Domain-Specific Languages. Addison-Wesley.*

Gamma, E., Helm, R., Johnson, R., and Vlissides, J. (1995). Design Patterns: Elements of Reusable Object-Oriented Software. Addison-Wesley.

Ghosh, D. (2010). DSLs in Action. Manning.

Hindley, J.R. (1987). Basic Simple Type Theory. Cambridge University Press.

Köhnlein, J. (2012). Xtext tip: How do I get the Guice Injector of my language? `http://koehnlein.blogspot.it/2012/11/xtext-tip-how-do-i-get-guice-injector.html`

Levine, J. (2009). Flex & Bison: Text Processing Tools. O'Reilly.

Martin, R.C. (2002). Agile Software Development, Principles, Patterns, and Practices. Prentice Hall.

Martin, R.C. (2008). Clean Code: A Handbook of Agile Software Craftsmanship. Prentice Hall.

Martin, R.C. (2011). The Clean Coder: A Code of Conduct for Professional Programmers. Prentice Hall.

Parr, T. (2007) The Definitive ANTLR Reference: Building Domain-Specific Languages. Pragmatic Programmers.

Pierce, B.C. (2002). Types and Programming Languages. The MIT Press, Cambridge, MA.

Schill, H. (2015). Using Xcore with Xtext. XtextCon, `http://www.slideshare.net/holgerschill/using-xcore-with-xtext.`

Steinberg, D., Budinsky, F., Paternostro, M., and Merks, E. (2008). EMF: Eclipse Modeling Framework. Addison-Wesley, 2nd edition.

Vlissides, J. (1996). Generation Gap [software design pattern]. C++ Report, 8(10), p. 12, 14-18.

Voelter, M. (2013). DSL Engineering: Designing, Implementing and Using Domain-Specific Languages.

Zarnekow, S. (2012). Xtext Best Practices. EclipseCon Europe, `http://www.eclipsecon.org/europe2012/sessions/xtext-best-practices.`

Zarnekow, S. (2012-b). Xtext Corner #8 - Libraries Are Key, `http://zarnekow.blogspot.it/2012/11/xtext-corner-8-libraries-are-key.html.`

Zarnekow, S. (2015). Extending the Xbase Typesystem. XtextCon, `http://www.slideshare.net/szarnekow/extending-the-xbase-typesystem.`

Index

Made in the USA
Middletown, DE
21 November 2019

79106641R00236